WHO IS MY BROTHER?

Facing a Crisis of Identity and Fellowship

F. LaGard Smith

Cover by Left Coast Design, Portland, Oregon

WHO IS MY BROTHER?

Copyright © 1997 by F. LaGard Smith
Published by Cotswold Publishing
24352 Baxter Drive
Malibu, California 90265

Library of Congress Cataloging-in-Publication Data

Who Is My Brother?/ F. LaGard Smith
Library of Congress Catalog Number 97-92480
ISBN 0-9660060-0-3

Printed in the United States of America

DEDICATED

To my mother, Mary Faye Smith—

Whose uncommon sense of universal fellowship
has blessed the rejected, the troubled, and the lost.

WITH APPRECIATION

For allowing me to invade their already busy schedules, and for their careful attention to various stages of the manuscript, I wish to thank John Acuff, Lesley Archer, Dan Chambers, Tony Coffey, Eric Heddon, Jimmy Jividen, Bob Owen, Brian Pederson, Scott McDowell, Bill Roper, Jeff Walling, and Jim Woodroof.

Nothing is more stretching than those special occasions when personal understandings can be challenged by groups of Christians thinking aloud together. I am particularly grateful for the opportunity to be challenged on the issues within this book by the faculty and students of both the Sunset School of Preaching and the Bear Valley School of Biblical Studies (particularly Denny Petrillo). Also, by those who participated in the Yellowstone Bible Camp in August, 1996; the Preachers Retreat at Pettijohn Springs in September, 1996; and the church leaders meeting in Glasgow, Scotland, this past spring. Those who contributed most to my own thinking were those who most disagreed. An author without diverse brothers and sisters in Christ who boldly share their convictions is an author robbed of perspective.

My appreciation goes to R. L. Roberts and Erma Jean Loveland for their generous research assistance. Special thanks as well to Dr. Minta Sue Berry for her gifted editing of the manuscript; and, as always, to my wife, Ruth, for her own editorial contributions and her gracious tolerance of all the late nights I spend writing.

CONTENTS

INTRODUCTION

This is a book about Christian fellowship. Who is a Christian? Who is not? With whom do we share kingdom participation as brothers and sisters in Christ? How should we regard those who have never been spiritually reborn in the same way as first-century believers? Indeed, how should we treat those who have in fact been born again into the kingdom?

For some years now, I have become increasingly concerned that our noble commitment to doctrinal purity has had the unwelcome side-effect of producing an unhealthy addiction to infighting and division. A pervasive party spirit, church splits, acrimonious brotherhood papers, and divisive issues of every kind have made a mockery of Jesus' plea for unity among his followers.

In fact, in the name of doctrinal purity many among us have drawn such exclusive lines of fellowship that so-called "erring brothers" on the other side of those lines might not even be regarded as genuine brothers at all. Hence the title question: Who is my brother?

There are also the more practical questions: How am I to regard my brother with whom I have doctrinal disagreements? Under what circumstances am I called upon to withdraw my fellowship from a sinning brother or sister? What does it mean to have the kind of sharing and caring *koinonia* fellowship that we read about in the first century church?

After a period of concentrated study, I began to share with others through lectures and occasions of mutual discussion what I came to call a "five-fold fellowship." My intent ultimately was to publish that material in book form, which I have now done in Part II of this volume.

However, as I was in the process of formulating my thoughts for such a book, it suddenly came to my attention that an equally compelling question was being asked by others from a completely different direction. With surprising rapidity and intensity, I began to hear calls for a wider Christian fellowship with all who have faith in Christ, whether or not they have been biblically baptized. To say the least, this extraordinary plea for unity with all who claim to be Christians gives new meaning to the question, Who is my brother? Virtually overnight, the range of fellowship issues had expanded far beyond the original scope, making Part I necessary.

In retrospect, I am thankful for the added perspective which the troubling questions raised in Part I gives to the already-difficult issues discussed in Part II. Reexamining the threshold question of who shares in kingdom fellowship with Christ himself reinforces what it means to be in kingdom fellowship with each other. In the final analysis, the bounds of the former determine the bounds of the latter.

Who then is my brother? Never in our time has the question had so many different implications. Never in recent history have those implications been more crucial.

Pausing for Perspective

So many, many questions lie ahead, about lines and boundaries and relationships. Almost needless to say, the complex issues surrounding Christian fellowship are not easy, and I can assure you in advance that we won't all agree on every issue. In fact, I suspect that there is at least something in the pages ahead to disappoint each and every reader. The last thing I want to do is to parrot anyone's party line.

My task has been to ask the hard questions and give you my own best understanding of God's will, regardless of where it might lead. Our task together is to think more critically than perhaps we ever have about issues that are becoming increasingly important as the church faces revolutionary changes at the dawn of a new millennium.

But before we ask even the first question about fellowship, we need to do some serious soul-searching as to why we're concerned about where the lines of Christian fellowship ought to be drawn. Are our motives pure? Are they as Scripture-driven as we'd like to think? Or is it possible that our interest in the matter of Christian fellowship reflects motives more human than divine?

Let me share with you a brief thought-provoking article as we begin our search for Christian fellowship.

Who's "We"?

News item:[1] Monday evening, Jews worldwide will gather for Passover and retell the story of freedom from slavery in Egypt and the journey to receive God's word at Mount Sinai.

Every year the story is told in the first-person plural: "We went forth from Egypt...."

This year the pronoun is the story. Who's "we?"

Who's a Jew?

In Israel this is a raging battle for political, religious and social power. In the USA, a tiny group of ultra-strict orthodox New York rabbis has proclaimed that the faith of 90% of American Jews is not authentic Judaism.

This rift among Jews raises fundamental questions for people of all faiths:

Who is a true believer? Who belongs to the community of faith? Who is a true Catholic? A genuine Baptist?

Who's "we?" And who's to say?

Nancy Ammerman, author of *Baptist Battles*, on dissension among Southern Baptists, says, "The minute you talk about defining yourself, you are talking about drawing lines and boundaries."

Then fighting over them.

Christians split from Jews. Eastern and Roman Catholicism divide. Islam fractures. Martin Luther protests....And so on and on.

---

1. Cathy Lynn Grossman, "Rabbis' stance raises issue for all," USA Today (International edition) April 18, 1997, p. 7A.

The quest for religious identity and community—the search for those like us in spirit, language, and culture—is not just for preachers, scholars, or theologians.

Every religion is concerned with identity, with delineating who is entitled to its privileges, who carries its burdens.

A Catholic is someone baptized into the church, regardless of parentage or practice, says R. Scott Appleby, of the Cushwa Center for the Study of American Catholicism at the University of Notre Dame.

A Baptist, says Dr. Mark Coppenger, president of Midwestern Baptist Theological Seminary, Kansas City, Mo., "has made a mature decision to accept Jesus as Savior and Lord and commit to the authority of Scripture and to salvation by faith, not by works."

He sympathizes with the orthodox rabbis' effort to maintain doctrinal order in a lax world of easy spirits.

"Southern Baptists and Orthodox Jews are swimming upstream in a culture that adores pluralism," Coppenger says. "We're saying that there is truth and falsity, that you can be dreadfully wrong and wonderfully right, and that it makes a difference."

Fellowship: A Universal Question

When it comes to the intricate issues surrounding Christian fellowship, it is easy for those of us in the churches of Christ to think that we are the only people of faith who struggle with such questions. Yet while we are asking, "Who is a Christian?" rabbis the world over are asking, "Who is a Jew?" While we are asking, "Who is a member of the church?" Catholics and Baptists are asking virtually identical questions. While we are drawing lines and boundaries, so is everybody else. Everywhere you turn the question is the same: Who's "we?"

That we are not alone in our quest for spiritual identity must surely tell us there is something far more fundamental at stake than merely our concerns about correct church doctrine, name, and practice. "Fellowship" has something to do with "identity," and "identity" may well address concerns having little or no biblical basis.

Is Who's "We" the Real Question?

When you consider that races, cultures, families, and nations have spilt centuries of blood in maintaining purity of the group (never more atrociously demonstrated than in the ethnic cleansing of the Nazi Holocaust), what emerges is not just the question, Who's "we?" The question everybody seems to be asking is, Who's *not* "we?"

Couched in the negative as it usually is, the question points to patently ignoble motives. Motives like fear and ego-driven pride. The family fears the ethnically-different outsider who is marrying into a clan. A post-Pearl-Harbor America fears Japanese-Americans to the point of illegal internment. Southern Californians, fearing an influx of Spanish-speaking Mexicans from south of the border, vote overwhelmingly for an anti-immigration initiative.

Call it a fellowship of the fearful, in which perfect fear casts out love. Lines are drawn only to show where walls are to be built as a fortress against all intruders.

As we enter into this study of Christian fellowship, we need to check our motives. Is there any chance that our interest in the bounds of Christian fellowship is tainted by the fear that others might be more acceptable to God than we might wish? Or the fear that says our own acceptability before God depends upon everyone else's being wrong?

In the ego column is the horror spun out from Hitler's fantasy of a superior Aryan race. In the Deep South it was the Ku Klux Klan lynching blacks so that "poor white trash" could claim superiority to *at least someone.*

Call it a fellowship of conceit in which power and politics exercised selfishly (often cruelly) permit the ego-driven to feel a heady sense of being "the chosen ones." With such elitists, lines are drawn to remind others that they don't deserve to breathe the same air as those who are putting on airs.

Again, it's time to be brutally honest with ourselves. Is there any chance that our interest in the bounds of Christian fellowship is tainted by the conceit that we are the only ones who *deserve* to be God's people? Or the conceit that we alone are acceptable to God because we alone have a perfect understanding of the doctrine of Christ?

Human line drawing (often under the pretense of merely articulating lines already drawn by God) is betrayed by its focus on the question of who is *not* "we."

In the field outside our English cottage, I've seen a bunch of little white lambs butt heads with one little black lamb for apparently much the same reason. His crime was simply being different. And, of course, the story is repeated time and again among us human beings when the little black lamb turns out to be a black family moving into an all-white neighborhood; or a Korean shopowner in a largely-black, east-Los Angeles neighborhood during the L.A. riots; or the Jewish tailor and his family who offended German sensitivities in the 1940s.

Self-identity seemingly requires exclusion of all who are different from ourselves. By color. By race. By gender. By education. By economic status. And, of course, by doctrine. We may appeal to doctrinal authority as the basis for refusing fellowship to others, but can we really deny that we are being swayed by an orthodoxy defined by our own particular doctrinal understanding—an orthodoxy which asks only Who's *not* "we?" and answers the question by settling simply for Who's *different*?

Who Then Are "We"?

Driven at times as we all are (even unknowingly) by fear, ego, and sheer difference, we would do well to restate the question in its original, positive form: *Who's "we"?* Who is "we" without having to declare who is *not* "we"? Who are "we" in our own DNA of faith?

What is our blood line? What is our spiritual race? From whence have we come?

Ours is a sublime heritage. We "are a chosen people, a royal priesthood, a holy nation, a people belonging to God" (1 Peter 2:9). Does that give us reason to boast or to exclude wherever we possibly can? Peter squelches any such notion, reminding us that "Once you were not a people, but now you are the people of God; once you had not received mercy, but now you have received mercy."

How dare we who once were *nothing* and *unworthy of mercy* draw lines of fellowship based upon little more than our own need for self-identity? How presumptuous can we be even to pick up the chalk!

It is God who does the choosing, not we. "Praise be to the God and Father of our Lord Jesus Christ....For he chose us in him before the creation of the world....In love he predestined us to be adopted as his sons through Jesus Christ, in accordance with his pleasure and will" (Ephesians 1:3-5).

Chosen. Predestined. Adopted.

All who are chosen. *All* who are predestined. *All* who are adopted—not just you and me. Listen again to Paul's salutation in his first letter to the Corinthians: "To the church of God in Corinth, to those sanctified in Christ Jesus and called to be holy, together with all those everywhere who call on the name of our Lord Jesus Christ—*their Lord and ours....*"

Certainly there are those who, having refused to call on the name of the Lord, are *not* chosen, predestined, or adopted. And certainly there are those who are outside the boundaries of Christian fellowship; who are not among the saved; who cannot participate in kingdom blessings; and who have no hope of heaven.

But the most wondrous thought is not who is *out* but rather who is *in*! Think about those of us who are God's children. For we were dead in our transgressions and sins. Unworthy. Undeserving. Unlikely. Yet "God raised us up with Christ and seated us with him in the heavenly realms in Christ Jesus."

Because of our own merit? Not a chance! Because we are something special? We know better! It is only by God's grace that any of us have been saved. Only by his grace are any of us within the boundaries of fellowship with God. For each and every one of us, God had to take the chalk and run the line behind and around our feet in order to include us within the circle of his kingdom. And he got down on his knees to do it!

No More Fear, No More Ego

If we could ever fully grasp *who* we are, and *whose* we are, and *why* we are, our perceived need or selfish desire to draw lines of fellowship would be so transformed in motive that we could not possibly draw such lines without tears and torment.

To see ourselves as unworthy, grace-saved, children of adoption is to put ourselves on notice that we, of ourselves, are in no position to draw *any* lines of fellowship other than those which God himself has drawn—either to exclude where God has included, or to include where God has excluded.

The best we can do is to make a conscientious attempt to recognize those whom God himself has chosen. Ours is to speak boldly about bright lines where there are bright lines (because they are *his* bright lines) and to proceed with deliberate, prayerful caution where the lines are more blurred, knowing that the areas painted in grey also come from a divine palette.

So who's "we"? We are the most wondrously blessed souls since the beginning of time, and the last people in the world who ought to take any delight in deciding who is *not* "we."

PART I

THE QUIET REVOLUTION

Putting all the ecclesiastical corpses into
one graveyard will not bring about a resurrection.

DAVID MARTYN LLOYD-JONES

CHAPTER ONE

A CLEAR AND PRESENT DANGER

Error is always in a hurry.

ENGLISH PROVERB

A n extraordinary thing is happening among the churches of Christ. In pulpit after pulpit, lectureship after lectureship, and congregation after congregation, a dramatic revolution has quietly been taking place. Never before in the history of the restoration movement has so dramatic a change occurred in so short a time with such little opposition. Who would have guessed that so many among the churches of Christ would abandon their distinctive understanding of baptism or welcome as fellow Christians all those whose focus is on Jesus regardless of whether they have been baptized?

Call it a theological coup.

Of all the doctrines unique to the churches of Christ, none has been more central than the absolute necessity of adult, faith-prompted baptism for the remission of sins. If the practice of early-youth baptism seems at times to overshadow our insistence on adult immersion, and if there is still less than unanimity regarding the literal indwelling of the Holy Spirit at the point of baptism, nevertheless the transforming, initiating nature of baptism has been a core doctrine throughout our particular restoration history. (Not that the restoration movement itself matters in the least—only its call to let the Bible be the sole authority in all things religious.)

Despite the restoration movement's captivating nondenominational appeal for unity, the grand irony was that our particular understanding of New Testament baptism became a wedge between us and others. That wedge, in turn, widely fostered an attitude of exclusivity which admitted no doubt that we were the only Christians.

Certainly it was said by some that we were "Christians only, but not the only Christians." Yet this typically suggested nothing more than that there might be other biblically-baptized believers who, although Christians, had not yet abandoned their denominational associations or sectarian thinking. For most, even that position has been considered a questionable concession. There has never been a general acceptance of the so-called "pious unimmersed," or those whose only "baptism" was as an infant, or even those who were baptized believing they were already Christians. Among the churches of Christ such believers were never commonly regarded as Christians or accepted as brothers and sisters in Christ.

Given our particular beliefs regarding baptism, therefore, it would have been unthinkable for us to fellowship as Christians anyone who did not share our view of baptism, both in understanding and personal experience. Consequently, ours has been a closely-drawn, exclusive circle of fellowship.

The Tie Between Baptism and Fellowship

By contrast, many denominations have the luxury of transcending doctrinal differences if they choose to do so. In response to Roman Catholicism, the resounding call of the reformation movement was *Sola Scriptura, Sola Fide*. If "Scripture Only" sounds more than faintly familiar (like our own rubrics "Back to the Bible" or "We speak where the Bible speaks and are silent where the Bible is silent"), the same was not as true of the rallying cry "Faith Only."

Among some groups "faith only" came to mean that immersion was not necessary in order for a person to become a Christian. In an overreaction to Roman Catholicism's sacramentalism (which included a kind of magical "baptismal regeneration" for infants), descendants of the reformers missed the New Testament's clear teaching about Christian birth. Hence the appearance of alternatives such as immersion by those who are already Christians as an outward sign of an inward grace (the basic Baptist position[1]); or no requirement of baptism whatsoever (just "know and love the Lord," or say the "sinner's prayer" and that's enough).

When becoming a Christian requires nothing more than a sincere profession of faith in Christ, there is obviously greater latitude for cross-denominational inclusion of all those who make that profession. (Whether a Christian is subsequently baptized may be a matter of serious concern for some, but one's failure to do so does not rob him of his status as a Christian.) Denominational differences have less to do with Christian fellowship than with sectarian preferences. In fact, the very word *denomination* suggests *names within the same class or kind*. Mere variations on theme. Divisions within a greater whole. Diversity within unity.

It would surprise many within the churches of Christ to be told that virtually all Protestant denominations—including Baptists, Presbyterians, Methodists, Episcopalians, and others—speak in their various liturgies of the *church of Christ* (meaning the universal body of Christ) almost as naturally as we do. That there is one body, one Spirit, one hope, one Lord, one faith, and one God and Father of all is in no dispute among Protestants. When it comes to the "one baptism" of Ephesians 4, however, there is a curious, almost inexplicable blind spot. On that one, believers are all over the board.

The point is that one's view of baptism contributes significantly to one's view of fellowship. The more narrow one's view of

---

1. Not all Baptists would agree that baptism is merely an ordinance which must be obeyed by those who are already Christians. This statement from a Baptist Declaration of Principle could easily have come from our own literature: "Christian baptism is the immersion in water, into the name of the Father, the Son, and Holy Ghost, of those who have professed repentance toward God and faith in our Lord Jesus Christ."

baptism, the more narrow the acceptable bounds of fellowship. Or to put it another way, there is an interdependent relationship between baptism and fellowship: An exclusive view of baptism prompts an exclusive view of fellowship; whereas an inclusive view of fellowship demands a non-exclusive view of baptism.

The importance of this last observation is that our own historic commitment to biblical baptism is particularly vulnerable to any felt need or desire for a wider ecumenical unity with other believers. If one's top priority is doctrinal purity, at some point ecumenical fellowship is necessarily diminished. Likewise, if one's top priority is unity, then the act of Christian birth must be interpreted as broadly as possible in order to accommodate all those who believe.

It is increasingly clear that achieving unity with others in the wider "Christian community" has become a crusade among a new generation within the churches of Christ, and with it has come a willingness to sacrifice clear doctrinal teaching on the matter of baptism. The result is a revolutionary sea-change in which over a century and a half of consensus regarding both baptism and fellowship is being jettisoned in a frenzy of ecumenical fervor.

Run Silent, Run Deep

Normally such a radical abandonment of settled doctrine could not occur without more controversy. One can only imagine what would happen if pianos suddenly appeared in one church building after another; or what reaction there would be if women preachers abruptly took to the pulpits in droves. Oddly enough, there would be a greater uproar over these more peripheral issues than there has been to date over the two core tenets of baptism and fellowship.

One reason for the difference is simply a matter of visibility: It's difficult to hide a piano or a woman preacher. Innovations which are that obvious would surely stir the hounds. By contrast, less tangible changes—even if more crucial—can easily elude close scrutiny.

A second reason is more subtle still. For the most part among those who are calling for change, baptism is still being spoken of in terms of essentiality. But let no one be fooled. If baptism is still considered to be essential, it is only because that for which it is essential has itself undergone a dramatic change. The adjective may remain the same, but it's being applied to a completely different noun.

Until now baptism has been understood as being essential to salvation, to becoming a Christian, to being a brother or sister in Christ. For a growing number of cutting-edge preachers, religion professors, and progressive congregations, baptism is now essential only to being fully obedient *as one who is already a Christian.* In other words, baptism is essential in the same way that most Baptists and many evangelicals have always understood it to be essential— as merely an outward sign of an inward grace and a command to be obeyed.

Listen closely these days and you will hear a lot of talk about *process.* For many in the church today, baptism is coming to be understood as something a believer does along the path of discipleship, as and when the light of that "essential Christian act" dawns on him in the process of maturing as a Christian. Some will be baptized earlier; others, later. Whatever the timing of one's baptism, the committed believer is nevertheless said to be a brother or sister in Christ.

No one seems to have figured out quite yet what negative implications lie for any brother or sister who *never* sees the light about baptism's "essentiality." If the process is never completed, does that which is supposed to be essential somehow become unessential?

A Process of Contradiction

So far, at least, the language and rhetoric still sound familiar. In fact, the uncritical listener will hardly be aware that anything has changed. All he hears is that we need to have a healthier theology of New Testament baptism than we have had in the past, particularly in contrast to alleged sacramentalism and baptismal regeneration (which some may have taught but most have not). He is even told with a straight face that we have never held a distinctive view of baptism—as if to say we would not really be giving up anything significant were we to begin articulating baptism as other believers articulate it. From all the window dressing, one would never suspect that dramatic change was in the wind.

There is no better example of such window dressing than that which was presented by a prominent speaker in a recent lectureship. With boldness and conviction he proclaimed that baptism is "a decisive dramatic confessional moment of faith." That "'dead' people need to be buried, and baptism is that burial." That "a different person came up out of the water from the person that went down into it." That "when raised from the waters of baptism, you're raised to a new life." That "baptism alters your past and future." That "baptism is your second birthday." That "it formalizes my relationship with Christ." That because of baptism "I have a new family." That "baptism is effective because there is a Word of God associated with it." And that "the New Testament doesn't know anything of an unbaptized Christian."

Sound biblical? Absolutely. Every word. But his three-lecture series was laced with inconsistency regarding the nature of baptism, none more shocking than this statement: "I was saved years after I was baptized. I became a Christian well after [being baptized]." What in the world is he telling us? Does he mean that he was raised to a new life years before he was saved? That his baptism was "effective" years before he was saved? That he had a formalized relationship with Christ and a new family in Christ well before he was a Christian?

The signal he is sending comes in loud and clear as we hear him saying repeatedly, "Salvation is a process, not an event." That's Morse code for the proposition that baptism and salvation are not necessarily packaged together—that salvation can come after baptism...or, by implication, even before.

If he were asked point blank, the speaker would deny that faith alone saves apart from baptism. He would say that he preaches baptism unto the remission of sins. But it is mystifying, to say the least, that anyone taking that position would feel compelled to talk in terms of "process."

Sure, our coming to God is a process. And reaching the point of faith commitment is a process. Even after one's baptism, being re-created in the image of God is an ongoing process which doesn't end until we are translated by death into the heavenly realm. But why talk about "process" when the issue at hand is baptism?

Commenting on Acts 2:38 and the phrase, "unto the remission of sins," the speaker asked: "Do you really believe that you can draw a line down the middle of the page and say, 'Do you believe you were saved on *this* side, or *this* side of the line (...the line is baptism...)?' I think that Paul would scoff at that cottage-meeting, home-Bible-study technique. I'm not sure Paul would have understood the question being asked."

Quite to the contrary, anyone writing about being "baptized into Christ" and being "clothed with Christ" would have understood the question perfectly. What would have dumbfounded Paul is the speaker's own belittling of the question, together with the obvious implication that salvation can precede baptism just as easily as it can coincide with it or follow after it. Which brings us to the next obvious question: What, if not the line of baptism, is the point at which salvation is assured to the one who seeks it? And the only answer can be the point of faith. Faith apart from baptism. *Faith alone*—a doctrinal position which the speaker disclaims!

What can possibly explain such schizophrenic analysis if not the dubious distinction between *event* and *process*—an unbiblical distinction which repeatedly led the speaker into an inextricable muddle of logic and doctrine. Consider, for example, the glaring inconsistencies in the following statements made throughout the three lectures:

Process: "I was saved years after I was baptized."

Event: "I got the gift of the Holy Spirit when I was baptized."

Process: "I became a Christian well after [being baptized]." "Salvation is a process, not an event."

Event: "Am I even saved? Am I even a Christian? I reference my baptism to erase my doubts. I say, 'I *did* give myself to the Lord.'"

How can one receive the gift of the Holy Spirit through water baptism without yet being saved? How can one look back on his baptism as a specific reference point for having been saved if salvation is not to be associated with any particular event? How can one say that he was not a Christian until well after his baptism, yet reassure himself that he is a Christian by recalling the experience of being baptized?

In today's lectures, sermons, and articles, the language is loose. The logic, dodgy. The implications, troubling. And to what end?

If the conversion experience is a wondrous, divine gestation process, baptism is a definitive, womb-departing point of birth. A fixed point. A precise moment in the life of a believer which parallels the very death, burial, and resurrection of our Lord that made the imparting of his grace to us possible.

Christ's death wasn't a process. It was a single, supreme act of divine sacrifice so awful that the earth shook and the rocks split! Nor was Christ's burial a process, but the pitch-dark, ominous dividing line between death and life. And "process" is hardly the word for Christ's resurrection, the most glorious, defining event in the history of the world!

When we are baptized into the likeness of Christ's death, burial, and resurrection, our salvation is not a process. It is a single, watershed event in which our sins are washed away by the blood of the Lamb. It is the moment we cross the line down the middle of the page between spiritual death and eternal life—the very instant in which the stone of captive sin is rolled away and we emerge into the light of salvation glory! Not a moment before. Not a moment later. As Everett Ferguson so elegantly has phrased it, "baptism is the appointed time at which God pronounces forgiveness."[2]

Why All the Doubletalk?

What could possibly explain all the contradiction and confusion in the treatment of baptism we are hearing from our leading lights today? My own guess is that many of them are "wavering between two opinions," as Elijah might put it. On one hand they are loath to abandon what they know intellectually to be the truth about New Testament baptism. Yet, on the other hand, they have a worthy desire to find some way to have unity as Christians with the many sincere, faith-prompted folks out there who have never been biblically baptized.

Whenever you witness this much logical chaos and doctrinal dithering, one good explanation is that there is a civil war going on between the head and the heart. But even that may not always be the case.

It seems that, for some, continuing to talk about the essentiality of baptism is just a comfortable way of feeling better about abandoning an orthodoxy in which one no longer believes. Indeed for others it may actually be a way of hiding the ball from those who might object if they really understood what is being urged. Whether wittingly or otherwise, it is only smoke and mirrors. That which is paraded out the front door as being essential, walks in through the back door as being unessential. At the back door, no

2. Everett Ferguson, *The Church of Christ* (Grand Rapids: Eerdmans Publishing Co., 1996), p. 183.

reference at all is made to baptism, simply to Christian faith and unity.

If—as we are now being told—we are faced with a biblical imperative to accept all who truly believe in Jesus Christ as our spiritual brothers and sisters, then practically speaking baptism becomes an irrelevance. There may be continued calls, as with the above speaker, for "the single dramatic bold movement of coming out that God requires of anyone who has faith in her heart to be publicly identified with Jesus." However, for a growing number of folks among us, there is nothing relative to salvation that is forfeited if a person of faith never gets around to participating in that "coming out."

The kind of wide-open fellowship now being urged upon us necessarily implies that our long lost brothers and sisters in Christ were saved solely on the basis of their faith. To maintain under these circumstances that baptism is somehow still "essential" is to say one thing but mean another. At the very least, we no longer mean what we've previously always meant by "essential."

At the moment, so it seems, the seductive talk about Christian unity is mesmerizing. It *sounds* biblical and certainly feels right. But in the rush to embrace our "Christian" neighbors, some are not stopping long enough to ask whether unity at the cost of doctrinal purity is the kind of unity for which Jesus prayed on his way to the cross.

What Engine Is Pulling This Train?

Why the sudden urge to pursue religious unity at any price? Sociologists might suggest that it's simply a "Buster" phenomenon. As products of broken homes and a fractured society, the so-called "Busters" seem to be searching for a sense of wholeness and community. They are also the most pragmatic, pluralistic, multicultural, and non-judgmental generation to come along in decades. They are non-confrontational, manage by consensus, have little political or church allegiance, and are more likely to form their personal judgments on the basis of opinion polls than upon any fixed ideology.

But it doesn't take a sociologist to figure out why there is so much talk about unity. Undoubtedly at least part of the reason is the very same thing which has prompted every other call for unity: sectarian, divisive, acrimonious, un-Christlike *disunity*! Can we in the churches of Christ honestly plead Not Guilty to such a charge? Having tasted the blood of exclusivity toward others, all too often we have devoured our own brothers and sisters with an equal, if not greater, passion. Could it be that a generation less tied to party affiliations and traditional allegiances is saying to the rest of us "enough is enough!"?

Certainly our own splintered fellowship would be sufficient reason alone to conduct serious unity talks among ourselves. However, the current call is not just for unity among those who identify with the "churches of Christ," or even among those in other fellowships having common roots in the restoration movement. The pendulum is now swinging from one extreme (where even baptized believers are often not regarded as brothers and sisters in Christ) to the other extreme (where virtually anyone and everyone is a Christian).

The most ironic aspect of the so-called *unity* movement is that there are some among us who are willing to push for a more inclusive ecumenical unity, even at the cost, if necessary, of further dividing congregation upon congregation among the churches of Christ!

Unity with others by means of further disunity among ourselves? It's almost as if there is a decided preference for association with those who are on the outside over those who are on the inside. Is that because some among us are embarrassed to be part of the churches of Christ? Are they fearful of appearing judgmental in an era which tolerates everything but intolerance? Are they really that desperate to be mainstream?

Maybe we have just gradually come to see ourselves more as

"evangelicals" than something as seemingly archaic and cliquish as "the brotherhood." Maybe it comes from going to "Christian bookstores" and reading "Christian books" by "Christian authors" and listening to "Christian artists" singing "Christian songs" on "Christian radio." How could all these folks whose music we listen to and whose books we read *not* be Christians?

Surely this brings us to the heart of the matter. How can we say that Chuck Swindoll is not a Christian, or that James Dobson is not a brother in Christ? Are we really to believe that God will send C. S. Lewis, Francis Schaeffer, and John Stott to hell? These men have mentored us, prompted us, and stretched us in our own Christian thinking, sometimes even more than our own preachers and writers.

Closer still are our personal friends and neighbors who are righteous, committed believers. More than just hereditary, nominal "Christians," they are active participants in their churches, are perhaps diligent students in one of the many community Bible studies, and are the kind of conscientious believers who take their faith to the streets of the inner city. Do we not see in them the same zeal for the Lord that we ourselves have—or, to our shame, an even *greater* zeal?

Hard Questions; Harder Answers

The next question ought to haunt us all. Who most appears to bear within himself the fruit of the Spirit: a godly friend in another church, or the biblically-baptized brother who is so materialistic and worldly that he doesn't have a clue what it means to be a Christian?

Sure, that brother sits next to you in the pew every Sunday morning and shares the communion, but you can be certain that he'll not be back Sunday night; and you'll never find him praying during the week, or reading his Bible, or sharing his faith, or "washing the feet" of those in need. Has God really called us to extend fellowship to this baptized brother yet refuse fellowship to our spiritually-minded friends simply because they have never been biblically baptized? Can that be right? Does that make any sense?

The closer to home it comes, the more complicated it gets. If New Testament baptism is to be the test of fellowship, with whom do you most closely relate spiritually: the ticket-punching, thoroughly-secularized brother we've just talked about or a committed, biblically-baptized woman preacher in the Disciples of Christ?

Would your answer change if she preached a sermon calling upon the church to recognize gay marriages? Should your answer change if our brother in the pew (assuming a completely new frame of reference) couldn't be more faithful in his worship and service to the Lord but turns out to be unfaithful to his wife? Surely, somewhere along the line fellowship must have different boundaries, depending upon whether we're talking about *doctrinal* or *personal* purity.

The mere fact that there's been a biblical baptism hardly eliminates problems of fellowship. If anything, it just raises more intricate difficulties. Consider, for example, this set of circumstances. Suppose that this adulterous brother (eventually divorced by his wife) marries the woman with whom he's had the affair. If one day he comes to his senses and wants to repent, must he put away his second wife? Suppose this woman was not a Christian when she married but now wants to be baptized. Can she do that without separating from her husband? If they continue living as husband and wife, are they "living in adultery"?

Surely by now you've guessed where this is going. Suppose your answer to any one of those questions is different from the answer given by a faithful, righteous brother sitting in the pew in front of you. Do your differences with him about any of the thorny questions involved in the matter of marriage, divorce, and remarriage require a separation of fellowship? It's no secret that there are many among us today who think so.

In fact, the issue gets even more complicated when we move from individuals to congregations. Suppose, for example, that there is consensus within one congregation about the issues surrounding divorce and remarriage. Must that congregation withhold fellowship from another congregation which has come to a different understanding? And would you be compelled to reach another conclusion if the issue were not divorce and remarriage but, instead, instrumental music?

What if the issue were women wearing veils, or women being appointed as deaconesses? Or church funds being used to support an orphans home operated by another congregation? Or clapping during the worship hour and using worship ministry teams singing contemporary praise songs instead of traditional hymns?

As you undoubtedly are aware, there is an endless list of issues over which we have parted fellowship through the years. Nor does it help in the least to maintain that we should divide only over matters of faith, not over matters of opinion. One brother's matter of opinion is another brother's matter of faith, and *vice versa*. Given such a simplistic prophylactic against brotherhood divisions, it's a wonder that any fellowship at all remains.

Finally comes what may be the most intriguing question of all: What does God say to us about fellowship when our brothers and sisters in Christ begin to teach and practice open fellowship with those who have not been biblically baptized? Or as they might remind us, What shall God say of us if we *refuse* to fellowship those with whom he himself is in fellowship?

Looking Ahead

In the remaining chapters we have much to think about, much to explore. For all who take God's Word seriously, the question of whom God has called us to fellowship may be both the easiest and the most difficult of questions. Just when we begin to think that the line of fellowship is clear and certain, we are suddenly whisked away into any number of fuzzy, shadowy areas of fellowship, many of which have already been suggested.

In the remainder of Part I, "The Quiet Revolution," we will

continue to assess the present crisis—what has led to it, what is actually being said, and how we ought to respond to it in a biblical way. Some things just couldn't be clearer.

Is fellowship really all that flexible?

Part II, "Five-fold Fellowship," is the heart of the book. Beyond even the present crisis the enigma of fellowship will continue to challenge us on five different levels, each of which presents us with a unique (perhaps surprising) set of fellowship ethics. Only when we come to see fellowship on the broadest possible scale will we fully appreciate the intricacies of any lesser part. And here's where it begins to get fuzzy.

Is fellowship really so simple?

Part III, "Rethinking Sacred Cows," invites us to dig deeper than we ever have into areas that have been either taken for granted or actually declared off-limits. When is a brother or sister to be disfellowshiped? Who is a false teacher? Is there any hope of heaven for believers who are not in the Lord's body? The time has come for open, honest, and critical thinking.

Is fellowship really what we've always taught it to be?

CHAPTER TWO

THE GHOST OF FAITH-ONLY ARGUMENTS PAST

Nothing is more harmful to a new truth
than an old error.

JOHANN WOLFGANG VON GOETHE

I f the theological coup sketched briefly in Chapter One is in fact the "quiet revolution" I've presented it to be, you may be wondering if the case hasn't been overstated. I can assure you, first of all, that the revolution is as much "grass-roots" as "pulpit-led." From the pew to the halls of academia, there is a growing acceptance of the notion that people in other faith groups are as much Christians as we are.

But perhaps you've not seen evidence of dramatic changes regarding baptism or fellowship in your own congregation or even heard about it in others. Therefore, it seems that at least some corroboration is reasonably in order. Without specific examples of what is actually being said, I fear some readers might regard my concerns as premature, or even groundless.

For the moment, then, let me give a fairly extensive review of just one of the many sermons which I could have selected. The speaker is a well-known, highly-respected preacher in one of our larger congregations. I appreciate the fact that within the setting of a local congregation a preacher does not always need to re-plow ground which he may have previously plowed with his church family. Consequently, their mutual assumptions may not readily appear in any given sermon. Nor is it likely that this particular sermon, some of which was obviously "off the cuff," had been honed and refined in the same way as a formal article or a book such as this. Nevertheless, I'm assured that what follows does indeed capture the gist of what was being said. By the time you read this, in fact, the full sermon in question will already have been published as part of a series on our heritage.

Focusing on this particular sermon is not really the point—only that it illustrates so well the approach being taken in the many other sermons, lectures, and scholarly articles which are providing impetus for the quiet revolution. It is the *approach* that is important. The analysis. The flow of the argument. The specific scriptures being used and the restoration sources being cited in support. Grasp that, and you will begin to understand what is happening along a broad front.

From Redemptive Baptism to Salvation by Faith Only

The preacher began by outlining (very much the same as I did in the opening chapter) the exclusivity which we have come to know and practice in the churches of Christ. He then proceeded to share his own personal crisis of Christian fellowship, which began with an eye-opening college course on the book of Romans and its teaching about God's grace and was followed by his exposure to other people outside the churches of Christ:

> But what are you going to do with all the wonderful
> Spirit-filled, Jesus-like, prayerful believers who don't go
> to church where we go, weren't baptized like we were
> baptized, and whose doctrine doesn't line up exactly
> like ours? That was the crisis for me.

Fleshing out that thought he referred to all the martyrs throughout history who had given their lives for Christ. And to those who prayed and wrote books on prayer, as if Jesus Christ were their closest friend. And specifically to men like Billy Graham (for the fervency of his evangelical message); Richard Foster (for his commitment to prayer); Tony Campolo (for his call to Christian service); Anglican preacher and writer John Stott (for his holiness and spirituality); and, of course, James Dobson (for trying to save our families).

His conclusion? "One day it hit me. I needed to come clean on this, because I believe these are God's people, even though they are not a part of my little bunch."

Quoting Romans 15:7 ("Accept one another, then, just as Christ accepted you...."), he suggested that there is a "circle of fellowship" having a central point—Jesus Christ—and a circumference defined by the way that we live and by what we teach about the central message of the gospel. His example of a central tenet of Christianity came in the form of a negative affirmation: "If someone said, 'I don't believe that Jesus Christ really came in the flesh,' that's a big one" (citing 2 John 7-9).

For this preacher the line of fellowship was to be drawn wherever "somebody starts messing with the essence of Jesus Christ and salvation in him alone." It is this line, he suggested, that has always been drawn in our particular heritage. "This is what our people said: 'In matters of doctrine, unity; in matters of opinion, liberty; in all things, love.' And this is what they said: 'Christians only, but not the only Christians.'"

Restorationist Barton W. Stone was then quoted for saying that unity would not come from either a creed, or a demand that the Bible be interpreted alike, or from the same form of water baptism, but rather from "the fire of God's presence among his people." Alexander Campbell, too, was quoted with what might seem to be a *coup de grace* on the issue at hand:

> Should I find a Pedobaptist [practicing infant baptism], should I find someone like that more intelligent in the Christian Scriptures, more spiritually-minded and more

devoted to the Lord than a Baptist, or one immersed on a profession of the ancient faith, I could not hesitate a moment in giving the preference of my heart to him that loveth most....

I cannot be a perfect Christian without a right understanding and a cordial reception of immersion in its true and scriptural meaning and design. But he that thence infers that none are Christians but the immersed, as greatly errs as he that affirms that none are alive but those of clear and full vision.[1]

The sermon came to a revealing high point in the observation that the early restorationists were as committed to unity as they were to biblical baptism. He urged that we, like them, should be committed to the ideal of non-denominational Christianity— "eager to study God's Word and obey it, in humility recognizing that we don't have all truth, in gratitude recognizing that [my own emphasis] *faith in Christ alone is what brings salvation.*"

Unity or Heresy?

That last line alone, in the context of a sermon dealing with how we should regard believers who may or may not have been baptized, ought to be more than sufficient evidence that a doctrinal coup has taken place. For any preacher in the mainline churches of Christ to make such a statement should be shocking in and of itself. That it was made by one of our high-profile preachers (and apparently went virtually unchallenged by his congregation) is more telling still. For as long as any of us can remember, salvation by faith only has been Public Enemy Number One in our many doctrinal disputes with others. And its twin corollary—that all who be-

---

1. "The Lunenburg Letter," *Millennial Harbinger*, September, 1837, pp. 411f., 414; November, 1837, pp. 506f.

lieve in Christ, therefore, are to be fellowshiped as Christians—follows as a close second.

The two implications of the sermon could hardly be clearer: 1) Salvation simply *must* be by faith alone, because there are Spirit-filled, godly people who have not been biblically baptized; and 2) since these Christ-followers in all the various denominations have been saved, we must fellowship them as God's people, as brothers and sisters in Christ, as grace-pardoned participants in the kingdom of God on earth.

With this message comes the calm assurance that we can hold to that position while simultaneously maintaining our historical view of baptism. ("You can. You can," the preacher emphatically insisted.)

A person could be excused for wondering how it is possible to maintain simultaneously two mutually-exclusive definitions of a Christian: one which predicates salvation solely upon a person's faith; the other in which faith alone without immersion cannot save. To say the least, attempting to maintain two contradictory positions on the efficacy of baptism makes a mockery of the restoration catchphrase, "In matters of doctrine, unity...."

And they all cry "Unity, unity," but there is no unity. Certainly no unity on the crucial questions of justification, salvation, and kingdom participation.

Will the Real "Faith Only" Please Stand Up?

If only all the current talk about salvation by faith alone were aimed at a different issue. If, for example, the question is whether our salvation comes via a *faith system* or a *works system*, the answer must be a resounding "faith only!" Of this there can be no dispute. "For it is by grace you have been saved, through faith—and this not from yourselves, it is the gift of God—not by works, so that no one can boast" (Ephesians 2:8-9).

Nor should we ever fall for the argument that baptism is a "work," as if it somehow nullifies salvation by grace. Are we to believe that *anything* we do in response to God's grace is a "work"? If so, coming to a faith in Jesus is itself a "work." When Jesus was asked by the crowd around Galilee, "What must we do to do the works God requires?" (John 6:28-29), Jesus answered, "The work of God is this: to believe in the one he has sent." That being the case, "faith-only salvation," as the term is popularly used, would be no less a "work" than baptism. (Equally, if an insistence upon immersion is legalistic, as many charge, then an insistence upon faith would be no less legalistic.)

The culprit here is a quite different use of the same terminology. One kind of (biblical) "faith-only salvation"—in marked contrast to "works salvation"—is being confused with a completely different (unbiblical) "faith-only salvation." The latter, unworthy imitation declares that immersion is not required for a person to be in the kingdom of Christ. It's a case of taking something genuine and making it counterfeit.

What's happening, I believe, is that an unseemly divorce is being brokered between "faith clauses" and "baptism clauses" in passages such as Romans 5:1,2 and Romans 6:3,4. It is clear from chapter 6 that Paul assumed baptism was part and parcel of the faith by which we have been justified (in chapter 5). For Paul, obedient faith *included* baptism. So to say that "faith in Christ alone is what brings salvation" is correct only if it is clear that baptism is necessarily included in that faith.

Similarly, divorce the "faith clause" in Galatians 3:26 from the "baptism clause" in 3:27 and you end up with the incongruous result that there are "sons of God" (through faith) who are not "clothed with Christ (through baptism)."

If perhaps in the past our emphasis on baptism has wrongly appeared to imply that confessional, penitent faith were somehow of only secondary importance, it would be equally wrong now to transform Paul's "package of responsive faith" into the single, saving element of faith alone. In Paul's view, salvation comes neither by baptism without faith nor by faith without baptism. Rather, God bestows his grace upon those who bow to him in submission through both the inner act of belief and the external act of immersion. As it was in the beginning, so it must be even now: "What God has joined together, let no man separate."

Lessons From Reformation History

It would shock a lot of people both in our fellowship and beyond to learn that when Martin Luther spoke of "faith only" he was referring to a *system of faith* as opposed to a *system of works*. (It was Catholicism's works-oriented religion against which the reformers protested.) Despite our differences with Luther about the form of baptism and its application solely to adults, the fact is that Luther—as well as virtually all the other reformers—believed that baptism was absolutely necessary for a person to be in the kingdom. In terms of what it takes to become a Christian, not even the reformers themselves believed in what is now being taught so widely as "faith-only salvation."

Beyond Scripture itself, perhaps the most compelling argument against salvation by faith apart from immersion is the very history of that notion. It was not until Ulrich Zwingli's break with Luther over the matter of the sacraments that baptism was thought to be merely symbolic rather than transactional. Having argued that the eucharist was symbolic, Zwingli erroneously applied the same reasoning to baptism. Thus commensed a doctrine of baptism which theretofore had been all but unknown, yet which has now become the dominant view among Baptists and most evangelicals.

I say "dominant," yet it is noteworthy in this regard that as late as 1977 the British Baptist Union gave serious consideration to renouncing the symbolic view introduced by Zwingli and to reaffirming baptism as "a personal transition from death to life." In 1983 Baptist scholar Michael J. Walker spoke of rescuing "the sacrament of baptism out of the Zwinglian shadows" and described baptism as "a place of rendezvous between God and man, an integral part of that process of conversion."[2] What irony, then, that we of all people should even think of adopting a view of baptism which only surfaced after some fifteen centuries of Christian teaching and still today is not even held unanimously by those who are Zwingli's doctrinal descendants.

Certainly as it is currently being articulated, "faith-only salvation" is hardly mainstream among the churches of Christ. What's more, you'd have to abandon all logic to think that our consensus understanding of redemptive, cleansing, confessional, transforming baptism can somehow be reconciled, harmonized, or synchronized with the kind of "salvation by faith alone" that has been pressed in our historical discussions with others.

That caution goes even for our great predecessor in the faith, Alexander Campbell, whose personal Odyssey over many years of exciting biblical discovery led him speak of baptism and fellowship in a number of different contexts which are not always as clear-cut and consistent as one might wish. Not even Campbell could escape the fellowship enigma. He, no less than any of us, was caught in an inescapable conflict at any point where his earnest desire to find fellowship with spiritually-minded unbaptized believers led him to say that they were Christians as much as those believers who had "a cordial reception of immersion in its true and scriptural meaning and design."

How Quickly the Water Has Evaporated!

If in fact the *true* and *scriptural* meaning of immersion is that baptism is an integral part of becoming a Christian, then Campbell's analogy of a person without "clear and full vision" fails. The only consistent analogy would be that of a person who was never born—never "born again" into the kingdom. Jesus' familiar answer to Nicodemus—"I tell you the truth, no one can enter the kingdom

---

2. Michael J. Walker, "Baptist Worship in the Twentieth Century," in H. Leon McBeth, *The Baptist Heritage* (Nashville, TN: Broadman Press, 1987), pp. 514ff.

of God unless he is born of water and the Spirit" (John 3:5)—raises the crucial question both to Alexander Campbell and to us: Can a person be a Christian without ever having entered the kingdom of God?

The obvious answer can only be sidestepped by taking the view held by some that the "water" of which Jesus spoke was not the water of baptism (a mistake which Campbell himself never made). Such an understanding of the passage is decidedly strained, especially since immediately after this conversation Jesus and his disciples went out into the Judean countryside, "where he spent some time with them, and baptized." As also did John, who was "baptizing at Aenon near Salim, because there was plenty of water, and people were constantly coming to be baptized" (John 3:22-23).

Water, water everywhere, and all the faith-only arguments did shrink.

Is it really so out-of-bounds to suggest to the person of faith that he, like Saul, should "get up, be baptized and wash his sins away"? Have we been so wrong in taking Peter's words at face value, that baptism—being an obedient response to God's grace—"saves you" (1 Peter 3:20,21)? If we have been completely off base on these texts, then why has there been no frontal attack on our flawed understanding of such pivotal passages? If, on the other hand, those texts actually say what they appear to say, then the further question is begged: Can a person be a Christian without having his or her sins forgiven?

And in light of Acts 2:38, where believers on the day of Pentecost were commanded to repent and be baptized *for the forgiveness of your sins,"* can it really be said that baptism has absolutely nothing to do with our being forgiven?

Getting the Cart Before the Horse

When one *starts* with Scripture and *stays* with Scripture, the texts pertaining to Christian birth are clear and unequivocal: baptism is an essential prerequisite to forgiveness, salvation, and kingdom fellowship. At that point Christian unity finds its natural boundary around all those who have been immersed in faith into the family of God.

By contrast, when one goes about it backwards—starting, instead, with subjective feelings about where the boundaries of Christian unity ought to be—the inevitable result is an end run around the many texts which speak so clearly about how we come into a saved, forgiven relationship with God.

To those who think otherwise I propose this simple challenge: Make the case *first* for salvation on the basis of faith alone, without any reference whatsoever to fellowship. If you can do that, then you are entitled to draw your conclusion that fellowship in Christ extends to all who truly believe. Not only is that approach more sensible, it is more honest. Backing into a faith-only conclusion solely because of a pre-commitment to a wider Christian fellowship ignores altogether what Scripture tells us about the meaning and purpose of baptism.

Barton Stone was absolutely correct, of course, in saying that unity does not come solely from the correct practice of water baptism but rather from "the fire of God's presence among his people." Form doesn't always produce substance. (For that matter there is plenty of documented division, strife, and exclusivity among those of the faith-only persuasion.) But when the apostle Paul rebuked the Corinthians for their squabbling and division (1 Corinthians 1:10-17), he called them back to their own individual baptisms as the very bedrock of Christian unity.

Whereas Paul based his plea for unity upon their commonly-experienced act of being baptized into the one body of Christ, today's plea for unity declares that baptism is no longer essential for Christian unity. Could Paul have been so mistaken?

Furthermore, as Barton Stone himself likely would have answered today's ecumenicals, *enthusiastic disobedience* is no more acceptable to God than *unenthusiastic obedience*. Need we be reminded of Samuel's rebuke to King Saul (in 1 Samuel 15:22) about the relative virtues of *sacrifice* and *obedience*? Or Paul's insistence (in Romans 10:2) that *zeal* and *knowledge* are not interchangeable values on the spiritual market?

Whatever else we or others may preach about the importance of baptism (whether for forgiveness of sins or for after-the-fact obedience), today's all-inclusive version of Christian unity necessarily implies that being a "wonderful Spirit-filled, Jesus-like, prayerful believer" precludes the need for baptism *in order to be a brother or sister in Christ.* Implicit in the call for unity among all who believe is the clear signal that baptism isn't really necessary *for being in Christ* as long as there is observable zeal in the name of Christ.

Apart from the obvious error in these subtle messages, what kind of unity could possibly be achieved when it is built upon the shifting sands of, at best, scriptural misunderstanding; or, at worst, wilful disobedience?

About that Center and Circumference...

There is yet another way in which the cited sermon got the cart before the horse. It happened when the preacher defined the circumference of his "circle of fellowship" by the twin criteria of "the way we live" and "the way we teach about the central message of the gospel." Certainly he was right in saying "You can't live in wilful disobedience to God's Word and remain in the church's fellowship." But the implied unity argument—that *living righteously* puts a person into Christ's "circle of fellowship"—simply does not follow. You can't describe the entry door by describing a separate exit door. In the New Testament, they are not the same door. What it takes to be *fellowshiped* is not simply the opposite of what it takes to be *disfellowshiped.*

For that matter not even living disobediently is alone sufficient to kick a person out of the kingdom. (If it were, none of us would be left.) Paul repeatedly rebuked sinful brothers and sisters, referring to them as fellow partakers in the kingdom. In his Ephesian letter, for example, he appealed to "fellow citizens with God's

people and members of God's household" that they put away the
sins of falsehood, anger, stealing, unwholesome talk, bitterness,
brawling and slander, sexual immorality, and greed, "because these
are improper *for God's holy people*" (Ephesians 2:19; 4:25-5:3).

For Paul the circumference of Christian fellowship is not defined by righteous living—as important as that is—but by whatever it takes to be "fellow citizens with God's people" and "members
of God's household." *Faith?* Indeed. "You are all sons of God
through faith in Christ Jesus..." (Galatians 3:26). *Faith alone?* Indeed not, "...for all of you who were baptized into Christ have
clothed yourselves with Christ" (Galatians 3:27).

The second part of the preacher's criteria for determining the
circumference is equally convoluted. To say that a person is *excluded* from the "circle of fellowship" for denying that Jesus Christ has
come in the flesh (2 John 7-9) tells us little about what a person
must positively affirm about the gospel in order to be *included* within the circle. Does affirming the opposite—that Jesus Christ *has*
come in the flesh—bring a person within the "circle of fellowship?"
I can point you to some New-Agers who believe at least that.

If the circumference of fellowship is to be determined by "the
central tenets of Christianity," as suggested, then how about Paul's
own list, which he specifically associated with keeping "the unity
of the Spirit through the bond of peace" (Ephesians 4:3-6)? If I'm
not mistaken, Paul listed seven central tenets, not just six. Is Paul's
"one baptism" any less central than his "one Lord," or his "one
faith?" Has his "one baptism" nothing whatsoever to do with the
"one body?"

It just won't do to define orthodoxy by describing heresy. Or
to determine who is on the inside of the "circle of fellowship" by
talking about who is on the outside.

Being Careful About Context

It is always convenient, of course, simply to assume the very
conclusions we want to reach. That happens every time the unity

advocates cite someone like Barton Stone referring to "the fire of God's presence *among his people*;" or quote such unity passages as Romans 15:7—"Accept one another, then, *just as Christ accepted you.*"

In such usage there is an uncritical assumption that all believers are in fact included "among God's people," or are encompassed within "those whom Christ has accepted." I can't be certain of Barton Stone's specific frame of reference; but it's no secret that in Paul's letter to the Romans there is explicit implication that all the saints in Rome have been "*baptized into* Christ" (Romans 6:3).

In recent years there has been considerable (legitimate) criticism of "proof-texting" out of context, with much of the censure coming from the same people who are now using the unity passages so indiscriminately. Careful scholarship demands that we not cite calls for unity within a specific target group and apply them loosely to unity between that group and those outside the group.

In each case we must ask, Who is being addressed? To whom is the plea for unity being made? Merely because Paul speaks of the need for unity, does it follow that he is calling for unity between baptized believers and unbaptized believers? Is there anything in the context to suggest that he has anything in mind other than unity among those believers whose baptism he takes for granted?

Of all the unity passages, John 17:20-26 would certainly be the easiest for someone to cite in support of Christian fellowship with all who profess to know Christ. (In fact, this text was read prior to the sermon under discussion.) Jesus, of course, prayed on that occasion for "those who believe in me...that all of them may be one." No mention of baptism; only faith. Yet there is nothing singularly peculiar about that. Because faith is the threshold commitment leading to a person's baptism, it is faith, not baptism, which is the linchpin of our conversion experience.

Undoubtedly this is why the so-called "Great Commission" is worded as it is: "Go into all the world and preach the good news to all creation. Whoever believes and is baptized will be saved, but whoever does not believe will be condemned" (Mark 16:15-16). If a person does not first believe in Jesus, there will be no personally-chosen baptism. That said, is anyone prepared to contend from this passage that baptism is not inextricably linked with salvation, and by implication with Christian fellowship? To suggest that Jesus prayed for unity among all believers without further qualification would force us back to the clearly unacceptable conclusion that the saved and the unsaved are to be one in Christ.

Understood in their proper context, all of the unity passages in the New Testament presuppose a mutual relationship with Christ in which faith-prompted, redemptive, salvational baptism has played an indispensable role.

Getting the Restorationists Right

Sadly it is not just the biblical writers who have been taken out of context. The same goes for men like Campbell and Stone who have been enlisted in support of the "faith-only" revolution. Naturally these uninspired, fallible men are not to be regarded as authoritative in any opinion which they might have held. But as long as they are being quoted, we owe it to them to set the record straight.

Of one thing there can be no doubt: Neither Campbell nor Stone would have any part in today's reincarnation of the old "faith-only" argument. In response to John Rogers in 1842, Stone observed that "We all, like others, once believed that a man must be saved before he should be baptized."[3]

Stone explained that he had formerly regarded himself as being saved without immersion in the same way that he understood Cornelius to have been saved on the basis of his godly faith and pious life.[4] But restudying Acts 11:14 ("He [Peter] will bring you a message through which you and all your household will be

---

3. *Christian Messenger*, vol. 12, June, 1842, p. 226.
4. "To Archippus," *Christian Messenger*, vol. 5, May, 1831, pp. 103-109.

saved"), Stone had been compelled to change his mind. "What! He so pious, so benevolent, so engaged in prayer, cleansed, and accepted of God, and yet not saved! So says the scripture...therefore Cornelius has not received the remission of sins...previous to his baptism."[5]

Having more fully grasped God's plan of salvation, Stone saw the issue in stark terms: There were not two plans revealed—one with baptism and another without.[6] For Stone at his prime, "faith-only salvation" was a wholly unbiblical notion.

All of this, of course, is light years away from where the preacher's reference to Barton Stone seemed to lead on the question of Christian unity. When Stone said that unity would not result from water baptism but rather from "the fire of God's presence among his people," he was by no means implying that "wonderful Spirit-filled, Jesus-like, prayerful believers" are saved apart from baptism or are to be fellowshiped as partakers of the kingdom. Had Stone been sitting in the audience when his full understanding was only partially represented, he undoubtedly would have risen to his feet in horror and amazement.

And then there is the Alexander Campbell quote which the preacher used. What he did not tell his audience was that Campbell later commented on that very statement by way of clarification.[7] "I wish," said Campbell, ruefully, "I should not have been addressed on this subject by the worthy sister so often named" (the one from Lunenburg, Virginia, who had asked the original question—Who is a Christian?). "But we are all learning and progressing towards perfection," he conceded.

Campbell attempted to extricate himself from the controversy which had arisen over his earlier statement by showing that the term "Christian" can be used in a number of senses: 1) As simply a

---

5. "Remarks on Elder D. Purviance's Communication," *Christian Messenger*, vol. 7, January, 1833, p. 17.
6. *Christian Messenger*, vol. 12, June, 1842, p. 291.
7. *Millennial Harbinger*, December, 1837, pp. 561-567.

follower of Christ; or 2) in a national sense (for example, those "Christian nations" which *profess Christianity*); or 3) in the special sense of *how one puts on Christ* (in which case it includes faith, repentance, and immersion); or 4) *the style of life which one leads.* This last category, said Campbell, is "the sense in which I used the term in the obnoxious phrase first quoted by our sister of Lunenburg." He had not, he stressed, used the term *Christian* "in its strictest biblical import," but "in its best modern acceptation."

Referring to those unimmersed believers whose lives were nevertheless lived in the *style* of Christians, Campbell reckoned that *"they should not enter into all the blessings of the kingdom on earth."*

What simply has to be remembered about the early restoration leaders is that they did not have the luxury of hindsight as we do. For them the very idea of trying to restore New Testament Christianity was a fresh enterprise. In the process of emerging from traditional denominational thinking, they quite understandably had many false starts.

As beneficiaries of their heroic struggle we do both them and ourselves a disservice to play fast and loose with our heritage. If we have reason to honor them for their commitment to Christian unity, we likewise have reason to honor their dogged search for the biblical basis on which that unity was to be achieved. In the end that basis was not "faith-only salvation." Nor was it the piety of professing believers. It was kingdom participation, granted by the grace of God and received through faith-prompted immersion into Jesus Christ.

What To Do With Our Godly Neighbors?

This brings us full circle to the preacher's opening question, What are we going to do with all the godly believers who haven't been baptized as we've been baptized? We simply have no option. We must honor their faith and then endeavor to teach them the way of the Lord more perfectly! It is not without some irony that the point of doctrine about which Apollos needed further teaching from Priscilla and Aquila (in Acts 18:24-28) was baptism. Could a better example be found of a fervent, committed believer in Christ than Apollos? Even so, his ignorance of Christian baptism warranted loving confrontation and corrective instruction.

The same was true of the disciples in Ephesus (Acts 19) who had not heard of the Holy Spirit. Paul didn't just say, "Don't worry about it. Because of your great faith you're automatically Spirit-filled." Instead he taught them more adequately about the meaning and purpose of baptism into Christ—particularly as it relates to receiving the Holy Spirit—and then baptized them in the name of Jesus.

How can we have loving unity with our godly friends without telling them frankly that they are not yet in the kingdom? How can we regard them as being "Spirit-filled" yet not introduce them to the "washing of rebirth" by which the true renewing of the Spirit takes place? How can we embrace them as fellow Christians and never once mention that they are not in a state of forgiveness?

Friends don't let friends continue under the illusion that they're saved when they're not.

If we are truly concerned about our godly friends who have never been baptized into Christ, we will not speak of family unity until we have spoken to them about how a person is *born* into the family. Merely wishing someone were your brother doesn't make him one.

Regrettably, current calls for ecumenical fellowship are conspicuously silent about the need for baptism as a prerequisite (like faith, repentance, and confession) to kingdom fellowship. But then, why should there not be silence? What reason do we have to teach anyone else about *redemptive* baptism if we ourselves see its significance in terms of discipleship and obedience, but unrelated to in-Christ, kingdom salvation?

Even if the melody nostalgically lingers on, for some among us the music has stopped. By transforming completely what it means for baptism to be "essential," they may still believe that baptism retains great significance, but they have given up on the precise significance which Scripture itself has given to baptism.

So don't fall for the latest headline, "Christ Calls for Greater Unity Among His Followers." The story isn't about the need for greater harmony among saved ones in the kingdom—a story which desperately needs telling. It's about a doctrinal departure of disastrous proportions—an appealing bit of fiction which never should have been told and which ought never to be repeated.

CHAPTER THREE

NOT BY OVERNIGHT EXPRESS

The sixteenth century said, "Responsibility to God."
The present nineteenth says, "The brotherhood of man."

CHARLES LEMUEL THOMPSON

Most coups seem to happen overnight. You pick up the morning paper and discover that the ruling government in some Latin American country was overthrown by a military junta in a midnight massacre. Of one thing you can be sure: behind the scenes the stage had already been set. It may look as though it happened overnight, but what led to the moment of truth was put into place over a much longer period of time.

What we are seeing now in our own theological coup has resulted from the convergence over time of several seemingly unrelated factors. To properly understand "the quiet revolution" we'd do well to go back and find out where it came from. If perhaps its timing was unexpected, its inevitability was predictable.

In the following pages, please allow me to paint with a broad brush without at the same time tarring every congregation with the same brush. Some of my observations may be apropos to us all; others may fit only a few. So when I use the word "we," I may not necessarily be describing "you."

Overall trends is that which is of interest here, not wholesale brotherhood bashing—itself a trendy enterprise. Although there is much which could be said positively about the church these days (especially a growing desire for spirituality and freshness of expression), there are also many disturbing causes contributing to the current crisis of fellowship.

Can You Spell Biblical Illiteracy?

Consider first of all the rampant biblical illiteracy evident among a fellowship of believers who once were known for being people of the Book.

In one Bible class after another the diligent quest for an authoritative "book, chapter, and verse" on such subjects as Christian fellowship has been replaced by banal discussion of *books about the Book* or, worse yet, by the latest psycho-babble on everything from marriage and parenting to dieting and codependency. The memorization of passages is all but ancient history, and adult classes rarely rise above the level of Scripture proficiency once expected in junior high.

Year after plodding year, fifty-, sixty-, and seventy-year-olds answer the same elementary questions about the text that they were asked as teenagers. Everyone knows the questions. Everyone knows the answers. Hardly anyone knows the point. Digging too deeply, or asking hard questions, or making relevant application to our own lives seems almost forbidden. What teacher today dares demand homework, or background reading, or even critical thinking during the class time?

From top to bottom in congregation after congregation, Sunday fare is milk, not meat. Make that *skim* milk.

In our time of worship the music ministry has invaded space once dedicated to the ministry of the Word. Lately we're so focused on praising God that we don't seem to have time to listen to what he's telling us. A sermon longer than twenty minutes is an affront to our collective attention deficit disorder. And any congregation with two morning services is a slave to the printed program and the ticking of the clock. We hardly "take time to be holy," or even to be informed.

It's not just a matter of minutes, of course, whether fifteen or ninety. The real problem is the lack of substance in our sermons. Are we taking God's Word seriously, or are we fearful of confronting our comfortable lifestyles? Are we preaching a steady diet of grace and love without due attention to obedience and commitment? Whatever the topic, do we take the time to mine the great depths of God's amazing revelation? The danger is that with each passing year the written Word becomes more and more marginalized by other, seemingly more inviting, forms of worship activities.

Sadly, the illiteracy begins early. Too many youth ministries, pressured by parents to entertain the troops, have dropped the ball when it comes to training young people in methods of doing serious Bible study. Of course many parents themselves have already dropped the ball—at home, where Bible stories and table talk ought to have laid a strong foundation by the time children get old enough to do serious study. It's television, videos, and computer games that grab the kids' attention in the home. When church kids know more about Barney than Barnabas and spend more time with soccer than with Scripture, their study habits for a lifetime have already been set as surely as if plastered in a splint.

Our people, both young and old, have been destroyed for lack of knowledge. When those in the pew are ignorant of the Word, it should not be surprising that those in the pulpit can wander from the Word unchallenged and unchecked.

When the popular young preacher urges us to accept our unbaptized neighbors as brothers and sisters in Christ because the apostle Paul told the saints in Rome that "whoever confesses that Jesus is Lord" is saved, who in the audience will think of Matthew 7:21? How many will greet the preacher as they leave the building with the usual, fawning "Fine sermon today," and how many will ask, "How do you reconcile Paul's words with Jesus' own warning that not everyone who says to him, 'Lord, Lord,' will enter the kingdom of heaven?"

Whatever the issue, a biblically-illiterate church is a church perpetually poised on the brink of doctrinal disaster.

Satisfying the Church-Growth Feeding Frenzy

The biblically-illiterate church is also likely to be a spiritually-dead church. And so we have been, across the board. Congregation after congregation just going through the motions. Just maintaining. No smoke, no fire. Not growing, only slowing. (Should the Boston movement have come as a surprise? Cult that they have become, no one can blame them for wanting to move most of us off dead center.)

So how do we stoke the fire? How do we breathe life into the corpse? How do we get the church growing again? Surely evangelism ought to be the key, but that brings us to an interesting story.

In the first century the New Testament church experienced phenomenal growth. Enthusiasm was in the air. It was an exciting time to be a Christian. And a dangerous time. The disciples faced something few of us have ever faced: persecution. Did that put an end to the growth, enthusiasm, and excitement? To the contrary. "Those who had been scattered preached the word wherever they went" (Acts 8:4). And the church grew by leaps and bounds.

In the days of the apostles, evangelism was accomplished by proclamation. The gospel was preached, and those who heard the good news with open hearts flooded into the church. It was like cloning. One became two; two became four; and four became eight. And much the same could be said of the early years of the restoration movement when the notion of following apostolic example to the "T" was a fresh, invigorating idea.

Over the years, however, the church began to ossify. By and large, we circled the wagons and hunkered down. Like the remnant in the days of Haggai, we left off building God's house and concentrated on putting fine paneling in our own homes. We moved from being an on-fire sect to a tradition-bound denomination. If we proclaimed the Word, it was from the pulpit, not from house to house or from heart to heart.

So how did we grow? In the period of the world wars it was evangelism by procreation. Quite simply, families in the church gave birth to the next generation of Christians. We "grew up in the church." And thanks to big families with five, six, maybe ten kids, the church grew exponentially.

But the advent of the modern family with 2.3 kids and a dog put an end to that. Unless we baptized the dog, we could hardly expect to maintain our own ranks, much less grow. We weren't even keeping all the kids. Some of them became converts to an ever-more-enticing material world. Some of them were simply bright enough to figure out that we weren't exactly the dynamic New Testament church we pretended to be, and off they went in their disillusionment.

So, what to do? How were we going to get the church growing again? In typical American fashion, many congregations first tried gimmicks. Everything from joy buses (which were bought from the denominational church down the street), to kitchens, to gymnasiums. Grab the kids and maybe we'll get their parents. (Sometimes, praise God, it actually worked!) If we just feed the older folks' stomachs and appeal to the young folk's insatiable appetite for sports, thought some, we'll keep the attendance high. Whether or not it actually made many converts, the country club approach was a definite drawing card.

But the competition became stiff. Every congregation in the area was vying for the same limited pool of church members. Besides, neighborhoods were changing, and white flight sent our people in panic out of the city centers and into the suburbs. Older congregations were abandoned, leaving their cavernous buildings to become empty mausoleums and their aging members mere caretakers.

It was then that the Wal-Mart Syndrome set in. Out in the suburbs, yuppie families began to look for churches that met their felt needs. Translate that: a church with a good youth program for the kids; a dynamic, cutting-edge preacher; and an upbeat, exciting worship format. Churches which fit that formula grew; churches which didn't, died. Typically that meant the rich got richer and the poor got poorer. Big churches got bigger; small churches got small-er. It became the era of the mega-church.

Of course, growth in the mega-churches was mostly an illu-sion. They weren't growing in real terms, only swelling. In a varia-tion on what Paul had in mind, they "robbed other churches." They were evangelizing not by *proclamation* or by *procreation* but by *amalgamation*.

It became the era of church growth. No, not great evangelistic crusades in which thousands of unbelievers were brought to Christ through the proclamation of the gospel. I'm talking about the cot-tage industry of church-growth seminars, church-growth books, and church-growth theories—complete with reverential pilgrim-ages to Bill Hybels' Willow Creek Community Church, the shrine of trendy church-growth thinking.

Dynamic congregations learned to do market surveys in yup-pie neighborhoods to find out what people wanted in their church. Careful attention was paid to the size of the parking lot, having been told that no church can grow larger than its capacity to park cars. "Seeker services" were introduced to make the church more inviting and user-friendly. That meant dramatic skits and more up-beat music.

For all that, we've begun to realize that we can't compete on the same terms as the other mega-churches outside the churches of Christ. For many among the uninitiated, *a cappella* singing can't match the musical extravaganzas of the big community church across town; nor, for the young people, the decibel level of their drums and guitars. Our concern with biblical guidelines regarding gender roles is out of step with a more gender-liberated "Christian community." ("How are we going to keep our young women if we refuse to let them participate in leadership roles?") And, most cru-cial of all, our historical insistence on baptism isn't sufficiently tol-erant to include just anyone who walks in the door claiming faith in Christ.

So once again many are asking, What to do? How are we

going to make the church grow in the current climate? In an era of non-ideological pragmatism, the answer is increasingly clear: become all things to all people that we might grow big churches. Talk less about specific "church doctrine" and more about a generic "Christian faith." Change the name on the sign outside. Mimic the hi-tech worship productions of the glitsiest churches.

Most important of all, figure out some way around our exclusive views on Christian fellowship even if it means rethinking our historic position on biblical baptism. That way, we can appeal not only to members of the church in the surrounding area but also to people from every other denomination as well. Everyone is invited. No questions asked. Whether it's dress or doctrine, the word is out: "come as you are."

And the more who come, the less objection there will be to accommodating others like themselves. It doesn't take long for the critical mass to shift. Who was it that said the church is always only a generation away from apostasy?

Apostasy happens when we pervert the idea of accommodation. Are we accommodating people for the sake of truth, or are we accommodating truth for the sake of people? When numerical growth becomes more important than faithfulness to the Word, you can be sure that it is no longer God who is adding souls to the church. It is not church growth like Pentecost, but church growth at any cost.

Rationalizing What We've Already Decided to Do

If the story I've just told you about church growth doesn't happen to fit your particular experience, don't immediately dismiss it. The story fits just enough influential congregations to have a Reaganesque trickle-down effect. In order for some among us to justify radical change, it has been necessary to radically re-tool our theology. For that, we have called upon (who else?) our theologians, and they have not disappointed us. An emerging generation of church leaders who sat at their feet is now fully equipped to rationalize whatever changes we perceive to be necessary in order to keep in step with the times.

I confess I could be wrong about the chickens and the eggs in terms of whether demands for changes in practice preceded theological innovation or vice versa. Some of my theologian friends insist that I've got it backwards, and I partly believe them. If the face-value meaning of biblical passages is undermined by a liberalized theology, it doesn't take long for apostolic practice to become just so much historical baggage. Although my best guess is that cultural commitments have driven our theology, and not vice versa, what I can say with complete certainty is that each washes the other's back.

No issue better illustrates the imperative for theological mutation than the call for a wider role for women. Those who are intent on women becoming more visible in leadership roles are immediately faced with Paul's injunction (in 1 Timothy 2:12), "I do not permit a woman to teach or to have authority over a man; she must be silent." (Not to mention numerous other passages, from Genesis onward, to the same effect.)

As I have suggested previously, if you don't like the message, you have to kill the messenger. In this case, the messenger is a particular way of interpreting Scripture. It's a matter of hermeneutics. What kind of lenses are you looking through when you read Scripture? What prior assumptions have you already made about the way in which Scripture is to be distilled and applied?

For anyone who may have been on Mars for the last ten years, much discussion has ensued regarding the so-called "old hermeneutic" and its replacement by a "new hermeneutic." In the old hermeneutic attention was given to biblical commands, examples, and any necessary inferences which might flow from either of those. Using that approach to interpreting Scripture, it is nigh unto impossible to justify a significant public leadership role for women.

Despite being referred to in one article after another (praised by some; pilloried by others), the "new hermeneutic" was most conspicuous by its lack of definition. While seeking to avoid abuses seen to be associated with the old hermeneutic, the new hermeneutic offered little by way of an alternative. (I live in hope that my own offering of Purpose, Principle, and Precedent—as a "not-so-new" hermeneutic—may yet be seen as a more responsible approach to Scripture than either old or new.[1])

When all the dust had settled, the primary difference between the two hermeneutics was mirrored in the very precision with which the old was defined and the nebulous imprecision which clouded any definition of the new. The old hermeneutic was accused of being too fact-oriented, too rationalistic, too systematic, too formulistic, too scientific. The new hermeneutic focused fuzzily on narrative, on story, on being cross-centered and Christ-centered. The resulting Herculean struggle was between two competing standards: the old, *objective*; and the new, *subjective*.

Future historians will look back on our time and point to the fork in the road. It won't be difficult to trace. When you view Scripture *objectively*, you come up with completely different conclusions from those you reach when you view it *subjectively*.

The truth is we need *both* the objective and the subjective. *Both* head and heart. *Both* facts and story. *Both* a church orientation and a Christ-centeredness. *Both* law and grace. We may no longer be people of the Book, but we are definitely people of the pendulum. Having an uncanny ability to swing from one extreme to the other, what we most desperately need today is *balance*.

The Seamless Garment of Scripture

The danger in moving from the extreme of objectivism to the extreme of subjectivism on any given issue is that no single issue stands alone in theological isolation. Take, for example, the issue of gender roles. If one person decides that Paul's injunction against women teaching in public assemblies can be dismissed as merely a

1. *The Cultural Church* (Nashville: 21st Century Christian, 1992), 148-189.

reflection of his first-century, patriarchal culture, then another person is entitled to make the same cultural argument relative to any other issue.

It has angered even some of my closest friends for me to dare suggest the parallel, but the fact remains that the cultural argument used by pro-feminist theologians is being used, word for word, by pro-gay theologians. It hardly matters that we ourselves would never use the cultural argument to justify homosexual behavior. The point is that, once the hermeneutical door is opened to *ecclesiastical* change, we should not be surprised to see other folks in search of *moral* change rushing through the same open door. For today's non-judgmental generation the cultural argument is the perfect vehicle to justify their now-instinctive penchant for wide-open, no-holds-barred social tolerance. ("Paul didn't understand what we now know about the genetic causes of homosexuality, etc., etc."—which reminds us that the cultural argument speaks as much to one's low view of inspiration as to anything strictly hermeneutical.)

Nor is it enough simply to point out a distinction between the legitimate and illegitimate use of any hermeneutic. With only rare exception (think long and hard about this...) every church that has expanded the role of women based upon the cultural argument is now struggling with pro-gay theology. Do we really think we are somehow different? Do we really think that we are immune?

That we are not immune was made eminently clear by more than one key speaker at one of our popular lectureships three years ago. To make the point that we need to be more grace-oriented and caring, one highly-regarded preacher told the story of a young man (not a member of the church) who kept dropping by his office for seemingly no particular reason. Just to talk. Just to visit...until the day came when he blurted out that he was gay.

The preacher then put the question to his audience of church leaders: "What was I supposed to say to this young man?" As if the preacher had been placed in some big dilemma. As if there were nothing for him to say about the condemning nature of sin or the forgiving nature of a gracious God. As if clear biblical teaching about homosexual behavior were no longer a loving, caring, grace-oriented response.

Admittedly there is a vast gulf between doctrine and morals, but hermeneutically it's a straight line. When, by a strangely subjective hermeneutic, the good news of Christ is turned into a pragmatic gospel of inclusiveness, legitimate concerns about gender roles have a nasty way of not stopping until we are forced to include even out-of-the-closet, practicing homosexuals.

Apparently we have forgotten that Scripture is a seamless garment. Pull out one thread and it all unravels. If Scripture can't be trusted in one part, there is doubt throughout. If we undermine its authority in the Epistles, we undermine its authority even in the Gospels. If what Paul wrote concerning women's roles and homosexual behavior is culturally suspect, what he said about baptism and Christian fellowship might at least be second-guessed.

It was left to another keynote speaker at the same lectureship to take us full circle to our present discussion. Taking his text from Galatians, the speaker launched out against legalism, but ended up having swung the pendulum to its opposite extreme. Suddenly we were hearing: "Paul's gospel was evangelistic." "Law-keeping erects barriers to evangelism." "Rules get in the way of the gospel."

What kind of laws and rules did the speaker have in mind? What were our unique "identity markers" which he said got in the way of the gospel? His examples included *a cappella* music, weekly Lord's Supper, and, incredibly enough, baptism! To insist on any of these, apparently, was to promote an exclusivity unbefitting Paul's inclusive gospel of grace. If we are going to evangelize as Paul did, came the message, we must eliminate anything that would be a barrier to someone coming to Christ—even if that means abandoning baptism as a required act of Christian initiation.

When baptism must be dispensed with because it is a barrier to evangelism, we have taken leave of our senses, and the seamless garment of Scripture has at last completely unravelled. The subjectivity of the new hermeneutic, unhindered by any need for objective analysis of New Testament teaching, has marched from seemingly innocuous issues like gender roles, to hints of moral compromise, to tossing out baptism in the name of Christian grace.

And with that, the cultural church has come of age. In numbers too large to ignore, we have moved from an objective to a subjective hermeneutic; from doctrine to pragmatism; from law crowned by grace to something more like antinomian, lawless grace.

It's not just the Chinese Year of the Ox; it's also the year of the theological oxymoron: lawless grace; "faith-only" salvation; and unbaptized Christians.

UNCOMMON COMMON CAUSE

When pulling together means pulling away from God,
a Christian must be willing to stand alone.

MARGARET TROUTT

If I were black, I almost certainly would have participated in Louis Farrakan's Million Man March. Forget that Farrakan is a Muslim, a demagogue, and a racist. All you need to know is that one in four black men is either in jail, just out of jail, or on probation. That two-thirds of all black children grow up without a father in the home. That black-on-black killings are snuffing out the lives of young black men faster percentage-wise than all the famines and plagues in Africa. That black boys have no male role models at home and no men to lay down the law.

Anyone who wants to place blame for the deterioration of the black family in America on political or economic causes is simply blind. The cause of the problem is moral and spiritual. It has nothing to do with race as such; it has everything to do with an absence of male spiritual leadership. In short, black men have gone AWOL.

So when Farrakan appealed to black men to quit blaming the rest of society for their problems and to take responsibility for their families and communities, he tapped directly into the heart of the black malaise. Whatever else he may be wrong about, he could not have been more right about the plight of the black male.

That is why I would have eagerly gone to Washington and joined hands with my black brothers, whether they were Muslims,

Christians, or nonbelievers. For that one day, such a noble cause would have trumped any other religious or doctrinal differences which might divide us.

The same could be said about most wars, in which men come together as one to fight a common enemy. It wouldn't matter whether we were black or white, rich or poor, educated or uneducated, Jewish or Christian. As Thomas Moore put it in *Come, Send 'Round the Wine*, "Shall I ask the brave soldier who fights by my side in the cause of mankind if our creeds agree?"

Common cause has a natural way of transcending diversity.

Common Cause Builds Unexpected Bridges

I see common cause at work when I join with others in the fight against abortion. No one has taken more initiative against this ungodly holocaust than Roman Catholics. Their participation in the right-to-life movement and particularly the Life Chains which they sponsor has kept the nation's attention focused on the issue when most other religious groups were happy to let it just fade away.

On several occasions I have been asked to speak at fundraising banquets for local Crisis Pregnancy centers supported largely by evangelicals. Their holistic concern for the mother and her child seems to me to be the best way to fight abortion. Sidewalk protesters outside abortion clinics may have their place, but in the long run this civil war will be won not on sidewalks or in the courtroom or in legislative halls but in the hearts and minds of America's people.

At each banquet I have been touched by the poignant expressions of Christian faith which have punctuated the evening. Sadly, members of the churches of Christ are nowhere in sight. Quite unbelievably, many among us are actually pro-choice. The rest of us are mostly just apathetic, or perhaps laboring under the false assumption that abortion is a political, rather than a spiritual, issue, and therefore off-limits to Christian involvement.

If the primary mission of the church—as the church—is preaching the gospel to lost souls, I as an individual Christian have an additional personal obligation to support that which is good and to fight against that which is evil. (Salt and light come in lots of different shakers and lamps.) In so doing, I find myself working alongside other believers who share a sense of that same responsibility. Conscientious, dedicated believers. In many cases, unbaptized believers.

On such occasions I don't preach about baptism. Rather, I speak about the unspeakable horror of abortion and about how it is killing America's soul. I do, of course, speak of God and his creation; of our being made in his image; and of our derivative responsibility not to take innocent life in the womb. But I don't speak of baptism. It's not the time. It's not the place. It is not what brings us together in common cause.

Much the same happens whenever I am asked by Christian media to talk about the evils associated with gay rights. The interviewers and those who listen to their programs have a mutual interest in countering a movement which poses a spiritual threat to all of us. If by official state action we are robbed of our ability to discriminate between right and wrong on the matter of homosexual behavior, we will not walk away personally unscathed. Moral compromise on any level fosters moral compromise on all levels. And so the "Christian community" comes out of its own closet to speak against a common enemy.

Linking arms with charismatics, pentecostals, and evangelicals of every stripe, I have joined in the crusade against this outrageous perversion—not only by book and lecture, but also on the airwaves. Sometimes uncomfortable airwaves. Each time I have walked onto the set of Pat Robertson's "700 Club," for example, I have wondered what in the world I'm doing there. For the sake of the cause, however, I put on a brave face and do the interview. (Christian television is one of few avenues I have to promote my books and my message to the kind of readers who care about what

I'm saying.) Despite yawning doctrinal gaps between us, on any number of issues I have common cause with Pat Robertson.

If, as it is said, politics makes strange bedfellows, sometimes moral issues can make equally strange bedfellows.

On the other hand, I often work with some of the most wonderful folks you could imagine. Because of my books on various issues of national moral concern, I have developed close relationships with such people as Beverly LaHaye (Concerned Women for America); D. James Kennedy (Coral Ridge Ministries); and Louis P. Sheldon (Traditional Values Coalition).

Regrettably, on issues such as gay rights, I have more common cause with believers outside the churches of Christ than within. We just don't seem to care. Others do.

As with abortion, when I am speaking out against the homosexual agenda I never mention baptism. Neither baptism, nor *a cappella* music, nor weekly observance of the Lord's Supper is germane to our collective interest in fighting homosexual activism. When specific doctrine is not the issue of the moment, common cause transcends it.

Lest I be misunderstood, I have in fact taken the initiative to discuss such doctrinal concerns as baptism with my comrades in arms on moral issues, doing so (in the manner of Priscilla and Aquila) off-mike and off-camera. Common cause does not create an exclusion zone for respected fellow travellers. To the contrary it ought to build bridges where sensitive doctrinal issues can be surfaced even more easily.

More Than Professional Courtesy

You've probably heard the one about the fellow who was walking through a cemetery and came across a gravestone with the inscription, "Here lies a lawyer and a Christian." Shaking his head in wonderment the man said, "There must be two men buried in this grave!"

Despite its great potential for joke and jest, there really is such a thing as a "Christian lawyer." In fact I belong to a national organization known as the Christian Legal Society. It is a group of lawyers and law students who prize their profession of faith in Christ while also valuing their chosen profession of law.

The CLS is not just a social organization. Members gather for prayer, Bible study, and lectures on matters of mutual spiritual concern. In support of religious causes, they write articles, make appellate arguments, and provide expertise when someone's exercise of religion is threatened. It speaks well of them that they are often in the trenches fighting against the American Civil Liberties Union.

Each year at the annual meeting of the prestigious American Association of Law Schools, there is also a separate gathering of Christ-professing law professors. Papers are presented; panelists discuss issues of common interest; and participants share times of faith and commitment to God-ordained justice.

What we have in common in both organizations is a fundamental agreement on Constitutional authority (not wholly unlike biblical authority); church-state and religious freedom concerns; social justice; and ethical and moral issues. If we sometimes differ regarding methods and means, nevertheless we begin from the same compass point. Believers all, we have common cause.

Keeping Promises, Breaking Commands

When I earlier said that I would have common cause with my black brothers, were I black, the truth is that, even being white, I share a similar common cause. It is not just the black family that is disintegrating. Whites are beginning to catch up with blacks on all the negative statistics: gangs, shootings, drugs, lower educational achievement—all the social ills once thought to be isolated in the black ghettos of the inner city.

Why are white suburbs increasingly facing the same problems? What happened historically to the black family *involuntarily* through slavery (the father being taken out of the home, leaving a matriarchal rather than a patriarchal family structure) is now happening to white families through *voluntary* divorce. And through workaholic fathers who, although technically still on board, might as well be living across town. (Not to mention increasing rates of childbirth out of wedlock, where there is little hope of a male presence.) When it comes to reneging on responsibility for male spiritual leadership, race is not the deciding factor.

For many years now I have spoken about God's role for Christian men more than on any other single subject. Our current controversy over what women may or may not do in our time of congregational worship masks a far more serious issue. The very well-being of the family, the nation, and the church is predicated upon male spiritual leadership.

It was with great excitement, therefore, that I began to hear about a burgeoning men's movement called Promise Keepers. Just imagine...football stadiums filled with 50,000-plus men, hugging each other, praising God, and committing themselves to male spiritual leadership. Unthinkable. Unheard of. An answer to prayer!

A further serendipity was the Promise Keepers' call for racial reconciliation. Here at last was a forum in which both blacks and whites could join together in confessing their abdication of male leadership. A Christian "Million Man March," if you will. Common cause on a spiritual level.

If only...(Why must there always be an "if only"!)...if only this crucial common cause hadn't also become an ecumenical call for interdenominational fellowship. Among the "Seven Promises of a Promise Keeper" (presented in the official book by that title[1]), is promise number six: "A Promise Keeper is committed to reaching beyond any racial and denominational barriers to demonstrate the power of biblical unity."

Can a New Testament Christian make such a promise? Is the language sufficiently nuanced that we could consider involvement

---

1 Contributing authors, *Seven Promises of a Promise Keeper* (Colorado Springs: Focus on the Family Publishing, 1994).

in Promise Keepers to be not a matter of Christian fellowship but a matter of common cause? (Surely no one would suggest that male spiritual leadership is less important an issue than abortion and gay rights—both of which, arguably, are often spinoffs from a lack of male leadership.) Can one be a member of the Christian Legal Society, yet somehow balk at being a Promise Keeper? And how could we possibly object to men assembling in the thousands to become better husbands, fathers, church leaders, and citizens?

This one is tough. We're not just talking about having common cause with other believers. What's different here is the specific promise that the Promise Keeper will ignore doctrinal differences and embrace all other Promise Keepers *as brothers in Christ.*

Is this simply a call (like our own restoration plea) to be Christians only? I would to God it were! But the fundamental question of Christian birth is completely lost in the appeal for interdenominational unity.

There is, for example, this statement (included as one of several to be evaluated in the group discussion guide): "I am ready and willing to meet with brothers in Christ from other denominations" (p. 179). And also this reference by the President of Promise Keepers: "In July 1993, men of all colors and denominations sang 'Let the Walls Fall Down' and then embraced each other as brothers in Christ" (p. 7).

Not much room for nuance there.

Interestingly, promise number seven could be the foundation for true unity in Christ: "A Promise Keeper is committed to influencing his world, being obedient to the Great Commandment (see Mark 12:30-31) and the Great Commission (see Matt. 28:19-20)." In fact Matthew 28:19-20 is specifically quoted by popular evangelist Luis Palau (p.194) immediately following his story of a businessman who was converted over lunch. "Right there in the restaurant, the man bowed his head, opened his heart, and prayed to receive Jesus as Savior. The transformation in his life was instantaneous. He finally had eternal life—and he knew it!"

No mention of baptism. No comment on its obviously signif-icant role within the Great Commission. Just further evidence of evangelicalism's incredible blind spot. Says Palau of God's forgive-ness: "He forgives all of us sinners the instant we believe Him with a repentant heart."

All the more troubling is the fact that, despite making a plea for transcending denominational creeds, Promise Keepers presents its own parachurch mission statement which itself is tantamount to a creed. As for what it takes to become a Christian, Promise Keep-ers replaces faith-motivated, penitent baptism with the so-called "sinner's prayer."

In a specially-marked-out box (p. 10), comes Promise Keep-ers' version of the plan of salvation:

Are You Sure You're A Christian?

You need to do five things to become a part of God's family. If you haven't already done these, I urge you, if you're sincerely ready, to do them now:

1. **Admit** your spiritual need. "I am a sinner."
2. **Repent.** Be willing to turn from your sin and, with God's help, start living to please Him.
3. **Believe** that Jesus Christ died for you on the cross and rose again.
4. **Receive,** through prayer, Jesus Christ into your heart and life. Pray something like this from the sincerity of your heart:

Dear Lord Jesus,

I know I am a sinner. I believe You died for my sins and then rose from the grave. Right now, I turn from my sins and open the door of my heart and life. I receive You as my personal Lord and Savior. Thank you for saving me. Amen.

5. Then **tell** a believing friend and a pastor about your commitment.

It hardly seems to matter that there is not one example in the New Testament of any believer ever becoming a child of God by praying such a prayer. Not one. There are references to belief, repentance, confession, and baptism on page after page of the Gospels, Acts, and the Epistles, but not a single reference to some so-called "sinner's prayer." Yet what else is evangelicalism going to do if it wants to be ecumenical? In order to transcend denominational differences, all that can be asked is a confession of faith.

Bill McCartney, founder of Promise Keepers and former head coach of the University of Colorado football team, wrote the chapter entitled "A Call for Unity" (pp. 157-167). McCartney cites Jesus' prayer for unity in John 17 and then quotes 1 Corinthians 12:13, where Paul wrote, "For we were all baptized by one Spirit into one body." But by the next page he has completely spiritualized away any role that water baptism might play in a person's becoming a child of God:

> There's only one criterion for this kind of unity: to love Jesus and be born of the Spirit of God. Can we look one another in the eye—black, white, red, brown, yellow, Baptist, Presbyterian, Assemblies of God, Catholic, and so on—and get together on this common ground: 'We believe in salvation through Christ alone, and we have made Him the Lord of our lives'? Is that not the central, unifying reality of our existence? And if it is, can we not focus on that and call each other brother instead of always emphasizing our differences?

The biblical answer is that we may *call* each other brothers in Christ, but we won't *be* brothers in Christ. Not on the basis of a humanly-conceived, clearly disobedient "sinner's prayer."

Where Paul pointed to New Testament Christians' common baptism as the very basis for the Christian unity which McCartney seeks, McCartney and his Promise Keepers apparently view baptism as merely a "quarterback option"—an ecclesiastical rite to be administered (if at all) by a convert's chosen denomination. Biblically, of course, that notion of Christian birth is a goal-line fumble. It's not the play which the Coach drew in the play book. How would Coach McCartney feel if his team ran a play other than the one he sent in from the sidelines? Would it make any difference if the players said they did it in the spirit of team unity?

I can't begin to tell you how much I hate having to be negative in any way about Promise Keepers. Take out the bits relating to the way one becomes a Christian, and both the book and the movement are inspiring. On the issue of male spiritual leadership we have common cause. But when the line between common cause and an unbiblical "Christian unity" is crossed, I simply can't join with them. It's that other promise I've got to keep—to be fully obedient to God's Word.

Sadly, I'm afraid Promise Keepers is more than just a little responsible for the theological coup we are currently experiencing. When our men (including many of our preachers) come home from an exhilarating, liberating week end at Promise Keepers, they have committed themselves to unity with "brothers in Christ" who supposedly have been saved, forgiven, and spiritually empowered apart from being born again of the water and the Spirit. Whether they discussed it explicitly or even gave it passing thought, they have just bought off on "faith-only" salvation. It is little wonder then that, on the subject of salvation, one cutting-edge preacher after another now speaks the language of Promise Keepers.

Today we are hearing that unbaptized believers are our brothers in Christ. Tomorrow we are likely to be hearing a flood of euphemisms currently being directed by the denominational world toward the penitent believer. Such phrases as "make a commitment"; "hand your life over"; "dedicate yourself"; "make a decision"; and "open your heart." Unless those phrases are accompanied by the divine command to "repent and be baptized for the forgiveness of your sins," they empty the gospel of its power.

Did Christ Pray for Unity Movements?

I confess it may seem incongruous to join with even nonbelievers in common cause, yet refuse to join in a movement specifically aimed at ecumenical fellowship among all believers. The difference, I think, is between *association* and *fellowship*. When I associate with others in common cause, I am making no statement (much less a *promise*) about kingdom fellowship. Even if the cause is righteous, the association is virtually as incidental as participation in party politics, business organizations, or the local Kiwanis Club's food drive.

By contrast, when the whole point of a unity movement among believers is to bridge doctrinal differences, care must be taken not to join in what amounts to a conspiracy of silence, especially regarding something as elementary as biblical baptism. Unlike other matters of doctrine (such as premillennialism, or tongue-speaking, or worship liturgy), Christian birth is a threshold question. Before there can be unity *among* the family of God, believers must first be *in* the family of God.

That is why the unity meetings which have taken place among baptized believers (generally coming out of the restoration movement) have every potential for good, while unity meetings with just any and every church along the road is immediately suspect. Unless interdenominational unity movements are open to seriously discussing what it takes to become a Christian then our participation only serves to paper over such crucial issues as salvation, forgiveness, and eternal destiny. It sends a wrong signal, both to our religious neighbors and to our own people, about what God requires of one in order to become his child.

In the latest fad—exchanging pulpits with denominational preachers—I find it intriguing that the exchange is invariably with a *Baptist* preacher. Certainly not a Catholic bishop or an Episcopal priest; and, so far, no Presbyterians or Methodists that I have heard of. The day will probably come for all of these; but why for the moment only Baptists?

Surely the reason is that Baptists pose the least risk. After all, they practice adult baptism, even if they've got the timing and purpose wrong. When you're making baby steps toward a radically new ecumenism, Baptists fall within a certain comfort zone. But if all those who confess Jesus as Lord are brothers and sisters in Christ, why not exchange pulpits with Catholics and Episcopalians?

In fact, why limit the unity movement to neighborhood congregations? Why not join up immediately with the National Council of the Churches of Christ (they've even got the right name) and with the World Council of Churches? Since their members now fit our new definition of Christians, are we not under an obligation to seek unity with them? Did not Christ pray that we have unity with them? If so, have they no need even to be taught the way of the Lord more perfectly?

What I think is happening is that some of us are so thrilled to be asked to dance that we don't want to spoil our welcome by posing hard questions. In our euphoria over being liberated enough to wash the feet (on at least one occasion, *literally*) of the celebrated denominational preacher, are we reserving time either publicly or privately to hammer out what Scripture really teaches about baptism?

I wish I could be unqualifiedly thrilled that a couple of our high-profile preachers have quietly engaged John Stott in a discussion about baptism. Unfortunately, these same two preachers happen to be among those who are now leading us away from a biblical view of baptism.

So we must observe this careful caution: Common cause and Christian fellowship are not interchangeable. Common cause may at times transcend doctrine; but Christian fellowship, wrongly assumed, makes a mockery of doctrine.

What's In a Name?

One final note. You may have noticed that throughout this

chapter I have used the term *Christian* in a number of different contexts. In virtually every instance I have used the term differently
from the way it is applied in previous chapters where the question
was, Who is a biblical Christian? Or, Who is saved? Who is forgiv-
en? Who is *in Christ*?

As seen in this chapter the term *Christian* (either alone or in
conjunction with other words) can be used in at least six different
senses:

1) "Christian," as distinguished from Muslims, Jews, Hindus,
Buddhists, atheists and agnostics. Those who profess to be follow-
ers of Christ, even if only nominally, or perhaps by default ("Since
I'm not Jewish, Muslim, or Hindu, and since I was raised in a
'Christian' family, I must be a Christian").

2) "Christian faith," that body of basic tenets to which virtually all who profess to be Christians would generally agree, including Christ's divinity; his incarnation; his redemptive death, burial,
and resurrection; and the eternal Judgment of all mankind in the
life to come.

3) "Christian community," composed of believers in all denominations and sects. Generally referring to active, rather than
merely nominal, believers.

4) "Christian causes," particularly tied to faith-motivated
benevolence and to moral crusades founded upon one's allegiance
to biblical morality.

5) "Christian radio and television," "Christian publishing,"
"Christian authors," "Christian books," "Christian book stores,"
"Christian artists," "Christian music," "Christian organizations,"
"Christian colleges and universities," "Christian Legal Society,"—
all of which operate uniquely from a Christian perspective, as dis-
tinguished from similar, but secular enterprises.

6) "Christian nation," one whose cultural heritage and found-
ing principles are distinctively Christian.

If a rose by any other name is still a rose, the converse is not
necessarily true. Calling a dandelion a rose doesn't make it one.

From the start, it is obvious that not everyone in a "Christian nation" is a professing Christian, much less a New Testament Christian. Nor do all "Christian books" truthfully proclaim the gospel in its fullness. Likewise, not all who sincerely profess to be "Christians" are in the saved body of Christ.

Is it improper then to employ the term *Christian* in these various contexts? Were we to substitute the terms *Israel* or *Jew*, we would easily recognize different usages of those terms even in Scripture, depending upon the context. Never is it better illustrated than in Paul's words (Romans 9:6), "For not all who are descended from Israel are Israel." Or in his reference to outward and inward Jews (Romans 2:28-29). Or even in Jesus' description of Nathanael (John 1:47) as "a true Israelite."

Sometimes these terms refer to the Jewish nation; sometimes, to the individual Jew. Sometimes we understand the context to speak of cultural Jews, who are not spiritual sons of Abraham; at other times, it speaks only of those faithful Jews who are Abraham's true spiritual heirs.

So yes, I believe it is proper to use the term *Christian* in a broader sense, given an appropriate context. The danger (and it is great) is that indiscriminate usage can be as convincing as the most cogent argument for wide-open Christian fellowship. If we merely assume that all things "Christian" are of biblical extract, then we are greatly misled. If we are to determine whom God has called us to fellowship as brothers and sisters in Christ based upon nothing more than the badge being worn on the lapel, then chances are we'll get it wrong.

Confusion about the term *Christian* may be as responsible as anything else for "the quiet revolution" regarding Christian fellowship. Yet apart from careful (even sophisticated) usage, I know of no easy way out. Within its limited meaning, America is indeed a "Christian nation" (or at the very least a *post-Christian* nation). And by virtue of their stated creeds, the Presbyterians, Episcopalians, and Methodists are indeed members of "Christian denom-

inations." We gain no ground by being overly technical in these
areas. It simply calls for greater discernment than is always easy or
comfortable.

In fact, it doesn't get any easier when we focus on the term *fellowship*. In Part II, next, I propose that there are varying levels of
fellowship, each with its own definable constituents, each with its
own unique set of difficulties. As we leave the more immediate crisis of "the quiet revolution," we will begin to explore an often-com-
plicated, overlapping "five-fold fellowship." Far from being a matter of "us and them," our call to fellowship requires nothing short
of the wisdom of Solomon. If there is black and white (and there
is), there is also grey. There are even multiple shades of grey.

At the end of the day Christian fellowship is not just about
bright lines but also (much to our chagrin) about difficult, challenging, fuzzy shadows.

To help us negotiate our way through all the shadows, the
next five chapters present five distinct categories of fellowship as
presented in the chart below:

Universal Fellowship:	The Family of Man
Faith Fellowship:	Like Family
Christian Fellowship:	The Extended Family
Conscience Fellowship:	Close Family
Congregational Fellowship:	Immediate Family

Universal Fellowship is the bond which we have with the
family of man—the good, the bad, and the ugly. By virtue of creation, we are all of Adam's race, all related to each other in the
brotherhood of man. More particularly among the throngs of humanity are those with whom we share a keen interest in things
transcendent and eternal. Together with these "seekers" from every
religion, we search for God knowing that "he is not far from each

of us. 'For in him we live and move and have our being.'" Although it is far removed from Christian fellowship, our shared quest for even "AN UNKNOWN GOD" (as in the case of the philosophers on Mars Hill) provides the very basis for our proclaiming more fully the God who "gives all men life and breath and everything else."

Faith Fellowship takes us one giant step closer to Christian fellowship but is still outside the boundaries of the kingdom. Within this category are all those who actively share our faith in Jesus Christ but who have not experienced rebirth according to the biblical pattern. Sadly, frustratingly, almost unthinkably—they are not part of the family of God. However, because of their great faith in Christ they are like family and may even be closer to us in many respects than brothers and sisters in Christ who are only nominal members of the church.

Christian Fellowship is fellowship with Christ himself, a relationship which comes into being when a person with penitent faith is baptized into Christ and thereby puts on Christ. In this category are all those who have this same "in-Christ" fellowship—all who are washed, forgiven, and saved. It is kingdom fellowship in relation to Christ the King. It is *koinonia* (sharing and caring) fellowship in relation to fellow Christians. For all who are brothers and sisters in Christ, it is fellowship of the entire extended family, based not upon total doctrinal cohesion but upon the wondrous fact that we are all children of the same Father.

Conscience Fellowship recognizes the fact that not all brothers and sisters in Christ have precisely the same understanding of how God has called us to work and worship within the kingdom. It provides elbow-room for the exercise of individual and collective conscience, even for enclaves of special "close family" fellowship among groups of congregations within the wider extended family. Not unlike the separate fellowships of conscience which developed between Jewish and Gentile Christians, this level of fellowship is an important subset within the overarching, more-inclusive "in-Christ" fellowship that all Christians share.

Congregational Fellowship brings us to the immediate family of Christians who work and worship together in local congregations. Under the oversight and leading of its elders, each congregation functions autonomously in good conscience before God. It is within the local congregation that *koinonia* fellowship most directly manifests itself in mutual edification, participation, and sharing. Table fellowship, both around the Lord's table and from house to house, makes possible a fellowship of heart and mind that binds the body together and even lays the groundwork for loving correction whenever discipline is made necessary.

Yet table fellowship is not limited to brothers and sisters in Christ. Table fellowship is a thread which runs throughout the entire tapestry of the human experience—with Christians and non-Christians, with believers and infidels, with saints, sinners, common folk, and criminals. It is a universal fellowship we share simply because we are human beings—a fellowship which we often forget in our haste to draw boundaries of faith. So it is here that we begin our focus on a broadly based five-fold fellowship.

PART II

FIVEFOLD FELLOWSHIP

*Brotherhood doesn't come in a package. It is
not a commodity to be taken down from the shelf with
one hand—it is an accomplishment of soul-searching
prayer and perseverance.*

OVETA CULP HOBBY

CHAPTER FIVE

UNIVERSAL FELLOWSHIP: THE FAMILY OF MAN

If I miss him in Christ, I'll hit him in Adam.

MARSHALL KEEBLE

When disaster strikes, who stops to think about the victims' faith: Were they Hindus, Muslims, Jews? Were they professing Christians? Baptized believers?

As the first reports hit network news about the bombing of the Federal Building in Oklahoma City, not one theological question crossed my mind. Only the question, Why? And who could have done such a thing? And what must the families of the dead and wounded be feeling? My heart went out to everyone involved, especially the family of little Baylee Almon, whose tiny, lifeless body was seen by the whole world as it was being carried away from the rubble in the burly arms of firefighter Chris Fields. Personifying horror on a grand scale, little Baylee gave a name and a face to tragedy. Were her parents Baptists, Presbyterians, or perhaps Catholic? As we all watched in horror, I'm sure none of us gave a thought to such identifications.

When it comes to tragedy, our own faces are reflected in each and every victim. When any part of humanity suffers, do we not all suffer?

The Brotherhood of Man

Hardly a day goes by without news reports of a famine in

some third-world country. Or more likely a civil war, forcing untold thousands of nameless people to flee their homes for crowded refugee camps where food and medicine are in short supply. Before peace returns and they are allowed to go home, countless children and old folks will die. Even today. This very day.

Only God knows how we can continue to live a life of luxury in prosperous nations while so many millions of people live in sub-human conditions. Who decreed that there should even be such a thing as "third-world" countries? Did God create three worlds?

When will we—no, when will *I*—ever really come to accept that these fellow human beings of every race, color, and creed are my brothers and sisters? If only you and I could somehow grasp the truth that we are all part of Adam's race. If only we could come to terms with the fact that in God's eyes we are colorless, cultureless, and classless—each individual a person of infinite worth to the God who has made us in his own image. If we could ever truly get a handle on that, wars would cease, economic disparity would end, and every human being would be treated with dignity.

The question is not so much the classic one, "Who is my neighbor?" The only really meaningful question can be, Who is *not* my neighbor? If I read Jesus correctly, among 5.3 billion people on the face of the globe there is no one who is *not* my neighbor.

I appreciate the fact that Cain was referring to his brother in the flesh, but his question "Am I my brother's keeper?" speaks as clearly to us today as it did at the dawn of Creation. The neighbor, the stranger, the foreigner, the inner-city dweller, the person of different color, the rich, the poor, the righteous, the sinful—all of them, each one—is my brother in the family of man. And to each I have been given all the responsibilities which go along with brotherhood.

Family-of-Man Fellowship

Our particularized use of the term *brotherhood* in the churches of Christ may have blinded us to a much wider fellowship which we share with all of mankind. Moses' law gave this ancient instruction: "Do not abhor an Edomite, for he is your brother. Do not abhor an Egyptian, because you lived as an alien in his country" (Deuteronomy 23:7). On the scale of eternity each of us is an alien, a wayfaring stranger in a world not our own. So do we not have a common bond with all our fellow travellers on the road of life?

"If you greet only your brothers," said Jesus, referring to ethnic, religious, and sectarian apartheid, "what are you doing more than others? Do not even pagans do that?" Loving our neighbors means loving those neighbors we like and those we don't. Sometimes our neighbors are folks that we'd love to hate. Or those we'd hate to love. You know—the "tax collectors and sinners" of our own day, like the ones with whom Jesus happily mixed. The rowdy, the rabble, and the riffraff. Am I to have fellowship with the ungodly of this world? Jesus did.

He also had fellowship with outcasts. The Samaritan woman at the well, for example, couldn't believe her ears. Imagine...a Jew lowering himself to ask her, a hated Samaritan, for a drink of water! "Don't you know," she virtually asked Jesus, "that Jews aren't supposed to have fellowship with Samaritans?" Jesus' response might well have been, "Don't you know that I can't serve you unless I first fellowship you?"

Jesus also had fellowship with those who suffered. When Jesus saw the widow of Nain, something within him struck a chord of human compassion. Nothing indicates that he stopped to question whether she was a righteous Jew, or perhaps a woman who might have harbored bitterness in her heart towards God. On the most fundamental level of human fellowship it simply didn't matter. "When the Lord saw her, his heart went out to her and he said, 'Don't cry.'"

Jesus was his brother's keeper—and his sister's. And he calls us to the same fellowship.

There is that story in Matthew 25:31-46 about the King on his judgment throne. The righteous were amazed and dumbfounded when the King said, "I was hungry and you gave me something to eat, I was thirsty and you gave me something to drink, I was a stranger and you invited me in, I needed clothes and you clothed me, I was sick and you looked after me, I was in prison and you came to visit me."

Looking around among themselves, puzzled, they turned again and asked the King, in effect, "Lord, when did we do these things for you? We don't remember seeing you hungry, thirsty, or needy." But they finally understood when the King said, "Whatever you did for one of the least of these brothers of mine, you did for me."

Which *brothers of mine?* The ones in "our brotherhood"? The ones who are members of the churches of Christ? The ones who are biblically-baptized believers? Or did Jesus have in mind a universal brotherhood among all humankind?

All in the Same Boat

Yet that raises a thorny question first asked by Paul in 2 Corinthians 6:14-15: What does a believer have in common with an unbeliever? If we're speaking of moral, doctrinal, or spiritual compromise, the answer is *nothing.* "Do not be yoked with unbelievers," said Paul. "For what do righteousness and wickedness have in common? Or what fellowship can light have with darkness?"

But if compromise is not the issue, then the answer is that we have the whole of human experience in common with believer and unbeliever alike. Like the rain which falls upon the just and the unjust, so ought also our love and concern to be showered upon the whole human race. It's all about the first part of Paul's encouragement (Galatians 6:10) which we typically run right past: "Therefore, as we have opportunity, *let us do good to all people,* especially to those who belong to the family of believers."

If we have a special obligation toward our own, we also have an obligation toward others. Believer and unbeliever. Baptized and unbaptized. As Paul also said, "Make sure that nobody pays back wrong for wrong, but always try to be kind to each other *and to everyone else*" (1 Thessalonians 5:15). Would that include abortion doctors? Yes. Homosexual activists? Yes. Republicans, Democrats, bosses, employees, postmen, store clerks, used-car salesmen, lawyers, and sweet little old ladies crossing the street? Absolutely. Every one.

To that extent we have Peter's lesson to learn—that we should not call any man "impure or unclean." Whom God has called us to fellowship we have no right to refuse. On the most basic threshold level we have universal fellowship with everyone who breathes.

"When pricked, do they not bleed?"

Just when we think that we have reason to write somebody off, we are reminded that we don't. This, in fact, is the amazing legacy of Jeffrey Dahmer. Not his sexual perversion, nor his horrid murders, nor his ghastly cannibalism, but his ultimate turning back to God. Dahmer's apparently genuine prison conversion is perhaps the ultimate reminder that even the most greatly distanced from us in the human race can never be "totalled" like some wrecked vehicle that is "written off" by the insurance company.

Not even the soul of the savage is beyond redemption. Not even the soul of the savage is beyond our love.

Not Without Limits

Universal fellowship does not mean, of course, that we can't have personal preferences. We don't have to choose everyone who walks down the street as a close friend. There is no law, spiritual or otherwise, that demands we invite just anybody and everybody into our home. In fact, we would be foolish to do so. Discretion is the better part not only of valor but of fellowship.

Nor does universal fellowship mean that we cannot "disfellowship" members of the human race who violate the law and become a threat to others. If as Christians we are encouraged to visit those who are in prison, we are also justified in putting them into prison in the first place. Fellow human beings though they may be, criminals have forfeited the freedom intended for them. In fact, where innocent life has been taken, there is biblical warrant for even the most extreme form of disfellowship—capital punishment. That a quick administration of capital punishment might have prevented Jeffrey Dahmer's prison conversion only makes a more difficult case for the death penalty. It doesn't rule it out biblically. Life for life was God's idea before it was ever man's.

By contrast with punishment for crime, universal fellowship does indeed ask hard questions about war and a Christian's participation in it. Given the number of innocent lives destroyed in forcibly resolving issues typically prompted by greed, power, and ego, war is one of the most troubling of all the issues related to conflict among the family of man. Yet, war between nations is not without biblical precedent, and its ethical resolution awaits another book for another day. Probably by another author.

Suffice it to say that universal fellowship is less likely to challenge us on some distant battlefield than on some sidewalk close to home where we are more likely to come into contact with the homeless and rejected of society. Difficult questions about capital punishment and war give us no excuse to ignore the crying needs of fellow human beings who daily stare us in the face.

How we deal responsibly with a person in each situation may vary according to the circumstances. Nevertheless, in the family of man, murderers, rapists, enemy soldiers, and common decent folks everywhere—including "the great unwashed"—are brothers and sisters all.

Table Fellowship With the Family of Man

Until only recently, we have tended to have a one-dimensional perspective of fellowship: If the other person is a baptized believer and agrees with us on all the issues of doctrine which we hold to be non-negotiable, then we are in fellowship; otherwise, we are not. Period. Plain and simple.

Well, maybe not so simple. In our everyday life we almost

never act pursuant to such a single, narrow perspective. I don't know of anyone—even the most conservative among us—who in a practical sense doesn't fellowship any number of folks on the road to spiritual perdition.

To begin with there are our literal neighbors—the ones who live next door on either side—with whom we share a fellowship of sorts. Certainly we don't snub them simply because they happen to be Methodists, or Presbyterians, or even New Agers. We rake leaves together, work in polling stations together, participate in condominium associations together, and join forces in the local Neighborhood Watch.

By and large it doesn't seem to matter if they are divorced and remarried unbiblically, or knock back a six-pack while watching the Super Bowl, or subscribe to *Playboy*. When it comes time for the 4th of July community barbecue, we plop ourselves right down next to them and have a hearty laugh together about the latest neighborhood happenings.

When we think in terms of Little League, or especially PTA, we might be tempted to make the distinction which I made earlier between *association* and *fellowship*. After all it is the Parent-Teachers *Association*, not even the *Fellowship* of Christian Athletes. Yet here we are not just talking about common cause where we become allies with others on a specific issue, then go our separate ways.

What's different about universal fellowship is our involvement with people *as people*. And I can think of no better indication of real, live fellowship than what we might call "table fellowship." At perhaps its lowest level is the venerable business lunch. "Let's do lunch" is a call, not just for association, but for fellowship. "He who has dipped his hand into the bowl with me" could provide an occasion for treacherous betrayal (as in the case of Judas). But business people are the first to recognize that fellowship over a shared meal is more likely an occasion when barriers are broken down and trust is developed. The same goes for romantic dinners, candles or no candles. How many "first dates" have been an invitation to dinner?

Jumping ahead for the moment, table fellowship in the form of the Lord's Supper is what brings the church together as a body in Christian fellowship; and the denial of table fellowship (in terms of both communion and ordinary meals) is symbolic of broken fellowship between brothers in Christ. As it relates to the family of man, simple table fellowship is an ongoing affirmation of our universal kinship with friends, neighbors, business associates—even strangers.

Multiple-Personality Fellowship

Here, however, is where it gets really interesting. Whether it be in our habits of shared table fellowship or simply in our everyday community relationships, we often apply a double standard when it comes to fellowship. In a variety of social settings we are more likely to share goodwill with non-Christians than with our own brothers and sisters in Christ—particularly if we disagree among ourselves over some (often esoteric) point of doctrine.

Unfortunately, our double standard hurts us in a variety of ways. First, of course, it suggests a preference for non-believers over believers. No matter how sharply we might disagree with a brother in our understanding of God's Word, surely a faith-filled brother in the family of God is due more goodwill than some faithless brother in the family of man.

Second, our fellowship with secular friends can actually become a barrier to evangelism. Have you ever felt as I have that you didn't want to mention anything about the Bible, or Christ, or eternal Judgment, because you were afraid it might ruin a good friendship? Isn't there an unspoken pact with our friends that we will not bring up anything that might cause unnecessary friction?

So most of us end up going to church on Sunday and talking about how our denominational friends are going to hell, but on Monday we have lunch with those same people and never once mention what we said about them on Sunday. Talk about your basic schizophrenia!

If there is any justification at all for our behavior, it may appear to come in Jesus' own ministry style. He was notorious for eating with society's sinners while condemning sin, or (more telling still) while berating the religious establishment. And yet when the religious establishment rebuked Jesus for his seeming hypocrisy, his response had a stinger in the tail: "It is not the healthy who need a doctor, but the sick," he reminded the Pharisees. Jesus wasn't just eating with sinners and conveniently ignoring their spiritual needs.

If our universal fellowship entails looking after those who are sick and poor, it also entails looking after those who are spiritually impoverished. At some point, table fellowship should lead to spiritual fellowship, and hopefully from there into true Christian fellowship. When given a chance, the road from the universal family of man leads to the spiritual family of God.

I'll never forget what someone said about my father at his funeral. "He first won a person's heart; then his head." The person telling me that was one of the many people Dad had brought out of the world into a new relationship with Christ. Looking back, I realize that the way Dad won hearts was simply by enjoying life to the fullest with everyone he met. He loved young and old; scholars and schoolboys; the well-to-do and the down-and-out. And table fellowship was often his sanctuary. He loved to eat and laugh and get to know people.

I started to say that Dad didn't come on like gang busters to cram religion down people's throats the first time he met them. And of course he didn't. But I also have to say that I distinctly remember his way of kidding folks about their lack of faith, or perhaps about any bad habits that might be apparent. In a light-hearted way he always let them know that he was thinking about their spiritual welfare. He gave them an opening. An invitation to talk further about their souls. And one after another they accepted both his invitation and the Lord's.

Universal fellowship is not a "no go" area where introducing

people to faith is off-limits. Universal fellowship is the very bridge
we cross in order to lead our earthly brothers and sisters to a heavenly fellowship in Christ.

When Fellow Man Has Faith

Another danger of having a blinkered view of fellowship is
that we can too easily dismiss the working of faith in the lives of
our fellow man. Our tendency is to say of others, either they are
Christians in the body of Christ or they are lost. Even though that
is true in a salvation sense, the fact that people are spiritually lost
does not mean that they are devoid of faith, or that they have not
grasped for God, or that they don't live lives prompted by what they
believe about God.

The plain truth is: there are other seekers out there besides
ourselves.

In the Bible we read about seekers who were not strictly associated with God's people. There was, for example, the Queen of
Sheba, who travelled long distances to drink from the wisdom of
Solomon. She was not one of God's chosen people, yet she was driven by her faith to know more about God.

And then there were the wise men who followed that wondrous star in search of the "king of the Jews." Who were these
magi? We don't really know. Some scholars think they could even
have been Zoroastrians from Persia. If so, they were hardly Jews.
Whatever their religious background, their search for Jesus was ev-
idently prompted by their quest to know a God powerful enough to
create that guiding star.

It's not just an ancient story. Even some of today's stargazers
have a heart for God.

Cornelius is perhaps our best example of a devout seeker
whose life was a model of faith—despite the fact that he was unsaved. In word, deed, and prayer, Cornelius was a true God-seeker.
Even so, Peter was quite willing to let him "go to hell" if it meant
having to give up his own narrow notion of acceptable fellowship.

Are we any different? Do we need a "large sheet" let down into our own thinking in order to have a new appreciation for faith wherever we find it—a sheet filled with God-seekers who don't fit our mold? God-seekers whom we sometimes actually penalize for having the wrong kind of faith, and whose currency might even be more valuable if they weren't religious at all?

Here's a reality check. To whom would we rather talk: a door-to-door vacuum salesman or a door-knocking Jehovah's Witness? With whom would we rather spend time: our secular friends from work who couldn't care less about anything spiritual or a devout Muslim down the street who is on his knees five times a day in prayer to Allah? Whom do we appreciate more: a Presbyterian neighbor who ignores his family and never goes to church or a Jewish co-worker who is dedicated to his family and faith?

In the family of man, some of the family spend time thinking about God and some do not. Some of our fellow human beings long to be in a relationship with God (in whatever way they know him) and some just don't care. For my money, I'd choose to fellowship a dedicated God-seeker over a faith-void secularist any day. At least with the true God-seeker—be he Hindu, Buddhist, Muslim, or Jew—I have a spiritual foundation on which I can build. If we don't speak precisely the same language, we at least have a common set of phonetics.

I think, for instance, of my friend Moses, a Muslim whom Ruth and I met on a recent trip to Jerusalem. Acquaintance quickly became camaraderie; camaraderie soon became friendship. Before we knew it, we were in his home on the Mount of Olives having lunch and talking about Mohammed and Jesus. It wasn't just a social call. It became a spiritual dialogue. We were seekers struggling to know God.

Of course, seeking is not salvation. But salvation comes from seeking. First things first. Baby steps, then big steps.

Oh, about that initial acquaintance. It began with mutual acts of kindness in the breakfast room of our hotel where Moses served

us our juice and corn flakes. A Muslim and a Christian bridged bul-
warks of faith on the common ground of nothing more than simple
humanity.

A smile. A laugh. A shared concern. An open heart. An invitation. A meal. A spiritual dialogue. It was a natural—make that a
*super*natural—progression.

Seeking Out the Seekers

I confess that I am overwhelmed by the awesome implications
of universal fellowship in the family of man. How by any means can
I fulfill my responsibility to seek the temporal welfare of the millions of people out there in the world, much less their eternal spiritual welfare?

Just today I took a long walk in Cheltenham, a town near our
home in England, and passed one stranger after another. Ordinary
folks, really. I couldn't help but think that I was walking past people who mattered to God as much as I do. People who, I suspect,
are basically good moral folks just trying to get on with life. Yet
people whose souls are in jeopardy of eternal condemnation.

So what did I do? Did I grab them and force-feed them with
the gospel? No. Did I even mention Jesus to them as I passed by?
No. In fact I didn't do anything. Like the priest and the Levite I
passed by on the other side. Just kept on walking and telling myself that they would think I was crazy for stopping them to talk
about their eternal destiny. It was surreal, as if I were watching a
procession of the damned marching headlong into an eternal abyss
and there was nothing that I could do to stop them.

Then came the question which I usually fall back on when I
find myself in perplexing situations: *What would Jesus do?*

It's one of those times when I wish I could have walked right
alongside Jesus when he travelled about in his ministry. What did
he do when he was among the multitudes scurrying around in the
busy streets of Jerusalem? Did he button-hole people and talk to
them about spiritual matters? In many cases (like the Samaritan

woman) we know he did. But did no one get past him without having to be confronted by the Galilean troublemaker?

And what did he actually do at those banquets besides eat? Did he invariably strike up religious conversations? Did he confront the sinners with their sins? Or was he content to build friendships that would blossom into an openness for later spiritual conversations?

I'm always tempted to say the obvious—that Jesus wasn't pushing his spiritual agenda through some kind of phony "friendship evangelism." But maybe that's just the way I rationalize my own woeful inadequacy. I'm good at making the social opening but pretty hopeless when it comes to making evangelistic closure. It's as if I'm waiting for those strangers on the street to turn suddenly to me and demand, "Tell me about Jesus!"

Knowing that people rarely beat a path to my door asking about their eternal salvation, I am forced to seek out the seekers. But that means leaving my comfortable pew and mingling with others of faith, perhaps in their own religious forums. That's why I speak wherever I am asked to speak. That's why I usually write with an eye to those outside the church. Limiting our spiritual fellowship solely to the family of Christ comes at the cost of never extending the family of Christ.

Still, I am overwhelmed....

Universal Fellowship; Universal Faith

The surprise really is how many of our fellow human beings at least pay lip service to God. They may be pagan idolaters, reincarnationists, or spiritists, but in their own way they all recognize "the Great Other." Even the most spiritually callous have some sense of God. Some sense of morality. Some sense of a greater accountability than to one's self. At the very least, a sense of conscience—that universal human attribute which more than anything else distinguishes us from lower creatures.

Referring (in Romans 2:14-15) to Gentiles who did not know

the Jewish law, Paul said that those who are not God's people "do by nature things required by the law." In doing so "they show that the requirements of the law are written on their hearts, their consciences also bearing witness, and their thoughts now accusing, now even defending them."

In my Law and Morality class each year we spend a lot of time discussing what morality is and where it comes from. Inevitably even my more skeptical students are forced to acknowledge universal moral laws which have been recognized by virtually every culture that has ever existed. (Social contract theory can't begin to explain it all.) Universal moral laws speak volumes about the sense of morality found within each human being.

The fact is that morality and faith are matters of *nature* as well as *nurture*. The man or woman without some basic, elementary religious faith is virtually non-existent. Some might call themselves atheists, but look hard enough and you'll find a spiritual bone somewhere. As the writer of Ecclesiastes reminds us (in 3:11), God "has set eternity in the hearts of men."

There is, then, no one with whom I have absolutely nothing in common spiritually. Where faith thrives in some, it is alive in many. Where faith is alive in many, it is at least latent in all.

Universal fellowship then is on a continuum. There are those whose own sense of faith (of whatever type) is as compelling as our own, and fellowship with them seems only natural. We may not be on the same channel, but we are on the same wave length. At the opposite extreme are those who seem to have little or no interest in matters of faith. Yet given man's intrinsic religious nature and moral consciousness, the human being does not exist whose soul is incapable of being touched. The only question is whether we value that soul sufficiently to desire having fellowship with it.

A Special Faith Fellowship

If as fellow creatures we have universal fellowship with the family of man—and particularly with those who, like us, are God-seekers—we surely must feel an even greater kinship with those who seek God exclusively through Jesus Christ. There is something special about those who acknowledge that Christ, and Christ alone, is the way to God.

I may appreciate the faith of fellow seekers who are devout Hindus, Muslims, and Jews (particularly the latter two groups, who worship the God of revelation), but I do not share the core of their faith as I do with those who profess to believe in Christ. Or, should I say, with those who *actively* profess to be Christians. (I'm not talking, here, about merely nominal "Christians." They are not true seekers.)

With actively professing "Christians" I share not just universal fellowship but a very special kind of "faith fellowship." An often *exhilarating* faith fellowship. An almost always *frustrating* faith fellowship. But whether exhilarating or frustrating, it's a unique fellowship of mutual faith in Christ. In the next chapter you'll see what I mean.

It's all the difference between being a believer and a Christian. Between putting one's faith in Christ and actually putting on Christ. Two different categories of those who seek God through Christ. Two very different levels of fellowship.

Universal Fellowship

- By virtue of creation, we are brothers in the family of man with every other human being on earth.

- Every person in need is our brother, for whom we are our brother's keeper.

- As people of faith we have something in common with all who actively seek God.

- No person is beyond the possibility of redemption nor our duty to evangelize the lost.

CHAPTER SIX

FAITH FELLOWSHIP: LIKE FAMILY

One language builds a fence.
Two languages can construct a gate.

BOYD A. MARTIN

Never is Christian fellowship more important than when you don't have it. Ruth and I do not live in the middle of a desert, or in some jungle compound, or in the frozen tundra of Siberia. But for six months each year we know the hunger for fellowship in a foreign land.

Perhaps when one thinks of England, it sounds somewhat overly dramatic to speak of being in "a foreign land." For most of us England is deep within our own roots, both in terms of America's British heritage and a (mostly) shared English language. If the number of American visitors who come our way is any indication, there are lots of closet Anglophiles across the Big Pond.

Yet even if England is about as close as one can be to home when living an ocean apart, nevertheless Ruth and I know something of the emotion behind the song of the exiles in Babylonian captivity: "By the rivers of Babylon we sat and wept when we remembered Zion" (Psalm 137:1). Christian fellowship in this land of pealing church bells is not exactly what you would expect in middle Tennessee, Texas, or even southern California. In all of England there are fewer than fifty congregations of the church, with the already small number of Christians reduced even more by the recent closure of American military bases which had accounted for many of the members.

Although we feel providentially led to a particular spot in this "green and pleasant land," which has been especially conducive to spiritual contemplation and Christian writing, on the downside it has meant that we are not geographically close to any congregation of the church. Over the years, driving across the Cotswolds to meet with the Christians in Oxford or driving south to Bristol has been our closest option. And this we have done periodically.

In the meantime we feel a great sense of being disconnected. With each Lord's Day that comes around we join the Babylonian exiles in asking, "How can we sing the songs of the Lord while in a foreign land?" (Psalm 137:4). Often, Sunday mornings begin quietly while we play one of the tapes featuring congregational singing with Frank Cleaver. These voices in song wing us across the miles to brothers and sisters in Christ with whom we join in singing familiar hymns. This helps but it is not the same as worshiping together with those of like faith. Finding that kind of fellowship has been a struggle for many years.

Learning About Worship from Other Believers

Before I met and married Ruth, I happened upon a small congregation of believers in a village some eight or so miles from the cottage. The first time I drove by the little "chapel" (as such buildings are known over here), the sign "Ashton-under-Hill Free Church" caught my eye. I was intrigued, first of all, by the name. As much as anything the word "Free" is meant to distinguish it from the only other church in the village, the established Church of England. I later learned that the congregation is not organizationally tied to any fellowship of congregations, but is local, independent, and autonomous.

More than just being intrigued by the name, I was impressed with the listing of meeting times. There was Sunday morning worship, of course, but also Sunday evening worship, Monday evening for praise and prayer, Wednesday evening for Bible study, and Thursday morning for mums and toddlers. To American ears that may sound unremarkable. But in contrast to mostly empty church buildings in this moribund "Christian nation," such a schedule indicated to me that here were some British believers who took their faith seriously. I decided to visit.

What I found was a mixed blessing. It was a congregation of some fifty souls, with committed, godly elders overseeing the work. Having no pulpit preacher, they often exercise a mutual ministry among the men of the congregation. These men are regularly augmented by outside speakers drawn from a wide variety of backgrounds. Each first day of the week they gather around the table for the Lord's Supper. And on one occasion I was present at a baptism which was done with such emphasis and thoughtfulness that it put our all-too-perfunctory baptisms to shame.

It occurred to me that we had been right all along to insist that the pattern of sound doctrine, wherever followed, would produce similar results. In fact, here was a group of people who had never heard of the "churches of Christ," yet they were very much like us. If they differed from us in any major respect apart from any particular doctrinal understanding, it was in what I sensed to be a much more profound worship experience.

Their special sense of worship comes across in any number of striking ways. For example, the prayers that are prayed are directed to God with an intimacy which I have never heard among ourselves. Although the believers at Ashton are far less articulate on doctrinal issues than we are, their memorized familiarity with Scripture far exceeds our own.

We could also learn much from them about the time-less-ness of the Lord's supper. Never is there any rush. Usually there are protracted periods of silence. Often there's an unplanned hymn, prayer, or Scripture reading. Almost always, it is thoughtful, meaningful, and moving.

Speaking of time, the clock is of secondary importance. Services begin at the appointed hour, but there is no particular ending time. If it's an hour, fine. If it's an hour and a half, that's fine too. No one is squirming or heading for the door. On one occasion, when a particularly devout woman in the congregation was dying of cancer, the congregation met for a *five hour* period of prayer! Never have I been part of such a touching gathering of believers. Certainly not among the churches of Christ.

The services at Ashton-under-Hill are an interesting blend of British formality and a disarming informality. As is typical of British worship (even among some of our own congregations), the one who is preaching is also the "presider." In addition to preaching, he usually chooses the hymns, leads all the prayers, reads the Scriptures, and presides over the Lord's table.

Any departure from that format, however, is taken in stride. The men are quite happy to be called upon to lead prayer from the audience, and songs are often led spontaneously from the congregation, mostly during the time devoted to the Lord's supper. The lyrics of those songs, incidentally, are invariably chosen to further illuminate the lesson of the hour. These folks know their hymns by heart—the *words*, that is, not just the melody.

Sound ideal? I said earlier it was a mixed blessing, and it is. Of all the similarities with our own doctrinal understanding and worship practice, there is one noticeable and, for us, disturbing difference: The singing is accompanied by instruments—at least primarily. When songs are led spontaneously as they often are, there is no accompaniment. But otherwise the instruments are a standard fixture of the worship.

For two or three years when I would periodically attend their services, I would slip into a side pew and worship pretty much in my own personal world. Little by little what I observed drew me more and more into what true worship ought to be. Their smaller worship intimacy was a refreshing contrast to the large, traditional congregations back home that seemed to be so stifled by routine worship ritual. Even their spontaneous informality was accomplished with such reverence that none of the clap-happy, trendy worship of more recent years could hold a candle to it.

As for the instruments, I tried to content myself with the thought that while everyone else was singing *with* the instruments, I was singing *without* them! Of course that didn't solve the problem for someone like myself who is so strongly opposed to musical instruments in worship. Their presence continually marred an otherwise enviable worship ideal.

A Surprising Sensitivity to Conscience

Over time word got around about the reason for my living in England (my writing of Christian books), and that eventually led to an invitation to speak—first at a home Bible study and then from the pulpit. As a discreet "aside" in one of my first lessons, I noted my doctrinal discomfort with instruments in worship. I'm sure it was that comment which led to an invitation to be on what was billed as an "Any Questions" panel one Wednesday evening. One of the questions which was submitted pertained to church music, giving me reason to believe that there was a good deal of curiosity about this "strange teaching." I obliged with a rather thorough treatment of the argument from silence and a brief history of how instruments had been wrongly introduced into Christian worship.

I don't know whether I had any instant converts to a new doctrinal understanding. (One of the three elders came from a non-instrumental background and already sympathized with that view.) But shortly after the "Any Questions" night, I was surprised when, on more than one occasion, someone suggested, "Could we just sing without the instrument on this one?" Quite obviously a tender sensitivity to my conscience had prompted the requests.

The most gratifying breakthrough came when I received a call from one of the elders, asking if I could come and "take the service" for them on a given Sunday. "And would you lead the singing *a cappella*?" he asked. Naturally I was delighted. I went, I preached, and I led the songs without any instruments. The congregation sang with its usual zest, hardly dropping a beat.

In the times thereafter that I have been invited to speak, it has come to be expected that the singing will be *a cappella.* It is fair to say that not everyone is happy singing without the instrument, but most find it at least tolerable if not actually refreshing. Ruth and I have been so encouraged that we have brought over a box load of our hymnbooks in the hope that one day perhaps we can teach them the kind of four-part harmony that can so richly enhance *a cappella* singing.

Appreciating Faith in Others

It would be enough in a book of this scope to use their concern for our consciences as an illustration of the attitude all of us ought to have when there are differences in understanding about New Testament teaching. How many of us are willing to forego a familiar worship pattern for the sake of others' consciences?

But for the moment there is a different point to be made. On the sliding scale of fellowship, there is much to be appreciated about the faith of others. Our legitimate fear of losing our way doctrinally if we begin to commingle with any and all professing Christians must be tempered with the recognition that we may have something (indeed much) to learn from those whom we normally consider to be "outside our fellowship." It works the other way around, as well. They have something (indeed much) to learn from us. But the only way that such a mutual learning process is going to take place is to honor shared faith, while openly and frankly discussing the differences.

What is most perplexing and frustrating about our association with the believers at Ashton-under-Hill is reflected in that intriguing phrase which we've already mentioned in two different contexts. Never in my own experience has the phrase "Christians, but not the only Christians" so precisely fit as in the case of some of the believers at Ashton.

Since there is no formally adopted denominational creed at the Ashton chapel, there are differing understandings about how one becomes a Christian. Some (few) of the worshipers appear to have been baptized pursuant to the New Testament pattern, and thus they are well and truly Christians. Others have been immersed with what appears to be a misunderstanding about the saving nature of baptism. Their baptisms were done as a matter of "obedience," not strictly "for the forgiveness of sins." Still others have never been baptized, yet they would certainly think that they are Christians.

I did not mention it earlier, but along with noting my concerns regarding instrumental music, I also raised the issue of Christian birth in my first lesson. Consequently, I was also asked at the "Any Questions" night about my understanding of baptism.

From what I can tell I have made some headway with at least a few of the believers who had never heard that baptism was anything other than a matter of obedience. Since they don't have a history of finely-honed doctrinal positions as we have, it's unusually difficult to know what the congregation is thinking. In this case, however, there have been positive reactions both to my earlier comments and to a recent sermon in which I preached point-blank about biblical baptism.

So I find myself among faithful, God-fearing, worshipful believers who have taught me much about the dynamics of worship, and yet their response to Christian birth is mixed at best.

What to do? How to regard them? How to regard so many other believers very much like them? We're back to the same question that we've been asking since the first chapter: What fellowship if any do we have with devout believers who have never been biblically baptized?

Like Family, But Not Family

With each passing day, I have a growing appreciation for the fact that there is such a thing as "faith fellowship" with those who believe that Jesus Christ is Lord. Although this fellowship clearly falls short of "in Christ" fellowship, it rises higher than the "universal fellowship" which I have with the family of man, even those who are spiritual seekers. Because of our mutual allegiance to the lordship of Christ, I have a fellowship with these believers which I could never have with the devout Hindu, Muslim, or Jew.

Yet the mere fact that these believers acknowledge Christ as Lord rather than Muhammad or Buddha is not the sole reason why I share with them a special kind of fellowship. As much could be said of *nominal* "Christians" who show no evidence of a commitment to Christ. Among *committed* believers in Christ, by contrast, there is an intimacy of faith and worship which I find enviable. Their hearts have the same yearning for Christ as does mine, and their lives have been truly transformed because of their faith.

What then am I to conclude? At least this: If they are not strictly "family"—and they are not—they are certainly very much *like family*. In virtually every way they think and act as those in the family would think and act. Anyone looking from the outside could be excused for assuming that they were in fact members of the family.

Is there someone in your own circle of friends who is so close to you and your family that you think of them "like family"? If so you'll understand what I mean when I say that it is possible for some folks who are "like family" to be even more like family to you than your own family! (I'm reminded of the proverb: "There is a friend who sticks closer than a brother.")

What makes the question of Christian identity more difficult, both for ourselves and for those who might be looking from the outside, is the disturbing fact that there are unimmersed believers who very often put to shame those immersed believers who ought to bear the fruit of the Spirit but don't. Spiritually speaking, these unimmersed believers can be more "like family" than our own Christian family.

As already suggested, none of this automatically changes family status. In ordinary human relationships we understand that those who may be "like family" are nevertheless not really and truly relatives. In like fashion it remains the painful truth that these faithful, God-fearing, worshipful men and women are *believers*, but not *Christians*. They are *believers* because of their faith in Christ; but they are not *Christians*, having not yet put on Christ through the saving act of baptism.

Yet let no one despise their faith! If we must regard them only as *believers* rather than fully as *Christians*, nevertheless we have much to honor about their commitment to Christ. Like the discerning Pharisee who asked Jesus about the greatest commandment (Mark 12:28-34), these our fellow believers are "not far from the kingdom." Show them nothing but contempt, and they probably will never become part of the kingdom. Treat them as if they were not just unbaptized, but ungodly, and we are as likely to push them away from the kingdom as to draw them closer to it.

It simply won't do for us to lump together in one indistinguishable mass all who are unsaved. That is no more safe than lumping together all who have been saved but whose lives may, or may not, reflect that salvation. We've simply got to be more discerning when it comes to faith fellowship.

A Case of Faith Fellowship

The level of fellowship which I have described as "faith fellowship" finds its scriptural basis in a passage which unfortunately has come to be greatly misused in support of wide-open Christian fellowship with all who trust in Jesus. Found in Mark 9:38-41, the passage records an incident in which John reports to Jesus that he and the other apostles rebuked a man whom they had observed driving out a demon in the name of Jesus. John's reason? "Because he was not one of us."

To John's great surprise Jesus said, "Do not stop him. No one who does a miracle in my name can in the next moment say anything bad about me, for whoever is not against us is for us." Notice that Jesus did not say, "Whoever is not against us is *one of us*." That would have been the appropriate response if Jesus meant to directly counter John's explanation that the man "was not *one of us*."

As if confirming that important distinction, Jesus goes on to say, "I tell you the truth, anyone who gives you a cup of water in my name because you belong to Christ will certainly not lose his reward."

Who did Jesus say *belonged to Christ*? It was John and the other apostles who *belonged to Christ*, not the one who gave the cup of water. There is no support here for some all-inclusive Christian fellowship based upon nothing more than "good works done in the name of Christ."

On the other hand, both the "demon chaser" and the "cup giver" are to be honored for the good deeds which they have done in Christ's name. They may not be *one of us*, but they are not our enemies. Indeed they may be in jeopardy of eternal condemnation, but they are not against us.

Is Jesus saying that these people should not be evangelized? Of course not. Is he saying that we ought to ignore their eternal jeopardy? Hardly! What he is saying is that we have a special kind of fellowship with all those who give honor to Christ in whatever they do. Not Christian fellowship, with all which that entails; but faith fellowship, giving honor to whom honor is due.

Surely our honoring them is part of "the reward" which Jesus said they would not lose. If "virtue is its own reward," their virtue of faith-motivated service to others will have both the reward of inner satisfaction and the reward of honor to whom honor is due.

The Benefits of Faith Fellowship

Another passage which seems to suggest something very much like faith fellowship tends to languish in obscurity. It is found in Solomon's dedicatory prayer at the completion of the temple (2 Chronicles 6:32-33). Solomon prays not only for the people of Israel but also for "the foreigner who does not belong to your people Israel but has come from a distant land because of your great name and your mighty hand and your outstretched arm...."

In the hope that all the peoples of the earth might know the name of Jehovah God and fear him, Solomon asks of God: When the foreigner comes and prays toward this temple, "then hear from heaven, your dwelling place, and do whatever the foreigner asks of you."

Have you ever prayed that God's blessings would rest upon all those who have turned their hearts and lives toward Christ? Do we, in judgment, pray only for that which is lacking (their salvation) and not, in appreciation, for that which they already have (their faith)?

If we can pray for national leaders who may or may not be people of faith, surely we can pray for those whose faith holds a nation together and whose faith—by its mere presence—bolsters our own.

What a different world it would be if everyone were a believer in Jesus Christ—even an unbaptized believer. Globally, it is hard to overestimate the good that has been done by Anglican and Roman Catholic missionaries in civilizing pagan cultures. (Their notorious errors and excesses pale when compared to the good done.)

I was struck recently by an editorial in one of the British newspapers paying homage to a retiring journalist by the name of Bernard Levin. Levin had predicted in August of 1977 the fall of Soviet communism, which he (a non-Christian) said would be brought about in large measure by people committed to faith in Christ. Ignoring for the moment his overly-broad use of the term *Christian*, listen to these insightful thoughts on what would turn out to be the real force behind the fall of communism:

Is it seriously to be believed that the only Christians in Russia are the ones we know about?...What do you suppose Christianity *is*?

Even when Christianity is spoken of in its widest possible sense, in all Christ-centered faith there is a leavening process wherever that faith exists. Faith itself is salt. Faith itself is light. Faith in Christ always has its reward, whether for an individual or for an entire society.

What is true of political freedom is equally true of personal freedom. One shudders to think, for example, how long it would have taken to rid the earth substantially of forced slavery had it not been for the Christ-focused commitment of such men in England as William Wilberforce and the man who gave us "Amazing Grace," John Newton. Even Abraham Lincoln's staunch opposition to slavery, although not specifically couched in Christian terms, was buttressed by appeals to a higher sense of religious faith.

Wherever it exists and in whatever form, faith, like righteousness itself, exalts a nation.

Songs of Fellowship

The mere mention of John Newton, former slave trader turned hymn-writer, ought to give us pause. In one breath we teach (rightly) that those who have been baptized only as infants are in jeopardy of eternal judgment; yet in the next breath we sing songs of faith written by those very same lost souls. Just leaf through our hymnbooks and you'll discover that one hymn after another—in fact, *most* of our hymns—were written by believers with whom we would claim no fellowship in Christ.

Consider, for example, Isaac Watts, a non-conforming Congregationalist whose only "baptism" would have been as an infant. It is his words of faith (written, incidentally, to be accompanied by instruments) which we sing in "Come Ye That Love the Lord"; "I'm Not Ashamed to Own My Lord"; "Alas! And Did My Savior Bleed?"; "How Shall the Young Secure Their Hearts?"; and "Am I a Soldier of the Cross?"

Certainly we may believe that Watts never went through the proper enlistment procedure to become "a soldier of the cross" and that there is a theological cloud on his claim that the Lord will own his "worthless name before His Father's face." But we can hardly deny that through his wonderful hymns we are caused to soar on the wings of Watts' own profound faith, no matter how uninformed and incomplete that faith might have been.

And how shall we regard Charles Wesley, whom we join in singing the transcendent sentiments of his majestic "Christ, the Lord, is Risen Today," his plaintive "Jesus, Lover of My Soul," and his exquisite "Love Divine, All Loves Excelling"? Do we not share a sweet fellowship of faith with anyone who can call us to such heights of celestial joy with these sublime words—

> Changed from glory into glory,
> Till in heav'n we take our place,
> Till we cast our crowns before Thee,
> Lost in wonder, love and praise.

Together with Sabine Baring-Gould we're "marching as to war, with the cross of Jesus going on before." Along with Horatius Bonar we have "heard the voice of Jesus say, 'Come unto me and rest'"; assuring us that, "Yes, for me, for me, He careth." And with William Cowper we glory in the fact that "there is a fountain filled with blood drawn from Emmanuel's veins" and that "sinners plunged beneath that flood lose all their guilty stains"—even if we associate that flood with faith-prompted immersion in a way William Cowper would never have understood.

All of which gives new meaning to Cowper's verse: "God moves in a mysterious way his wonders to perform." It doesn't get more mysterious than when we are singing about Christian unity among ourselves, using the words of John Fawcett, a devout believer with whom we would claim no fellowship. Historically we've never had Baptists like Fawcett in mind when we've joined our voices in singing: "Blest be the tie that binds our hearts in Christian love."

Week in and week out we are brought closer to God and to each other by singing together the anthems of praise and the musical prayers of those who strictly speaking were not Christians, "only believers." We may not have true Christian fellowship with these faith-filled hymn writers, but surely we share a common fellowship of faith in the One who died for us all.

The Practical Meaning of Faith Fellowship

If indeed there is such a thing as "faith fellowship" apart from true "in Christ" fellowship, the next question is, How does that fellowship operate in practical terms?

It means, first of all, that we must be bold enough to acknowledge Christ-centered faith wherever we find it—even in those who may be outside the boundaries of Christian fellowship. We must come to accept that it is not wrong to fellowship *as believers* others who wear the name "Christian" but aren't. Without giving anything away we can honor their faith, learn from their faith, be rebuked by their faith, be prompted by their faith, read the words of their faith, and sing the feelings of their faith.

Committed believers in groups outside our own Christian fellowship are not to be seen as spiritual lepers. We can benefit from their proclamation and teaching of the Word, whether it be in books, or over the radio, or even in a time of worship within their own buildings. Perhaps we have forgotten that only a couple of generations ago our forebears in the church used to attend whatever "gospel meeting" was in town, whether Baptist, Methodist, or Presbyterian. And the denominational folks attended ours. (Of course, it was also the era of religious debates, when doctrine was taken seriously, not just glossed over with saccharin calls for cheap grace and discount unity.)

I believe there is also something to be gained by thinking about blind spots. Not theirs but ours. It's easy for us to see the blind spot which virtually all other believers have regarding biblical baptism. But are we so presumptuous as to think that we ourselves have no blind spots?

It has taken a group of believers in a little English chapel to arrest my attention and teach me more perfectly the meaning of worship. What else do I need to learn, perhaps from Pentecostals, about what it means to give myself over to a more emotional expression of my faith? Or from Quakers, about listening more closely to God through meditative silence? Or from Anglicans, about a greater zeal for doing social justice? Or from the Dutch Calvinists, about thinking more Christianly in all that I do? Or from Catholics, about a greater need for confessing my sins before God?

I've often wondered if the various denominations haven't come into being because they each focus on something that other believers may have missed. Like university students we all seem to major in some things while minoring in others. Which isn't to say that all "majors" are of equal importance or that any aspect of Christian faith should be considered a "minor." Because what it takes to become a Christian is a threshold question, we've simply got to get that right before we do anything else. To complete the analogy, majoring in any subject is impossible without first being accepted into the university.

But what about the rest of the curriculum? What have we not yet learned? What blind spots do we still have? Acknowledging a wider faith fellowship can help us to answer those questions.

Seeking Out the Spiritually-Minded

More than anything else, perhaps, appreciating a distinct circle of faith fellowship may encourage us to choose our daily associations more carefully. In the opening chapter we posed the possibility—even likelihood—that we may have more in common, spiritually speaking, with one who is a Christ-centered "believer" than with a thoroughly-secularized brother in Christ. In this chapter we revisited that idea by talking about those who are not family, but who are so much "like family" that they can actually out-family our own family!

I recently shared with my colleagues on the law school faculty my distress at having come to the conclusion that I had more of a spiritual bonding with a visiting professor who is Catholic than I have with some of my colleagues who are baptized members of the Lord's church. In the year that he was with us, Doug and I had almost daily conversations about our mutual faith in Christ and about how we could best express that faith in ourselves, in our families, and in society at large. It has been years since I have had such deeply spiritual conversations with other colleagues who worship in the churches of Christ.

The respect which Doug and I had for one another's faith did not preclude candor about Christian birth. It's hard to look someone of Doug's deep faith in the face and say, "I can't count you as a brother in Christ," but that is one of the ironies of genuine faith fellowship. Sometimes we can say harder things to spiritually-minded outsiders than we can say to the unspiritual brother who sits next to us in the pew or who might work alongside us.

Like-mindedness doesn't make families; nor do families necessarily possess like-mindedness.

Sometimes choosing those with whom we most want to associate can end up crossing arbitrary lines of fellowship. As we will see even more clearly in the next chapter, the boundary of "in Christ" fellowship does not include those who are outside the family of Christ. Outside that boundary, there is no vested hope of salvation and no promise of participation in kingdom fellowship.

On the other hand, when mutual faith binds two spiritually-minded believers together, the spheres of faith fellowship and "in-Christ" fellowship begin to overlap in terms of preferential association.

At this point it is not enough simply to be members of the same church, even if it is the Lord's church. At this point the issue is not kingdom fellowship, but a fellowship of the spiritually-minded. Where "in-Christ" fellowship speaks to issues of justification, salvation, and sonship, faith fellowship by contrast speaks to the issues of commitment, vision, and spiritual devotion.

If possible, give me a friend and brother who is all of the above: justified, saved, committed, and spiritually devoted to his

Savior. If not possible, give me a believing friend whose faith is on fire, rather than a brother who is justified, but not electrified.

With such a friend, the door to the baptistery is probably left open, whereas the worldly-minded brother has symbolically slammed the door shut on his way out of the baptistery. Now that his ticket has been punched, he can't be bothered with being spiritually-minded.

How different it is with a spiritually-committed believer. A mutually shared faith fellowship with such a person edifies, encourages, and protects in ways which a more isolated fellowship with lukewarm brothers and sisters could never do. Just as evil companions corrupt good morals, unspiritual kinfolk in the kingdom can limit our spiritual horizons and quench the Spirit. In such a case, surely, better a supportive believer than a brother who hinders.

So where does all this leave us? Suffice it to say, faith fellowship will never be a substitute for genuine "in Christ" fellowship. There is an eternity of difference between the two. But being part of a family is such a blessing that finding others who are "like family" can only enhance that blessing.

Besides, the Father wants all the children he can get. If we love our believing friends *as if they were brothers and sisters,* by His grace they'll want to do whatever it takes to be fully adopted. Then they'll be brothers and sisters indeed!

Faith Fellowship

- Wherever it is found, whether in individuals, families, or nations, faith in Christ always has its reward.
- We have a unique fellowship of faith with all those who fervently seek God through Jesus Christ.
- Although they are not our brothers and sisters in Christ, other devout believers are "like family."
- We can be encouraged, taught, and even rebuked by their faith.
- Their faith provides a natural bridge to teach them more perfectly about the significance of baptism.

CHAPTER SEVEN

"In Christ" Fellowship: The Extended Family

God calls us not to solitary sainthood but to
fellowship in a company of committed men.

David Schuller

Recently in final preparation for a book on Israel, Ruth and I journeyed to Jerusalem, where we spent three weeks travelling throughout the country. We walked where Jesus walked. We followed in the footsteps of the apostles. We saw the tombs, touched the stones, smelled the profusion of competing aromas in the marketplace, listened to the cacophony of the crowds, and, yes, of course, tasted the exotic local delicacies.

We also worshiped with a congregation of Messianic Jews who assembled both on Shabbat (the Jewish Sabbath) and on the first day of the week. Except for references to Yeshua Machiach—Jesus, the crucified and risen Messiah of prophecy—their worship is not altogether unlike that of any other synagogue. It is Jewish in expression, right down to the traditional yarmulkes, prayer shawls, and the Torah scroll being reverently passed around the room to be touched by all who wish.

On the first day of the week these Messianic Jews meet again for more prayer, more singing, and more teaching from the Scriptures, but especially for gathering around the Lord's table in memory of the crucified Messiah.

For anyone accustomed to traditional Christian worship, the

worship of Jewish Christians can be jarring. It's like being hurled back 2000 years to the first century, complete with the chanting of the Hebrew Torah; the singing of the psalms, accompanied not with instruments but often with vigorous clapping; the openness to discussion (even debate!) following the sermon; and the informal passing of the matza (unleavened bread) and wine during the Lord's supper.

As it happened, we were in Jerusalem during the Passover and were invited to attend the Passover seder with these same Jewish Christians. Ruth helped prepare food in the kitchen, and I rubbed salt on the lamb to remove the blood. That night, as the ram's horn was blown throughout Jerusalem at the precise hour, we joined in the traditional ceremonies associated with the seder—celebrated differently by these baptized believers only in their recognition that Jesus was the lamb who was slain for the sins of the world.

After three weeks of sharing in fellowship with these Jewish brothers and sisters, I almost had to pinch myself to make sure that I was not back in the first century attending the crucial "Jerusalem conference" in which significant differences between Jewish and Gentile believers had to be hammered out.

The Extended Family
Never is one more keenly reminded of the diversity within the family of God than when sharing in worship with the Messianic Jews in Jerusalem. As a Gentile Christian, all of my theological nerve endings were on edge. Could these Torah-chanting, yarmulke-wearing, Passover-observing Jews really be my brothers and sisters in Christ?

The apostle Paul certainly thought so. In his Roman letter (15:7-9), Paul enjoined mutual fellowship between Jewish and Gentile Christians because we have a common Savior. "Accept one another, then," wrote Paul, "just as Christ accepted you."

When you and I were united with Christ through baptism into his death, at that same moment we were also united with his entire body—with all believers who have ever been baptized into his death and are thereby united with Christ.

The words of John Oxenham's great hymn come ringing to my ears:

In Christ there is no east or west,
In Him no south or north;
But one great fellowship of love
Throughout the whole wide earth.

Join hands, then, brother of the faith,
Whate'er your race may be.
Who serves my Father as a son
Is surely kin to me.

In his letter to the Ephesians (2:19-22; 3:6; 4:16), Paul paints the most vivid picture possible of the unity which we have with our brothers and sisters in Christ—Jew and Gentile; black and white; rich and poor; male and female; old and young; educated and uneducated; liberal and conservative; traditional and contemporary. Look closely at the words that I've emphasized and see how wonderfully God has knit his children together in one universal extended family:

Consequently, you are no longer foreigners and aliens,
but *fellow citizens* with God's people and *members of
God's household*....In him the whole building is *joined
together* and rises to become a holy temple in the Lord.
And in him you too are being *built together* to become
a dwelling in which God lives by his Spirit....This mystery is that through the gospel the Gentiles are *heirs together* with Israel, *members together* of *one body*, and
sharers together in the promise in Christ Jesus....From
him *the whole body, joined and held together* by every

supporting ligament, grows and builds itself up in love,
as each part does its work.

Let those words describing "in Christ" fellowship sink in. We
are fellow citizens. Members of God's household. Joined together.
Built together. Heirs together. Sharers together. Held together in
one body.

Fellowship Is God's Decision

What we tend to forget is that it is God, not we, who determines the boundaries of "in Christ" fellowship. Neither "in Christ"
fellowship nor "in Christ" unity is something we ourselves can define, limit, or regulate, since being "in Christ" involves the forgiveness of sins and reconciliation with God. That is why biblical baptism is such a watershed act of obedience. It is the point at which
God has chosen to call us into his fellowship.

"God is faithful," said Paul to the Corinthians (1:9), "who has
called you into fellowship with his Son Jesus Christ our Lord."
Therefore, says the aging apostle John, "We proclaim to you what
we have seen and heard, so that you also may have fellowship with
us. And our fellowship is with the Father and with his Son, Jesus
Christ" (1 John 1:3).

Our charge is not to *create*, but to *maintain* the unity already
created by the Spirit. "For we were all baptized by one Spirit into one
body." Our one baptism, prompted by our one faith in the one Lord,
has, by the one Spirit, made us not only part of the one body but also
children of the one Father, giving us the one and only hope we could
ever have to be one with each other, both now and in eternity.

Note carefully the word Paul chooses with reference to "in
Christ" unity (Ephesians 4:3): "Make every effort to *keep* the unity
of the Spirit through the bond of peace." That's *keep*, not create, orchestrate, or manipulate.

By God's Spirit we have been called into one new community
of people, one body, and one extended family. This being the case,

we must accept the fact that God has placed within the fellowship of his children all sorts of people. Numbered among us are the strong, the mature, the well-balanced folks who come from stable backgrounds. There are also the weak and those who struggle through life. Others are sensitive individuals whose consciences are tender and vulnerable.

Among the family there will be people of petty preferences and strong dislikes. Brothers and sisters with personality conflicts and doctrinal disagreements. Hand raisers, hand holders, and hand wringers.

Yet as different as we all may be, we have one thing in common: we all belong to Jesus Christ. We are his people; he has adopted us into his family; he has made us subjects in his kingdom, members of his body, and living stones in his holy temple.

Who Are My Brothers?

We are not the first to ask, With whom do we share "in Christ" fellowship? Jesus himself asked virtually the same question on that curious occasion (recorded in Matthew 12:46-50) when he was talking to the crowd and someone interrupted him to say that his mother and brothers wanted to talk to him. "Who is my mother, and who are my brothers?" Jesus asked. Answering his own question, Jesus said, "Whoever does the will of my Father in heaven is my brother and sister and mother."

Since my brothers and sisters in the family of God are determined by whoever does the Father's will, I'm in no position to make that decision—either to include or to exclude. We have no choice about our Christian siblings anymore than we do regarding our biological brothers and sisters. If God has made them his children then we must accept them as brothers and sisters.

Are there any biblically-baptized believers that you would be ashamed to call your brothers? How about the leaders of the Boston movement? Or those who worship in congregations of the Disciples of Christ or the Christian Church?

When it comes to being ashamed of our brothers, we must exercise great care. "Both the one who makes men holy," says the Hebrew writer, "and those who are made holy are of the same family. So Jesus is not ashamed to call them brothers" (Hebrews 2:11).

If Jesus calls them "brothers" who have been made holy through faith, repentance, and baptism, can we call them anything less? If Jesus is not ashamed to accept them as brothers, have we any right *not* to accept them? Unless they have demonstrated behavior sufficient to warrant treating them "as a pagan" (a matter of congregational discipline), we have no option but to accept all those whom Christ himself has accepted.

The Surprising Glare of the Bright Line

One of the most difficult challenges of "in Christ" fellowship is embracing the fact that the bright line between Christians and non-Christians is both *inclusive* and *exclusive*. It's a line of demarcation: no unbaptized believer is a Christian; no biblically-baptized believer is *not* a Christian.

Until recently we have been very good at *excluding* from "in Christ" fellowship all those who have fallen short of a proper biblical initiation. If they have never been born into the family of God, then they are not brothers and sisters in Christ. Period.

However, rarely have we come to grips with the necessary inference which leads us to the flip-side of the coin—that all those who have in fact experienced a proper biblical initiation must be *included* as Christians. As fellow citizens in the kingdom. As brothers and sisters. As part of the extended family of God.

You mean, even if for reasons of conscience we cannot maintain a worship fellowship with them? Yes. Even if, like Demas, they have forsaken us, having loved this present world? Yes. Even if some local congregation has had to disfellowship that brother or sister as a matter of discipline? Yes.

If that seems shocking, merely consider the parable of the prodigal son. Was the young man no longer his father's son when he was elbow-deep in pig slop? Did he somehow tender his resignation as a son when he huffed away to seek his fortune? He may have been a *prodigal* son, or even a *lost* son, but whether in rebellion or in repentance, he remained his father's son. As so do we.

I confess to you here and now that, like the prodigal son, I have been "elbow-deep in pig slop" in the eyes of my Father. Yet, my Father has always kept the light on for me, hoping I would return to my senses and to his open arms.

Which is not to say, of course, that none of us can fall away from our salvation and be eternally lost. Hebrews 6:4-5 fires a warning salvo across the bow of anyone who thinks otherwise. If the prodigal son had ended his life still in rebellion, there would have been no welcome-home party. If my life is lived in open rebellion before God in word, doctrine, or deed, then—son or no son, brother or no brother—I have no hope of heaven. And, of course, it may be necessary for the family to shun a prodigal brother or sister.

Even given the tragic possibility that a brother might fall away from the faith and become "captive to sin" (as was Simon the sorcerer before he repented), we've simply got to take more seriously each and every person who is in the extended family. As we've previously tried to make clear, Jesus' prayer for unity was not directed at the unforgiven but the forgiven. But if we really believe that, then we also have to accept the truth that Jesus has called us into a special relationship with *all* those who have been initially forgiven by his blood through the mediation of faith, inclusive of repentance and baptism.

Being a biblically-baptized believer is a watershed line of fellowship. At the point of becoming a Christian there are no degrees of fellowship. No "first-class Christians"; no "second-class Christians." Either a person *is* a Christian, or a person is *not* a Christian. Either a person's sins *have* been forgiven, or they *haven't*. Either a person *is* a brother or sister, or *not*. There is no such thing as a half-brother or half-sister.

If what we mean when we say someone is "an erring Christian" is that, because of some doctrinal position he holds, he isn't really a Christian after all, then we have just accepted the possibility that a son or brother can be shoved back into the womb as if he never had been born. Make no mistake, a son may ultimately be disinherited. *Becoming* a Christian is no guarantee of an eternal relationship with God. But a son is a son is a son. And a brother is a brother is a brother. Like it or not. Love it or hate it.

Kinship with black sheep in the family was a hard lesson which the prodigal son's older brother had to learn. Is it a lesson you and I have yet to learn?

A Rare and Special Case

Speaking of black sheep, in the rare case there are also goats. Several passages speak of the exceptional situation in which someone who may have been accepted as a baptized believer in the family of God is no longer a brother. These unique cases have been misused in so many ways that we've lost all coherence about them.

I'm referring here to men like Hymenaeus, Philetus, and Alexander (to whom Paul refers in 1 Timothy 1:20 and 2 Timothy 2:17), and to unnamed "anti-Christs" (such as those mentioned by John in 1 John 2:18). What had these men done that merited Paul's "handing them over to Satan"? They had blasphemed God. But in the buildup to Paul's condemnation of these men, he admits that he too was once a blasphemer. So what was different in their case?

They rejected, says Paul, both faith and a good conscience— "and so have shipwrecked their faith." We are not talking here about men of faith who happen to disagree with us doctrinally. (There is much more to say about this in later chapters.) What these men were teaching was anti-faith and anti-Christ. Among their teachings was the heretical notion that the resurrection had already taken place—a belief which apparently denied the very core of the gospel of Christ—Jesus' own resurrection.

John further clarifies the kind of person Paul is talking about. "Who is the liar?" asks John. "It is the man who denies that Jesus is the Christ. Such a man is the antiChrist—he denies the Father and the Son."

Two things tell us that we are no longer talking simply about black sheep in the family or about brothers with whom we have doctrinal differences. First, says John of these traitors, "No one who denies the Son has the Father." How can someone be a brother if he has disclaimed Christ, the Son, and therefore doesn't have the Father? Here's a person who has audaciously walked into some court and officially disclaimed his own sonship!

If you're thinking that a son can't just walk into court and deny his blood line (because a son is a son is a son), John himself gives the explanation. "They went out from us," says John, "but they did not really belong to us. For if they had belonged to us, they would have remained with us; but their going showed that none of them belonged to us." In other words, the odds are that such people were never *genuinely* baptized believers in the first place. Theirs was a sham wedding ceremony. They were never really sons; they were never really brothers.

But such "goats" among the flock are rare indeed—these "brothers" who are only *faux* brothers. They're not just *prodigal* sons, but *illegitimate* sons—made illegitimate by their own feigning perversity. How could a person be a *Christian* when he has denied the most rudimentary teachings about *Christ*, whose name he presumes to wear?

About the Word "Christian"

We've been speaking a lot about "Christians" and "non-Christians"; "believers" and "non-believers." But to be honest, the terminology of fellowship can get confusing. At times we've talked about believers who have not been biblically baptized (those with whom we have "faith fellowship," for example), who are not fully-adopted children. They are *believers* because they *believe*, but they are not Christians.

At other times our use of the word "believer" parallels the

New Testament's use, where faith-prompted baptism is assumed, as is one's status as a brother. There is Peter's admonition, for example, "Love the brotherhood of *believers*" (1 Peter 2:17). Or consider Acts chapter 5, where, within just a few verses, reference is made to "the whole church" and to "all the believers."

"Believers" in this latter sense are *saved believers*, most often referred to in Scripture as "disciples." Acts 6 makes several references to "disciples," but in verse seven Luke tells us that, as the word of God spread, "the number of *disciples* in Jerusalem increased rapidly." Denominational names aside, we are indeed "disciples of Christ." (To be distinguished is the use of the term "disciples" in Acts chapter 19, where it is used with reference to men who were John's disciples, perhaps on "the Way" but not far enough along to have been baptized into Christ and receive the Holy Spirit.)

Perhaps the oddest thing about fellowship terminology found in Scripture is the rarity of the term "Christian." We've used that popular term repeatedly in connection with fellowship, but never once does the phrase "Christian fellowship" actually appear in Scripture. All we know is that "the *disciples* were called *Christians* first at Antioch" (Acts 11:26). And that Agrippa put that famous question to Paul (Acts 26:28): "Do you think that in such a short time you can persuade me to become a *Christian*?"

Finally, Peter consoles all potential martyrs for Christ, saying, "If you suffer as a *Christian*, do not be ashamed, but praise God that you bear that name" (1 Peter 4:16). Nailing down exactly whom we are talking about, Peter goes on to say in the next sentence, "For it is time for judgment to begin with *the family of God*."

No question about it, those who are our brothers and sisters in the family of God are "disciples," "Christians," and, at the time of their spiritual rebirth, "saved believers." By whatever biblical name they are called, their initiation into the body of Christ was always the same. And when our own initiation follows the New Testament pattern, then we are brought together with them in believer fellowship, disciple fellowship, and certainly the Christian fellowship of which we primarily have been speaking.

On the Cusp of Fellowship

To this point we've talked boldly and confidently about the bright line of "in Christ" fellowship as if there were no shadowy edges at all to that line. I wish that were completely true, but I'm afraid it's not. Even where there are bright lines, the enigma of fellowship remains an enigma.

Few passages pertaining to fellowship can make our heads swim more than Acts 19:1-7, where we encounter those dozen "disciples" whom Paul found in Ephesus—the ones who had received John's baptism, but had not experienced the Holy Spirit because they had not been baptized in the name of Jesus. The passage tells us a number of things (for example, that technicalities do, indeed, matter when it comes to Christian birth; and that faith honored is faith taught more perfectly); but it also leaves us with many unanswered questions.

If there is anything close to a modern parallel with the situation described in Acts 19, it may be the relatively modern practice of baptism as a matter not of salvation but only of obedience. I say "close," recognizing that the example is not a perfect analogy. Unlike these men, whose faith in God had been claimed through John, rather than through Jesus, today's Baptists, for example, are fully convinced about the necessity of being baptized *in the name of Jesus*. Yet with Baptists (as well as with other baptized evangelicals) there is a certain similarity in their misunderstandings about the purpose and meaning of baptism.

Those today who are baptized as an obedient, after-the-fact symbolic act of a saved believer fall into a unique and altogether difficult category of fellowship. Clearly their form of conversion (getting the cart of salvation before the horse of immersion) is not consistent with the pattern of apostolic baptism. In the New Testament there is not one case where salvation preceded baptism.

That said, there is an important distinction to be made between one's act and one's understanding. Even if I may not always fully or accurately understand why I'm doing what I'm doing, being obedient to God is obviously what matters most. Yet that subtle distinction is as troubling as it is difficult.

What it suggests is the possibility that—despite their misunderstanding of baptism's purpose—believers who are immersed in order to obey the command to be baptized might nevertheless be regarded in God's eyes as saved believers. As Christians. If so, of course, they would not have been saved at the point of faith (as they, themselves, think), but only at the point of their baptism—an odd situation to say the least.

Two compelling questions are raised by that rather bizarre possibility. First, must a person have a completely correct understanding of the doctrine of baptism in order for his adult, faith-prompted immersion in the name of Jesus to "count"? I know of no passage which gives us a useful answer. Certainly, those who were baptized on the day of Pentecost knew full well that their baptism was for the forgiveness of sins. But that doesn't answer the quite separate question of how God views a person who obeys the Lord's command to be baptized, while under the mistaken belief that he is already a Christian. We're simply not told.

The second question is, Does God penalize false starts? It may not be decisive, but what would our answer be if, instead of baptism, the question were regarding the validity of a marriage between two people who had previously been living together? Would the fact that they had been wrong to live together outside marriage invalidate a subsequent wedding ceremony?

In fact, the closer analogy would be a man and a woman who incorrectly believe that they are married as common law husband and wife. If subsequently they should desire to formalize their assumed marriage as a demonstration of their love and commitment to each other, the wedding ceremony would actually legitimize a relationship which they thought they already had but didn't.

These analogies at least partially explain, incidentally, why "re-baptism" in such situations doesn't fit the same mold as in Acts 19. The men from Ephesus had to be re-baptized, not merely because of a misunderstanding about timing and purpose, but because their baptism was not based upon the redemptive blood of Jesus.

For those who are baptized in the name of Christ, however, the issue must surely be different. If unbaptized believers are only "living together" with Christ (as it were), do they not become wed to him in the believer's wedding ceremony of baptism? If so, their act of obedience has moved them from a qualified "faith fellowship" into full "in Christ" fellowship.

What makes such an hypothesis so awkward is that there is no express biblical warrant for guaranteeing salvation on the basis of such "time-delayed" baptisms. Search with a fine tooth comb and you'll never find New Testament believers or disciples being baptized *because they were already Christians.* So why would anyone want to fly stand-by when they can just as easily fly confirmed? And how can any collective body of believers resolutely perpetuate so unbiblical an understanding of baptism?

More to the point in our current push for all-out ecumenical unity, how can we fellowship these baptized believers as Christians and yet never engage them in urgent discussion about their seriously flawed perception of Christian birth? Even if God should ultimately overlook their ignorance, surely the minimum required on our part is scrupulous honesty about what the Scriptures actually teach.

Having written so strongly in earlier chapters about the error of "faith-only" salvation, it certainly gives me no comfort to now suggest that such error might nevertheless be overcome at the point of baptism. But I see no brighter line to follow. Given a type of baptism which is unbiblical in understanding, yet biblical in obedience, we are caught on the horns of a dilemma in a grey area between "faith fellowship" and "in Christ" fellowship.

It would be simpler, of course, just to say what we have usually said all along: that unless a person has been baptized *for the right reason*, he or she is not a Christian. I can only say that such a position is a tougher brief to argue than we've ever before admitted. Worse yet, if we've been wrong about it, then we have wrongly withheld fellowship from those with whom God himself is in fellowship.

My great concern is that, in trying to correct any mistakes we may have made in this shadowy area, we don't begin promoting a clearly unbiblical view of baptism. It is one thing to give someone the benefit of the doubt in terms of fellowship; it is another thing altogether to give that doubt doctrinal legitimacy. It is one thing to honor a fellow believer's incorrectly understood obedience; it is another thing altogether to think that God will honor us for our own quite-well-informed disobedience.

What that translates into, I think, is an obligation to be as vocal regarding baptism's true significance and purpose as we might be vocal in calling for fellowship with those who have been baptized under the mistaken illusion that they are already saved. Not wholly unlike what has come to be known as "tough love," call it "tough fellowship." If there is to be more than faith fellowship with these baptized believers, then let it not be without corrective confrontation.

Is there any bottom line to all of this? At the level of current ecumenical dialogue it surely means never talking about brotherhood with immersed "faith-only" believers without at the same time insisting that salvation prior to the point of baptism is an unbiblical notion which must be abandoned once and for all. On the congregational level it undoubtedly means that extending the right hand of fellowship must be made conditional upon an Apollos-like re-education regarding this crucial issue. Anything resembling a "Don't ask; don't tell" policy will be a leaven of doctrinal error that will corrupt any congregation it touches.

Where bright lines have become fuzzy over time, it's not for us to squint and make well-intentioned attempts to force them into a scriptural focus. Rather, it's time to get out a biblical brush and paint them bright again.

Does Jesus Have Other Sheep?

One final caution regarding the outer boundaries of "in Christ" fellowship. If there is in fact a special case to be made for those believing adults who are immersed with less than a correct understanding regarding the nature of biblical baptism, there is clearly no biblical basis for extending that special case to all forms and modes of baptism (such as sprinkling, pouring, or infant baptism), nor, less yet, to just any and all who look to the cross and put their faith in Jesus. Perceived exceptions have a way of tempting us to reach even farther afield for overbroad generalizations.

One passage that has every potential for abuse in this regard is John 10:1-16, where Jesus tells the Pharisees, "I have other sheep that are not of this sheep pen. I must bring them also. They too will listen to my voice, and there shall be one flock and one shepherd." If a person isn't careful he might jump to the conclusion that Jesus was referring here to all those with whom we have faith fellowship. That they, in fact, are the "other sheep" which are part of the "one flock."

Given the context, however, Jesus is telling the self-righteous Pharisees that his flock will be made up of more than just Jews, like themselves. He is obviously pointing to the universal nature of his kingdom, in which faithful Gentiles would also share. Certainly there is nothing in Jesus' words to support today's well-intended, but misguided, efforts at achieving Christian fellowship with those who are not yet fellow Christians.

From "In Christ" to Koinonia Fellowship

After our exploration of the boundaries of "in Christ" fellowship, the question of the moment is, What does that fellowship mean in practical terms? To begin with, we must retrace our steps to two passages which we cited earlier regarding universal fellowship.

This time it is the second part of Paul's encouragement (Galatians 6:10) that begs our attention: "Therefore, as we have opportunity, let us do good to all people, *especially to those who belong to the family of believers.*" Just as we have an obligation toward others, we have a special obligation toward our own. As fellow Christians we have a "family obligation" toward our brothers and sisters in the same way that we would understand a "family obligation" in any other context.

We must also express a special kindness toward those who are in the extended family of God. Remember when Paul said, "Always be kind to each other and to everyone else" (1 Thessalonians 5:15)? Clearly, Paul is differentiating between those who are Christians and those who are not. If we are to be kind to everyone else, surely we have a higher duty to be kind *to each other.*

Would that include those who have different ideas about worship style? Yes. Those with whom we disagree doctrinally? Yes. Even those who may have wrongfully abused us? Yes. For Paul, kindness isn't just a matter of our saying, "Have a nice day," to anybody who walks by. Says Paul as he begins his plea for kindness, "Make sure that nobody pays back wrong for wrong" (1 Thessalonians 5:15). He's not talking merely about normal courtesies here. He's talking about the often-difficult dynamics of give and take within a family relationship.

Speaking more precisely, we are now entering the realm of *koinonia* fellowship—not to be thought of as a separate category of fellowship but the *nature* of our fellowship which God has called us to share with all others who are "in Christ." The Greek term *koinonia* is used in a number of different senses, including fellowship based not only upon the mere fact of relationship but also upon conscious, voluntary, mutual participation.

It is the kind of Christian fellowship which followed in the wake of all those Pentecost baptisms. Acts 2:42-46 is a familiar passage, but it certainly bears repeating. Read the passage again. Slowly. Try not to think in terms of some special situation that called for extraordinary action. Ask yourself if we *ever* come anywhere near to approximating the kind of radical fellowship being described here:

> They devoted themselves to the apostles' teaching and to the fellowship, to the breaking of bread and to prayer....All the believers were together and had everything in common. Selling their possessions and goods, they gave to anyone as he had need. Every day they continued to meet together in the temple courts. They broke bread in their homes and ate together with glad and sincere hearts, praising God and enjoying the favor of all the people.

"In Christ" fellowship (something which God determines) doesn't automatically guarantee *koinonia* fellowship (something which we ourselves must make happen). Do we care enough for our brothers and sisters in Christ that, should an emergency arise, we would happily sell what we own in order to share with those in need?

This isn't the only passage which speaks about the early Christians' extraordinary fellowship of sharing. There is, for example, Acts 4:32, where Luke tells us that "all the believers were one in heart and mind. No one claimed that any of his possessions was his own, but they shared everything they had."

We might think that these days we are off the hook because there is no "present emergency" like the one presented by the explosive growth of the church in those early days. But in John's first letter (3:17), he suggests otherwise: "If anyone has material possessions and sees his brother in need but has no pity on him, how can the love of God be in him?" The fellowship of sharing never ends.

Money and possessions aside, can we honestly say that we have ever experienced the kind of excited, daily interaction with fellow believers described in Acts chapter two? Do we really enjoy being with each other and praising God together on a daily basis as they did? Do we revel in the company of our Christian family so much that even outsiders take notice?

From Caring to Conscience

Yet another aspect of *koinonia* fellowship bridges us to the next chapter and to the matter of "conscience fellowship." At base, *koinonia* fellowship has to do with how we treat each other as brothers and sisters. From *sharing* to *caring*, Peter calls us to "live in harmony with one another; be sympathetic, love as brothers, be compassionate and humble" (1 Peter 3:8). And James further admonishes us: "Brothers, do not slander one another. Anyone who speaks against his brother or judges him speaks against the law and judges it" (James 4:11).

Never are we more tempted to abandon the caring part of *koinonia* fellowship than when we differ with our brothers on some matter of doctrine. Far too often we not only act in distinctly uncaring ways (effectively withdrawing *koinonia* fellowship), but we also come very close to renouncing even "in Christ" fellowship.

The question for the next chapter, then, is this: What is the effect of matters of conscience on "in Christ" fellowship? Put differently, can there be multiple fellowships of conscience within the extended family of God? If so, do we continue to share "in Christ" fellowship? And, equally important, how should we treat each other?

This is where the rubber of Jesus' prayer for unity in John 17 meets the road of present conflicts among us. It is here that all the biblical calls for church unity and Christian harmony are put to the test. Whereas today's trendy ecumenism is mostly dressed-up humanism, maintaining "in Christ" fellowship in the crucible of doctrinal conscience is nothing short of divine.

"In Christ" Fellowship

- "In Christ" fellowship is the fellowship we have with all those who have accepted God's grace through faith, repentance, confession, and immersion.

- All who are thus united with Christ are united with each other as brothers and sisters in the family of God.

- There are no degrees or classes of Christians based upon differences in doctrinal understanding.

- Each child in the extended family is called to exercise the *koinonia* fellowship of sharing and caring to all other children in the family.

- If a child of God renounces faith in Christ or turns to an unrepentant life of sin, he forfeits his eternal inheritance.

CHAPTER EIGHT

CONSCIENCE FELLOWSHIP: CLOSE FAMILY

*Toward no crimes have men shown themselves so
cold-bloodedly cruel as in punishing differences of belief.*

JAMES RUSSELL LOWELL

I mentioned earlier worshiping with the congregation in Bristol, England. Ruth likes to arrive early. Nothing to do with punctuality. Nothing to do with any particular eagerness to greet our wonderful brothers and sisters there, though we always look forward to being with them. No, for Ruth its all part of a strategy to deal with the one cup which they use in the Lord's Supper.

The cup itself is an old cup. Some might even say a cankered cup. At best, it's a cup from which everyone present sips, including the sweet old sisters with their many ailments who have staked out the front row. So whenever she can, Ruth makes every effort to position herself so that she's among the first to receive the cup. Particularly, during flu season.

This last winter the threat of contagion got so bad that three of the dear sisters who had gotten the dreaded "lurgy" were thoughtful enough (here comes a picture to be conjured) to bring straws and discreetly sip from the cup!

Appreciative as she was, Ruth did wonder whether there was something theologically inconsistent about being *one*-cuppers but *three*-strawers.

Only recently I learned that using one cup is more a matter of doctrinal belief for some of the members than the mere tradition to which I had always attributed it. Others in the congregation would have no hesitancy at all in using a tray of individual cups. The Bristol congregation is certainly not one of the "one-cup, non-Sunday-school" churches with which we are familiar in the States.

Speaking of that group, I'll never forget attending one of their services in Birmingham, Alabama. They had the perfect solution for the folks in Bristol, particularly during flu season. As I've shared before, when it came time for passing the fruit of the vine, a brother blessed a rather large cup which he then poured into a device that had finger-like protrusions into a tray of individual cups. The multiple cups having thus been filled, they were served to a congregation of folks apparently content in the thought that they had maintained doctrinal purity *and* good hygiene.

Both in Bristol and on that one occasion in Birmingham I have joined in communion with brothers and sisters who put more stock in the literal meaning of "the cup" than I do. Although we differ in our understanding regarding this matter of doctrine, it does not violate my conscience to drink from a single container.

I find it fascinating that those who insist on a literal reading of "the cup" do not generally insist that it contain wine (the kind of wine which actually had made some of the Corinthians drunk, because they were taking more than a few pre-*koinonia* swigs before everyone else arrived). As you probably know, there are many Christians, mostly in Europe, who do, in fact, use wine—not just grape juice—for the cup. And there too I have joined in taking of the cup with no challenge to my conscience. Yet I know other brothers and sisters who would be uncomfortable in conscience were they to drink wine at the Lord's table.

A Laundry List of Doctrinal Differences

So one cup or many? Wine or grape juice? We've only begun to touch the hem of a very long garment in suggesting the many doctrinal differences which exist among Christians in the church today. Unlike preferences regarding worship style, doctrinal differences very often involve matters of conscience, particularly when those differences affect the time of "gathered" worship.

One might have biblical scruples about any number of issues which are matters of personal conscience but which do not have an immediate impact on a larger body of believers. Consider, for example, the question of going to war. One brother could go off to fight, having a clear conscience that he is doing God's will in overcoming an evil force. Another brother might conscientiously refuse to fight, believing that he should not kill his fellow man, no matter how compelling the cause. Each will answer to God for his own decision.

As much could be said about whether it is right to vote, or run for public office, or pay taxes, or salute the flag, or recite the pledge of allegiance. It wasn't all that long ago that such issues were the subject of considerable contention among our predecessors in the faith.

Even apart from personal decisions such as these, we might also have different understandings on a wide variety of biblical questions, beginning in Genesis with whether the days of Creation were literal, 24-hour days; or perhaps even whether the Flood of Noah's day was local or global.

Turning to Revelation, one could form many different views about events at the end of time. What say the Scriptures, for example, about those classic "Second Coming" scenarios? Should we be premillennial, postmillennial, or amillennial?

And what is the nature of heaven and hell? In heaven, will we be given back our present bodies, only somehow "glorified"? Or will our celestial bodies be so markedly different that we won't recognize them? Will the eternal punishment of hell be continuous, conscious burning, or will the "second death" of hell be something else? And what is the state of our existence between death and Judgment? Are we to be immediately in heaven with Jesus after we die, or only in a "waiting room" of some kind?

All of these questions about the past and the future raise yet further questions pertaining to our present fellowship. Does the fact that we might disagree on any of these questions mean that one or another of us has forfeited "in Christ" fellowship, or even *koinonia* fellowship? (Suppose we disagree on the answer to that very question itself—the one about forfeited fellowship!)

More Complicated Yet

One might suggest that there are more immediate doctrinal beliefs which pose a greater threat to "in Christ" fellowship than beliefs about either the remote events of Creation or the yet-to-be-known events at the end of time. Beliefs, for instance, like Calvinism's predestination, or original sin, or the impossibility of apostasy. Could "in Christ" fellowship embrace biblically-baptized believers who happen to believe any of those classic doctrines?

The fact that the penitent believers on Pentecost would not have had the remotest idea what any of those doctrines were all about probably tells us something about how much leeway must be given for doctrinal misunderstanding, at least as it relates to issues of fellowship. When sinners respond to Christ's commands to believe, repent, and be baptized, what additional theology must one know in order to become a Christian?

If in the process of becoming a Christian a person is not required to make a credal confession about predestination, original sin, or the impossibility of apostasy, how can "in Christ" fellowship possibly be put in jeopardy by error about such issues? (Knowing that there is little if any acceptance of these Calvinist doctrines among the churches of Christ, I use them simply to establish the principle that even significant doctrinal differences do not automatically disenfranchise a person from body fellowship.)

What the penitent believer must confess is not whether he believes in literal 24-hour days of Creation, or continuous conscious burning in hell, or the possibility of apostasy—but only that he believes Jesus is the Christ, the Son of God. Obeying the gospel in response to that simple confession is what "in Christ" fellowship is all about. As discussed earlier, it would take a subsequent denial of the very heart of the gospel—Christ's nature and mission—for someone to be excluded from "in Christ" fellowship solely on the basis of doctrinal error.

However, "in Christ" fellowship is not the end of the story where doctrinal error is concerned. There is always "conscience fellowship" to consider as well. Inevitably, as we have already seen, there are certain doctrinal teachings which of necessity will separate brothers and sisters whose consciences are violated by those teachings. Conscience fellowship is *fellowship within fellowship*, with those in each sub-fellowship, as it were, continuing to recognize their part in the greater family of God. It is fellowship which says, "We are brothers, but we must take separate roads."

Must We Divide Over All Issues?

Yet that only begs further questions. If, for example, anyone were to hold that fellowship must be broken because of disagreements about origins, or our future destiny—or perhaps more immediately compelling points of doctrine—why *those particular issues*? Why not also such issues as whether a widower can remain an elder after his wife dies; or whether it is right for an evangelist also to be an elder; or whether it is proper (perhaps even required) that elders anoint the sick with oil?

If, on the other hand, someone else were to hold that fellowship should *not* be broken because of disagreements related to questions of origins and future destiny, then why have other issues brought an end to fellowship? Issues like the missionary society, musical instruments, and cooperative schemes for supporting orphans homes?

Surely the initial answer must be that some issues directly affect us only as individual Christians, while other issues affect us corporately as a body of believers.

What you or I happen to believe about the "days" of Creation, or the extent of the Flood—or possibly even about premillennial-ism—has no direct impact on the church. If you or I might be wrong about the nature of our celestial bodies in heaven, or the form which eternal punishment will take in hell, the church at large will not suddenly be brought to a standstill.

By contrast, if musical instruments are used, every worshiper is affected If there is a missionary society, the whole organization of the church is affected. If we decide to support orphans homes out of the church budget, then everyone's contribution is affected.

This distinction between the private beliefs of individual Christians and corporate acts of the whole church goes a long way toward explaining why we have divided over certain issues, but not over others.

Enclaves of Conscience

The question arising at this point is whether it is biblical to have enclaves of conscience within "in Christ" fellowship? (By "en-claves" I mean groups of congregations which share a common un-derstanding on certain matters of conscience, such as the use or non-use of instruments. I'm not talking here about individual "church splits.") Does Scripture permit such segregation among brothers? Indeed, does it perhaps *demand* it?

Put differently, in light of our extended family, is there such a thing as "close family"? That is, tight-knit sub-groups of fellowship determined on the basis of mutually-shared consciences? Perhaps surprisingly, the answer is "yes."

Merely consider the great "conscience divide" between Jews and Gentiles in the first century church. Although brothers in Christ, united together in the same body, Jewish Christians and Gentile Christians had significant differences in both worship style and doctrinal understanding. Yet they were each given apostolic lat-itude to worship and live before God according to their respective consciences.

For Jews it meant continuing to observe circumcision, feasts, and Jewish dietary laws. For Gentiles it meant the freedom not to observe Jewish customs. Yet they remained brothers in Christ. Distinct but united. Separate but equal. Playing different notes, yet called to harmony.

When the Judaisers tried to impose their own consciences on everybody else, the apostles called for peaceful coexistence and mutual acceptance. At the Jerusalem conference of Acts chapter 15, Peter made a plea for unity that is as applicable to us today as it was to those who differed doctrinally in the first century:

> God, who knows the heart, showed that he accepted
> them by giving the Holy Spirit to them, just as he did
> to us. He made no distinction between us and them.

If there are to be enclaves of conscience fellowship, the broader boundaries of "in Christ" fellowship must be acknowledged at all times. Freedom to interact more intimately with those who are "close family" does not mean that we can deny, denigrate, or even ignore the wider extended family.

Which is not to suggest that we simply ignore or condone teaching, for example, which affirms gay marriages to be of God. That there are some doctrines too obviously ungodly to leave to others' conscientious understanding is underlined when the letter going out from the Jerusalem council highlighted certain sins (including sexual immorality) as being beyond the pale of other doctrinal differences.

Among such sins are not just homosexual marriages (too easy a target), but also heterosexual re-marriages that violate Jesus' clear teaching. For the moment, set aside the complicated questions surrounding the marital and spiritual state of those who come to Christ after already having been unscripturally divorced and re-married. There is nothing complicated about Jesus' teaching that a man is not to put away his wife and marry another woman unless his wife has committed adultery. How then can we ignore or condone the widespread practice of accepting unrepentant divorce and remarriage by those who were *Christians* at the time they broke covenant with their spouses without biblical cause?

Such obvious sin cannot simply be a matter of individual or congregational conscience. A contemporary version of the letter from the Jerusalem council would not urge us to "live and let live" regarding such fundamental moral error. That would be error in need of sharp rebuke.

The Heart of Conscience Fellowship

Chapter 14 (and the beginning of 15) of Paul's letter to the Romans is a virtual textbook on conscience and fellowship. Although Paul is specifically addressing the question of how individual Christians ought to deal with each other when matters of conscience arise, the principles are equally applicable to enclaves of Christians who differ with other Christians doctrinally. Listen again carefully, then, to Paul's instructions regarding conscience fellowship:

> One man [has a particular doctrinal understanding]; another man [has a different understanding]. Each one should be fully convinced in his own mind.

> So whatever you believe about these things keep between yourself and God.

> Who are you to judge someone else's servant? To his own master he stands or falls.

> You, then, why do you judge your brother? Or why do you look down on your brother?

> Accept one another, then, just as Christ accepted you, in order to bring praise to God.

Let us therefore make every effort to do what leads to
peace and to mutual edification.

May the God who gives endurance and encouragement
give you a spirit of unity among yourselves as you follow
Christ Jesus, so that with one heart and mouth you may
glorify the God and Father of our Lord Jesus Christ.

Few passages have been the subject of as much dispute as Romans 14, which itself begins with specific reference to "disputable matters." Does the passage address all disputed matters of doctrine (such as divorce and remarriage, instrumental music, and premillennialism) or only the two specific issues of eating meat and observing special religious days? Or indeed does the passage refer only to "authorized liberties" which are "matters of indifference" to God?

In the context of both the immediate chapter and the entire Roman letter, Paul was dealing with two specific issues—the first being the overarching issue of whether Gentiles were bound by the same restrictions once applicable only to Jews under the old law. It's all about doctrine, nothing that would be of *disinterest* to God.

The second issue, beginning in chapter 14 and continuing into chapter 15, is the question of how those who are "strong" are to forbear with those who are "weak." It's all about attitude, nothing to do with "authorized liberties" as opposed to "doctrine." For "the weak," eating only vegetables and observing special days were not just matters of personal scruples but dead serious doctrine—doctrinal practice associated with doctrinal belief.

Moreover, this second issue is aimed at individuals, not congregations. The individual "strong" Christian was not to cause an individual "weak" Christian to violate his conscience regarding his doctrinal understanding and practice.

That said, there is a principle inherent in the passage which applies across the board—whether to doctrinal understandings separating Jews and Gentiles; whether regarding meat eating and special days or regarding other doctrinal beliefs and practices; whether the "disputable matters" involve individuals or whole congregations. The principle is that *all matters of conscience will ultimately be judged not by us but by God.*

Does Romans 14 teach that either individuals or congregations are to tolerate sin in the name of Christian fellowship? Certainly not. The danger here, of course, is that one person can confuse sin (e.g. adultery) with doctrinal differences (e.g. whether a particular remarriage constitutes adultery). This can lead, in turn, to accusing others of tolerating adultery without acknowledging that, if the other person is right about the remarriage not being adulterous, then there is no sin at all being tolerated.

I appreciate that those who believe the remarriage to be adulterous will insist that it cannot be other than adultery, but it just brings us back to a frustrating doctrinal standoff—one of the very "disputable matters" about which Paul was writing. You can be sure that those who conscientiously refused to eat meat believed that those who did eat meat were doing so in violation of God's law. To them, eating meat was not a matter of scruples but sin. That is precisely why it was a matter of conscience.

What Romans 14 teaches is that 1) there will inevitably be disputable matters over which conscientious brothers and sisters in Christ will disagree; 2) that each Christian must practice that which his own conscience leads him to practice; 3) that each Christian is accountable to God for what he conscientiously believes and practices; and 4) that whenever a particular matter of conscience is seen as "silly" by "more mature" Christians, they have an obligation to avoid causing a violation of conscience on the part of the "weaker" brother.

For Paul it wasn't a matter of choice as between either unity or purity of doctrine but an imperative to maintain *both* purity of doctrine *and* unity. The balance was to be maintained by simultaneously honoring *submission* to conscience and *freedom* of conscience.

If we wish to be granted elbow-room for our own understanding of God's will, then we must grant that same elbow-room to all of our brothers and sisters in Christ. In that way we honor and protect both our consciences and theirs. Let there be no doubt: *We will not answer eternally to anyone else for what we believe or for how we worship God; and no one will answer to us.*

"Elbow-room," incidentally, may be something as simple as allowing time for others to mature in their understanding of what the Scripture teaches. Have we not all grown in our understanding over the years? Can we really expect every Christian—especially those who are babes in Christ—to have each and every point of doctrine absolutely correct all at once?

Contending for the Faith

This appeal for honoring the consciences of others is not a call for a moratorium on doctrinal purity or ecclesiological debate. Both in our own individual congregations and throughout the family of Christ, we must still "contend for the faith that was once for all entrusted to the saints," both regarding the person of Christ and his body, the church. Honoring the consciences of others does not mean that all doctrinal understandings are of equal merit. Nor does it mean that doctrinal error on the part of a baptized believer can never preclude eternal fellowship with God. Nor (for that very reason) that we should never challenge each other over doctrinal issues.

Anyone who thinks that after a person is biblically baptized virtually every other doctrinal issue is petty has missed the point. Anyone who thinks that all God cares about is moral purity in the lives of his children has forgotten what the inspired epistles have to say about such things as church organization, gender roles, benevolence, and Christian worship.

I honor the consciences of those who use instruments to accompany singing, but I believe that they are wrong to do so, and I will take every opportunity to convince them that temple music was part of a package of temple worship practices done away with under Christ. Likewise, I honor the consciences of those who believe that women may be appointed as elders and deacons or be given the freedom to teach men in public settings, but I believe that they are wrong in that belief, and I will continue to be outspoken in opposition to this rejection of God's call for male spiritual leadership.

Admittedly, honoring each other's consciences ("keeping what you believe between yourself and God"), yet still contending for doctrinal purity, stretches our comprehension. Yet I believe this twofold duty is a corollary to "speaking truth in love." Conscience fellowship doesn't muzzle doctrinal discussion; conscience fellowship shapes its form and makes it clear that, in the end, God is the One who will decide who is right.

Conscience fellowship never says, "How we worship and practice is of no ultimate consequence." It only says, "We must each be free to worship and practice conscientiously before the One who will bring every thought, deed, *and doctrine* into account.

Parting Company Peaceably as Brothers

If the extended family must at times be separated into enclaves of conscience fellowship, it can never be at the expense of *koinonia* fellowship. We must still care. We must still share. (Did not Gentiles contribute generously to the needs of their Jewish brothers?)

It is not diversity within the family of God that breaks fellowship—only our attitude about that diversity. Nor is continued *koinonia* fellowship to be seen as endorsing the actions of others in areas where we might differ. It simply affirms that, despite those differences, we recognize and appreciate brothers and sisters in Christ who are as much a part of the extended family as we are.

When we have sharp disagreements and feel compelled by conscience to part company, we are not wholly unlike Paul and Barnabas in their disagreement over John Mark (Acts 15:36-41). Although theirs was not strictly a doctrinal difference of opinion, the attitude with which they parted company is of immediate importance. They parted amicably, as brothers, each going his own way as he felt led.

Their *koinonia* attitude was like that of Abram and Lot, whose herdsmen became embroiled in rancorous turf wars when grazing land became scarce (Genesis 13:7-12). "So Abram said to Lot, 'Let's not have any quarreling between you and me, or between your herdsmen and mine, *for we are brothers*....Let's part company. If you go to the left, I'll go to the right; if you go to the right, I'll go to the left.'"

We see something of that same attitude again in the midst of the civil war between David's men, led by Joab, and Abner, commander of Saul's army (2 Samuel 2:12-29). In the heat of the battle Abner called out to Joab, "Must the sword devour forever? Don't you realize that this will end in bitterness? How long before you order your men to stop pursuing their brothers?" So Joab blew his trumpet, and the fighting stopped.

Surely it is time to blow the trumpet and stop our ungodly, unchrist-like infighting! No, not our ever-present obligation to "contend for the faith." But our *contentiousness*. Our *bitterness*. Our *biting* and *devouring* of one another. If we keep on doing that over matters of conscience, we will end up destroying one another, to no one's benefit, least of all God's. (Galatians 5:15)

As Moses said to the two Israelites who were fighting, "Men, you are brothers; why do you want to hurt each other?" (Acts 7:26)

At the Core of Conscience

In fairness, we have not always divided over such seemingly petty things as cups, classes, and clapping. Issues of conscience run far deeper than pianos, missionary societies, and orphans homes. What grabs the headlines is not always the full story.

I vividly remember an eye-opening discussion which I had with a group of brothers from the conservative Christian Churches in the northwest. They had asked me to come and speak with them about some of the issues I addressed in *The Cultural Church*. Their congregations were experiencing many of the same problems as ourselves relating to changes in doctrinal thinking and practice.

When at one point I mentioned the restoration rubric, "We speak where the Bible speaks and are silent where the Bible is silent," it was as if a lightning bolt had struck. What I had always read into that restoration phrase as *restriction* was, to them, *liberty*. No wonder we had always understood "the argument from silence" to forbid the use of instruments, while they had understood "the freedom of silence" to permit instruments! We didn't just disagree over instruments. At a much more fundamental level, we disagreed over hermeneutics.

Having grown up among the "non-institutional" (or "anti-co-operation") congregations, I was well aware too that the support of orphans homes was just the "corporate logo" in that infamous split. Deeper down, the fight was really about the principle of congregational autonomy—a fight which the "non-institutional" brothers were warranted in waging. Had they not raised a hue and cry, who knows what organizational superstructure might now exist among the churches of Christ?

Unfortunately what should have been a victory for conscience fellowship has turned out to be a colossal defeat in terms of our attitude towards those on the other side of the doctrinal fence. In the fight over institutions and autonomy, both sides were guilty of animosity. If a parting of the ways was probably inevitable, a lack of mutual love and respect was inexcusable. More serious yet—if conscience fellowship inexorably meant a separation, still, it should never have prompted the doubts which continue to linger in the minds of some about "in Christ" fellowship.

Conscience or Party Spirit?

Sadly, something insidious and sinister seems to happen whenever enclaves of conscience are formed for quite legitimate reasons. It's the eventual development of a party spirit. As time passes, the issues which originally raised concerns of conscience are long forgotten, and only a sense of exclusive correctness remains. "We are the faithful remnant." "We are the *true* Christians." "Surely, we are God's chosen ones."

At that point pure sectarian thinking sets in, and "in Christ" fellowship is reduced not just to a "close family" of shared conscience but to a wall-building, war-like clan of folks living in complete denial of anything like an extended family.

It's that air of superiority that gives the game away. We see it, for example, in the Pharisees and the Sadducees. They were more than just separated enclaves of conscience within the Jewish faith. Both groups were elitist snobs. Paul gives us an inkling of the smugness of the sectarian mentality when he said, "according to the *strictest sect* of our religion, I lived as a Pharisee" (Acts 26:5). The Pharisees weren't just right. They were *sure* they were right!

The same party spirit was also rampant in the church at Corinth (1 Corinthians 1:10-17). When Paul made his appeal that "all of you agree with one another so that there may be no divisions among you and that you may be perfectly united in mind and thought," he wasn't ruling out those situations where sincere conflicts of conscience might require a parting of the ways within an ongoing larger fellowship. What he was facing was a secular mindset of power struggles, personality cults, and a party spirit fostered by arrogance, not conscience.

The quarreling among the Corinthians appears to center around certain individuals—either Paul, Apollos, Cephas, and Christ, literally, or perhaps unnamed local leaders for whom Paul substitutes the more widely known personalities in order to better make his point. But from what we know about our own splits, the disputes undoubtedly ran much deeper than "preacheritis." They weren't just saying, "I am of Max"; or "I follow Rubel"; or "I follow LaGard." Deeper down, the Paulites probably identified closely with Paul's "intellectually-articulated" position on Gentile liberty;

and the Cephasites with a Jewish legalism more likely associated with Cephas (Peter).

But not even those underlying doctrinal affinities appear to be the cause of Paul's rebuke. By the time of Paul's letter, what apparently mattered most to the Corinthian brothers was an identifiable allegiance not simply to a particular doctrinal position (does Paul mention any specific issues?) but to a particular party, identified by their chosen standard-bearer.

When a party spirit takes over from issues of conscience, then separation into "close family" enclaves has lost its legitimacy. At that point the hallmark of clan warfare is power and pride. No wonder Paul quoted Jeremiah's warning: "Let him who boasts, boast in the Lord" (1 Corinthians 1:31). No wonder he employed the admonition, "Do not go beyond what is written," saying, "Then you will not take pride in one man over against another" (1 Corinthians 4:6).

Separation motivated by the constraints of conscience is sometimes necessary. Division motivated by ego, arrogance, power-struggles, and pride has no place. Such division serves only to destroy "in Christ" fellowship.

A Party Spirit Is No Picnic

Nor should anyone assume that either one of the two extremes in our extended family is more or less inclined to withhold fellowship because of doctrinal differences. From the wounds of personal experience, I can tell you that the extreme right and the extreme left can be equally divisive and mean-spirited. What I experienced in my earlier years among the conservatives, some of whom pride themselves on being guardians of truth, has been duplicated in kind in my more recent associations with liberals, who tend to pride themselves on tolerance and unity.

If you take our continuum of fellowship and bend it in a circle, you'll find that the radical right and the radical left meet on the back side of the continuum. The liberals may be more subtle in their divisiveness, but they can be no less exclusivistic and judgmental in their own sophisticated way than the hard-core, in-your-face fellowship police on the radical right.

When conscience fellowship is displaced by a party spirit—whether right, left, or center—you can be sure that there "ain't gonna be no party." Only hatred, spite, and ill will. Not even America's Civil War, fought between brothers in the flesh, engendered such enmity. In most instances it was a more *civil* war than our own vicious skirmishing over biblical doctrine.

Just how wrong can that be? Character-assassinating preachers, bow your heads in shame! Editors of venomous, warmongering brotherhood papers, fall on your knees! "Brothers, do not slander one another!" (James 4:11).

What in the world must God think of his children? What must a sin-stained, love-starved, spiritually-lost world think of us? How, by any means, do we expect the church to wage war against Satan and to save souls if we are consumed with consuming each other?

Let me share with you a great quote. It's from Bishop Burnet's preface to Henry Scougal's late seventeenth century work, *The Life of God in the Soul of Man*. [Emphasis mine.]

> There is scarce a more unaccountable thing to be imagined, than to see a company of men professing a religion, one great and main precept whereof is mutual love, forbearance, gentleness of spirit, and compassion to all sorts of persons, and agreeing in all the essential parts of its doctrine, and differing only in some less material and more disputable things, yet *maintaining those differences with zeal so disproportioned to the value of them*, and prosecuting all that disagree from them with all possible violence....
>
> They must needs astonish every impartial beholder, and raise great prejudices against such persons' reli-

gion, as made up of contradictions; *professing love, but breaking out in all the acts of hatred.*

What a convicting commentary! Could it be us— "maintaining our differences with zeal so disproportioned to the value of them?" Could it be us—"professing love, but breaking out in all the acts of hatred?"

Father, forgive us. We know not what we do.

A House Divided

Earlier mention of the Civil War reminds me of Jesus' words (Mark 3:25) that "if a house is divided against itself, that house cannot stand." Having decimated our own brothers through years of infighting, we have rendered ourselves unable to fight the real enemy and have left ourselves vulnerable to the world.

Which brings me to this thought. Surely it is not mere coincidence that God's family, Israel, was divided into twelve tribes. Twelve "close families," drawing strength from diversity. As long as they continued to see themselves as part of the larger family, Israel was united, strong, and victorious.

We see that spirit of "one for all and all for one" in the opening verses of the book of Judges, where, upon the death of Joshua, the Israelites planned their final strategy to rid the land of the Canaanites. When God indicated that the tribe of Judah was to lead the way, "the men of Judah said to the Simeonites their brothers, 'Come up with us into the territory allotted to us, to fight against the Canaanites. We in turn will go with you into yours.' So the Simeonites went with them."

Separate tribes though they were, they joined together to fight a common enemy. "How good and pleasant it is when brothers live together in unity!" (Psalm 133:1).

Of course we know that it was not always love and kisses between the tribes. Like us, at times they too had strong disagreements—even to the point of armed conflict.

Having opened on a high note of inter-tribal unity, the book of Judges closes with civil war between the tribe of Benjamin and the rest of Israel. What caused the conflict could not have been further removed from something so noble as maintaining doctrinal purity. Judges chapter 19 tells of an incident (strangely reminiscent of Lot and the men of Sodom) in which the men of Benjamin rape and kill a concubine belonging to a Levite who is staying for the night in the city of Gibeah.

It's a gruesome picture, but the Levite was so incensed at the way he had been treated by the men of Benjamin that he cut his concubine's body into twelve pieces and sent them all over Israel. The remaining eleven tribes got the message and vowed to avenge the wrong—at the point of a sword. A great struggle ensued.

On the first day of battle the tribe of Benjamin scored a huge victory, leaving Israel wondering if they might be doing the wrong thing in fighting against their brothers. So they inquired of the Lord, "Shall we go up again to battle against the Benjamites, *our brothers*?" And the Lord answered, "Go up against them."

There are times when we have little choice but to cross swords with our brothers. I believe that our present crisis is one of those times.

After losing again on the second day, and inquiring again whether it was God's will to fight against Benjamin, Israel was finally given the victory. With a vengeance! So great was their victory that the men of Benjamin were almost completely wiped out, leaving the future of that tribe in serious jeopardy.

It is here that the most amazing thing happens (Judges 21:2-3). "The people went to Bethel, where they sat before God until evening, raising their voices and weeping bitterly. 'O Lord, the God of Israel,' they cried, 'why has this happened to Israel? Why should one tribe be missing from Israel today?'"

Can you imagine what it would be like if those of us committed to *a cappella* music were to gather in Nashville or Dallas and grieve for our instrumental brothers, "because the Lord had made a gap in the tribes of Israel" (Judges 21:15)? Talk about a unity meeting!

And for the people of Israel, it wasn't just an ecumenical photo op. So great was their concern for the extended family of God that they devised a way to repopulate the tribe of Benjamin—even despite an earlier vow that none of them would ever give his daughter in marriage to a Benjamite. Incredibly enough, they managed this gesture of peace without having to break that vow.

Having thus honored *conscience* and *unity* simultaneously, "the Israelites left that place and went home to their tribes and clans, each to his own inheritance."

In today's terms—each to his own doctrinal understanding. Each to his own conscience fellowship. Each to his own "close family."

The Greatest Threat to Conscience Fellowship

Today there is a grand irony at work among us—or a stroke of pure genius on the part of Satan. The current call for wide-open "in Christ" fellowship with all "whose faith is in the cross and whose eyes are on the Savior"—regardless of baptism—presents the most challenging threat of all to conscience fellowship.

Think about it. Since conscience fellowship can only take place *within* "in Christ" fellowship, the move to accept unbiblical forms of Christian birth stretches to the breaking point our ability conscientiously to maintain "in Christ" fellowship with those who advocate and practice such a departure from Scripture.

How in good conscience can we have fellowship with brothers and sisters who are *undermining* "in Christ" fellowship? More serious yet, what fellowship would we be expected to have with those who might be accepted into churches of Christ without ever having truly become Christians?

We're no longer talking about the usual controversial issues. Nothing (apart, perhaps, from acknowledging Christ himself) could be more fundamental to "in Christ" fellowship than what it means to be "in Christ." Nothing (apart from the good news of God's saving grace) could be more "essential" to the gospel than how God has called us to respond to the good news.

With so much at stake the time is almost certainly coming when conscience fellowship will demand a separation from those who are currently advocating wide-open "Christian" fellowship with those who have not been united with Christ in biblical baptism. When that teaching is finally acted upon, it will not be solely a matter of personal conscience. It will be a corporate act affecting all the rest of us. Given such an impact on the whole body, division is not just probable; it is inevitable.

Further division among us—all in the name of Christian unity—will be reprehensible enough. But, stranger still, is the prospect of something we've never before encountered: the open acceptance of non-Christians within the churches of Christ.

Just how messy is fellowship going to get when we can no longer assume that someone who comes into our midst from another congregation of the churches of Christ is in fact a Christian? When the one thing we've always had in common (our baptism into Christ) is no longer commonly shared, the greatest division possible will have taken place.

If there is any silver lining to the dark clouds on the horizon, maybe, just maybe, we (on all sides) will finally be forced to make a distinction between the denominational Church of Christ and the non-denominational body of Christ, which is his church. It may be that we have erred to one extreme in the past. At that extreme only a denominational Church of Christ could have denied fellowship to those who were well and truly Christians. Now it appears that we are moving to the opposite extreme, where only a denominational Church of Christ can offer Christian fellowship to those who have never become Christians.

Before some of us go that far, it is left for the rest of us to draw a line in the sand. When it comes to conscience fellowship over the matter of Christian birth, previous controversies are penny ante.

Never will our various "close families" within the universal body of Christ be at greater distance than when we must separate from our ecumenically-minded, body-threatening brothers and sisters in the extended family.

If only it didn't have to happen. Is there not time even now to turn back? Is there not something within good conscience that we can do to prevent having a "missing tribe" among us? It's no secret that Satan's battle plan is to divide and conquer. Are we merely going to sit back and let him win? Or will today be the day that we cross swords in truth and love, then bind up our wounds and walk home together as brothers?

Conscience Fellowship

• Differences of conscience may require that we worship apart from other brothers and sisters in the extended family.

• Only those issues which affect our gathered worship typically require separate sub-groups of fellowship.

• Since matters of conscience will be judged by God, not by us, we must permit others the same freedom of conscience which we ourselves exercise.

• Honoring freedom of conscience does not lessen our responsibility to stand against doctrinal error either in our home congregation or in the church at large.

• Rancorous church splits honor neither freedom of conscience nor doctrinal purity.

• When divided by conscience, we remain brothers and sisters in the extended family of God.

CHAPTER NINE

CONGREGATIONAL FELLOWSHIP: IMMEDIATE FAMILY

A happy family is but an earlier heaven.

SIR JOHN BOWRING

Of the five different levels of fellowship, congregational fellowship is the most comforting—and can be the most confounding. It is comforting because it embodies the *koinonia* fellowship of caring and sharing at the most personal and intimate level. It is family. The *immediate* family.

Congregational fellowship is God's sublime answer to *Cheers*, "where everybody knows your name." No, not people whose emptiness is filled by nothing more than beer and banter, but people who worship together, pray together, study together, eat together, laugh together, cry together.

The local congregation is a spiritual "Neighborhood Watch." We look out for one another. We protect each other. Pull for each other. Encourage each other. Remind each other. And if need be, rebuke each other.

Both physically and spiritually, God put us in families for a purpose. Somebody has to know us, warts and all. Somebody has to love us, warts and all. Week in and week out. Year in and year out. Mistake in and mistake out.

Congregational fellowship may not be "'til death do us part," but it certainly encompasses "in sickness and in health." It means pot lucks for the healthy and bowls of soup for the sick. It means hospitality in the home, prayers in the hospital, sympathy at the graveside, and hugs whenever we need them.

Congregational fellowship is God's answer for loneliness. It is his way of telling us day in and day out that we are loved. That we have brothers and sisters who think we are important. And that they, in turn, are important to us. The best antidote to loneliness is not being served but serving; and congregational fellowship is tailor-made for having people to serve.

In the immediate family of a local congregation even single Christians can share the joys of being with children. And older folks can be "grandparents," whether or not they have grandchildren of their own. For those who are far away from their physical families, the church family near at hand is a serendipity of faith. Need a family? Find one in your local congregation.

Blurred Visions of the Cozy Family

Having an immediate family in the church can be all that and more. My own spiritual family for the past twenty years has been such a family. Lots of caring and sharing. Lots of serving and being served. Lately, lots of tears and shared pain at the loss of those we have loved, and lots of prayers for those still battling cancer and other life-threatening diseases.

Support comes in many different forms. Who but family could have tolerated my quirks, forgiven my mistakes, and seen the best in me when there was ample opportunity to dwell on the worst? Who but family would have allowed me such space to grow spiritually during times when I had so much growing to do?

Single for most of those years, I was also the beneficiary of more table fellowship than any bachelor ever deserved. And who could have asked for more precious "little people" in my life?

But it hasn't always been an easy fellowship. Over the years, the elders have received more than my fair share of letters, expressing concerns about a number of different issues. We've talked bluntly, prayed fervently, and disagreed often. It's not by accident that I've become known as the congregation's token conservative. Yet despite the fact that I often write issue-oriented books, I don't really enjoy the process of protest.

I could wish that my concerns were raised only by threats to my personal comfort zone. I confess that trendy contemporary innovations in worship style have made me want to run screaming out of the auditorium on more than one occasion. During one period it seemed we couldn't have a time of worship together unless we could assure ourselves that we were doing *something* different! But as in many congregations today, a growing sensitivity to personal preferences has led to a truce brokered by dual services—one, contemporary and lively; one, more traditional and solemn.

Unfortunately, far more serious matters of doctrine have presented a greater struggle. I've come to live with the feeling that I'm always just one crucial issue away from having no more room to manoeuver within the parameters of my conscience.

So what shall it be? Stay or go? Fight or withdraw? Maintain unity in the bonds of peace or abandon unity in the same spirit of peace? I can't tell you how many times I've revisited these tough questions.

Of course, it is not just I who am struggling with "immediate family" fellowship. Wherever I go these days, the questions I'm most frequently asked pertain to congregational fellowship: "What should we do now that our congregation has gone off the rails?" "Can we stay where we've been worshiping for years, now that they've introduced worship teams, drama skits, and Saturday night seeker services?" "Is there any way that I can keep my membership in a congregation that has appointed deaconesses?"

The anguish in the faces can hardly be described. Especially the older faces. The faces of men and women who don't understand why change is necessary. The faces of men and women who have given years of their lives in service to the congregation—who have paid for the building which they now see as being desecrated by unworthy worship.

Sure, maybe they *are* traditionalists. Maybe they *are* too concerned about a piece of real estate and not sufficiently concerned about what kind of worship is being lifted up to God. But at least they have earned the right to ask those anguished questions. They too are part of the immediate family. In fact, in most congregations they are the very backbone of the family.

So, questions, questions, and more questions. These days, so it seems, almost everybody has questions.

At What Point My Departure?

I don't know whether I'm the best person to talk about congregational fellowship, or, in fact, the last person who ought to speak out about it. I'm well aware that there are plenty of folks who would be critical of my staying as long as I have with a congregation which has posed so many questions of conscience over the years. I suppose they would call it compromise of the worst sort. Selling out. Caving in. Sometimes I've felt that way myself. The line in the sand seems ever shifting.

On the other hand, I can't help but think that learning to honor differences of conscience and style within an immediate family of brothers and sisters in Christ is a noble quest. Indeed, a spiritual imperative. In a very real sense it is not unlike coexisting with siblings in our own physical families. Even if we sometimes do an abysmal job of honoring the differences we have among us, it is always the aim, always the goal.

With our physical families, of course, we can't exactly just walk out and become part of some other family. That being true with flesh and blood, perhaps it is not such a good thing that we can do it so blithely with our church family. It doesn't take much these days to see that there is too much church-shopping and church-hopping going on.

Perhaps we're just cursed with success in some areas of the country, having unlimited options from which to choose. Yet maybe we shouldn't have the right to decide which congregation we will become a part of—especially if our decision is based upon nothing more substantial than a sense of aesthetics, or size, or worship style, or youth programs, or who the preacher happens to be.

If the process of attaching ourselves to a congregation were more exacting, perhaps our reasons for leaving a congregation would have to be more demanding. Imagine how much more cautious we might be in parting ways if becoming a member of the congregation involved more than just filling out a card expressing a desire to be recognized as a member. Nor is there much incentive to be deliberative about jumping ship when all it takes to withdraw from a congregation is simply no longer to show up!

Unfortunately, we have frustratingly little biblical instruction in this area. But if "the right hand of fellowship" were *extended* with more reflection, we might actually give more serious thought before *unclasping* the fellowship represented by that same "right hand."

As one who has faced the dilemma of what to do about congregational fellowship, I can tell you that running away is always a great temptation, but that refusing to run away has its own rewards for those who persevere. The list of questions which follows is by no means exhaustive, but I'll share with you some of the private thoughts arising out of my own struggle.

1) Is my discontent a matter of **conscience** or **comfort zone**? The wider latitude which ought to be given to others instead of insisting on my own personal comfort zone begins to narrow quickly when I can no longer worship in good conscience. But on this one I've got to be truly honest with myself. The particular way in which I feel most comfortable worshiping God has a funny way of turning into a "doctrinal issue" when no real doctrinal issue may be at stake.

Nor are all legitimate doctrinal differences in themselves matters of conscience. What are we doing as a congregation that crosses the line from *mere style* to *biblical error*? I may or may not like the raising of hands in worship, for example, but I could hardly deny that there is biblical precedent for raising holy hands to God!

2) **What efforts have I made to effectuate change?** Have I tried to resolve whatever issues are troubling me? Have I talked with the elders? Have I come up with possible solutions to the problem? Sometimes it may even require some soul-searching on my part to discover how *I myself* might need to change!

3) **What endorsement am I lending by my continued presence?** Guilt by association is not always legitimate, but it is almost always assumed! "No man is an island," or something like that. Others are watching. Inquiring minds want to know why I worship where I do—especially those who are in the same congregation. Do they assume that my membership in the congregation is an endorsement for what takes place there? Has my mere presence become for someone else a tacit reason for their supporting something I am personally opposed to?

4) **What good influence might I have by staying?** Maybe every congregation needs a token conservative (or a token liberal) to help stay the course. If all the whistle-blowers leave, who is left to hold the others accountable? It's possible, of course, to fool myself into thinking that I'm having an influence for good when I'm not. It's also possible for me to be the one who ends up being influenced! Sometimes it's the rescuers themselves who are lost during a rescue operation.

5) **What are my alternatives?** As with those who divorce and remarry, the likelihood is that I am merely going to exchange one set of problems for another. As someone has said, "the grass may indeed be greener on the other side, but you still have to mow it!" Usually what's on offer is a tradeoff between doctrine without spirit and spirit without doctrine. That Hobson's choice is simply unacceptable. God calls us to both.

Nor does a change in congregations guarantee freedom from conflicts of conscience. How many New Testament congregations, much less congregations today, were free from all doctrinal error?

Usually it's a matter of whose doctrinal faults you want to put up with most!

And sometimes there are simply no other options. If, for instance, there is only one congregation in town, the door is pretty much closed. Even driving to the next town is rarely a good solution. With each additional mile away from home, the opportunity for up close and personal *koinonia* fellowship recedes further and further. It's hard to be part of an *immediate* family when one is only a commuter Christian.

6) **Is my discomfort worth the cost of broken fellowship?** If a doctrinal issue is what most concerns me, I mustn't forget that unity among brothers and sisters in Christ is as much a matter of conscience as any other point of doctrine. Is the issue at stake sufficiently important that I must shatter the intimacy of a family which has nurtured me and supported me through thick and thin? Will my leaving cause disruption among others in the family?

And if I must leave, are there perhaps either better or worse ways to make an exit as a Christian concerned about unity? Leaving in a huff hardly captures the spirit of a principled departure; and—who knows?—if more people would leave with tears in their eyes, fewer people might actually end up leaving!

Having struggled with these complex questions for many years now, I have somehow managed to maintain a continuing, if rocky, fellowship among brothers and sisters with whom I sometimes disagree almost as much as I love. Yet staying on board has not just been an exercise in maintaining body unity. It has also made it possible for me to be part of a vital outreach to those who don't know Christ in the area where I work and live. It's easy to be so consumed with the problems of family fellowship that we forget our far greater responsibility to bring others into the family. Although immediate-family fellowship is important, it means nothing if extended-family "in Christ" fellowship is made to take a back seat.

Church Splits and Personality Power-Struggles

What goes for the lone Christian goes for the many. I speak here of the far-too-numerous "church splits" which have plagued us throughout our history. It is telling that in the entire record of the New Testament church, there is not one mention of anything like what we know as a church split. Enclaves of "conscience fellowship," yes (as between Jewish Christians and Gentile Christians); but church splits, no. Even the *divisive* church in Corinth was not a *split* church in Corinth. We mustn't forget that Paul says, I hear that there are divisions among you *"when you come together as a church"* (1 Corinthians 11:18). The church in Corinth was not always a harmonious church, but it was nevertheless a unified church.

If there were quarrels, they were between brothers and sisters within the immediate family, not among several other immediate families splintered off from the first. As far as we can tell, those who were "of Paul" did not worship separately from those who were "of Apollos" or those who were "of Cephas."

Church splits of the type we have today—complete with ungodly law suits over which group gets to keep the building—are unheard of in the early church. Maybe that's because the church in a given area was referred to collectively (as, for example, "the church in Jerusalem") which might have included a large number of congregations meeting and working separately. Or maybe there were church splits of which we simply aren't told. Whatever the case in the first century, today we enter into uncharted scriptural territory when we participate in any such split.

Presumably there are certain doctrinal issues which, as a matter of conscience, might require—as a last resort—that two distinct groups within a given congregation go their separate ways. Yet if it were truly a matter of conscience that made such a separation necessary, there would be no cause for the kind of rancor that typically accompanies church splits. Each group, respecting the conscience of the other, would part in tears and continue to respect each other as fellow Christians doing their very best to follow in the steps of Christ.

That church splits are more likely to end in tearing apart than in tears suggests that genuine doctrinal concerns are probably on the back burner. More likely on the front burner are personality rifts. Perhaps rifts like the one between Euodia and Syntyche (Philippians 4:2-3)—a rift which never reached the point of dividing the church in Philippi. Could that be because "the loyal yokefellow" did what Paul pleaded with them to do—to "help these women" resolve their differences? Does that not suggest what needs to happen long before a congregation gets to the point of a split?

The thing about splits resulting from personality conflicts is that virtually any point of doctrine can be used as an excuse to do what folks want to do in the first place. Show me a congregation whose members are not happy with each other for whatever reason, and I'll show you a "doctrinal dispute" just waiting to break out!

So let there be no talk of bitter divorce within a congregation, only sorrowful separation. If the latter is sometimes made necessary by conscience, no one's conscience ought ever to permit the former.

Where We May Have It All Wrong

Constantly aware of how difficult immediate family fellowship can sometimes be, I am haunted by the thought that those difficulties may exist in large measure because we've misunderstood what it means to be a member of a congregation of the Lord's people. What is a congregation anyway? How does it form? Why does it exist? To whom is it responsible, and who is responsible to it? For the next few moments it's back to basics.

When the body of Christ is referred to in Scripture in anything less than its universal sense, it is generally attached to a particular geographical location. We see references, for example, to "the church of God at Corinth," "the church in Cenchrea," "the church at Jerusalem," and "the church at Antioch." And we all know about the seven churches in Asia to whom John's Revelation was given—the churches in Ephesus, Smyrna, Pergamum, Thyatira, Sardis, Philadelphia, and Laodicea. In a variation on theme, we also see references to "the church of the Laodiceans" or to "the church of the Thessalonians."

Sometimes we even see a large number of churches in the same area, as with "God's churches in Judea" (1 Thessalonians 2:14) and "the churches in the province of Asia" (1 Corinthians 16:19), and the more generic "All the churches of Christ send greetings" (Romans 16:16).

At other times the association is with someone in whose home the congregation gathers for worship, such as "the church that meets in your home," referring to Philemon (Philemon 1:2); or "the church that meets at their house," referring to Priscilla and Aquila (Romans 16:5); or "the church in her house," referring to Nympha (Colossians 4:15).

The church was never meant to be exclusively universal. By God's own design, the church was meant to be gathered into smaller units of fellowship through which his work on earth could be accomplished.

We can learn much about congregational purpose and function by observing how these local churches were organized and run. In the beginning of his letter to the Philippians, for example, Paul directs his thoughts "to all the saints in Christ Jesus at Philippi, together with the overseers and deacons." Each congregation was composed of Christians under the leadership of both "overseers" (elders) and deacons—whose qualifications are more particularly set forth in Paul's letters to Timothy and Titus.

Rather than merely providing a forum for weekly corporate worship, these local congregations were structured in such a way as to provide spiritual leadership and Christian maturity for each member. The evidence for this is found in a number of different passages, including Acts 14:23, where "Paul and Barnabas appointed elders for them in each church"; and Acts 20:17, where "Paul sent to Ephesus for the elders of the church" and told them (20:28) to "keep watch over yourselves and all the flock of which the Holy Spirit has made you overseers." In his first letter (5:1,2), Peter also addresses elders and commissions them to "be shepherds of God's flock that is under your care...."

From these passages it is hard to come away with the notion that there was anything like our smorgasbord of congregations from which to choose. Those who became Christians met together for worship and study and table fellowship with the Christians who were closest to them, and they were all fed and led by those who had been appointed to lead that local body of God's people.

As far as we can tell, it wasn't so much a matter of *choosing* a congregation (and maybe changing one's mind later) but rather *submitting* to the spiritual oversight of those who had been put in positions of leadership in a given locale.

Immediate family fellowship in the days of the apostles wasn't anything like being a member of your local Rotary or Kiwanis club. The congregation didn't exist for one's own convenience or enjoyment. You didn't just join one Lord's day because you liked what you saw and then quit the next Lord's day because you changed your mind.

Having enlisted as a member of the Lord's army, the New Testament Christian was put into a platoon where he could be trained, disciplined, and molded into a cohesive fighting unit for the spiritual war being waged all around him. Or, to change the metaphor, each new sheep was separated into a smaller flock where he could be watched over and nourished and safeguarded by a shepherd who knew his flock individually by both name and need.

It is inconceivable that anything like today's noncommittal congregational affiliations existed in the first century. It wasn't so much a matter of *choosing* as of being, in a sense, *chosen*. Certainly it wasn't the composition of the congregation (much less its youth programs, facilities, or preacher) which had to pass muster, but rather one's commitment to an "immediate family" of brothers and sisters, whatever its makeup and whoever its leaders. Except where there was a change of address, only matters of conscience (such as those which existed between Jewish and Gentile Christians) suggested anything like our current practice of leaving one congregation for another.

Is Congregational Autonomy Just So Much Talk?

There are both internal and external implications which flow from the New Testament model of congregational fellowship. Internally, it means that we have much to reconsider regarding when and under what circumstances we can "change membership." Are we sheep with wandering rights, permitted to roam freely in search of greener pastures, or have we been called into flocks closest to home where spiritual shepherds have been given the responsibility to watch over our souls?

Externally, it means that we need to reaffirm our stated commitment to congregational autonomy. Oh, how we honor it with our lips, but our practice is far from it! When God gathered us into local congregations, he gathered us into immediate families responsible only to him, not to anyone else. Under the oversight and leading of its shepherds, each congregation must worship and function within its own collective conscience. The principle of family autonomy hasn't changed through the centuries. Together with Joshua we must continue to affirm that, while others must choose for themselves, "as for me and my household, we will serve the Lord" (Joshua 24:15).

Ever since the restorationist controversy over the missionary society, we have talked a good line about congregational autonomy. "No synods, conventions, or other organizational hierarchy for us, thank you very much!" But that hasn't stopped the brotherhood police from making congregations toe whatever line they happen to have drawn, at the risk of certain censure and castigation if they don't.

Let one congregation step out of line and you can be sure that there are plenty of others who are ready to "withdraw fellowship" from it. As if congregations can withdraw from each other. As if congregations were ever tied together in the first place.

It's one thing to have doctrinal enclaves of close-family "conscience fellowship" (where we ourselves may be compelled to withdraw). It's another thing altogether to shun some congregation in the same way the Corinthians were to shun the man who had his father's wife. Lest we forget, *only God can remove lampstands!* (Revelation 2:5,6). "He who has an ear, let him hear what the Spirit says to the churches."

Autonomy Doesn't Mean Total Independence

This is not to say, of course, that we are without biblical precedent for interaction among the various churches of Christ. At the direction of the apostles, local congregations in the first century shared benevolence with other congregations who had need. The very basis for our practice of taking up a collection on the Lord's day comes from 1 Corinthians 16:1-4, where the money being collected was being sent from one congregation to another. Or more correctly, from *several* congregations to the needy Christians in Jerusalem. ("Do what I told the Galatian churches to do.")

The same is true of financial support which was given in aid of evangelism. Paul thanked the Philippians for their "partnership in the gospel," an obvious reference to how they had supported Paul through their generous contributions as he travelled about on his missionary journeys. "Even when I was in Thessalonica," said Paul, "you sent me aid again and again when I was in need" (Philippians 4:14-19). Although this contribution was not strictly "congregation to congregation," we have here an example where one "immediate family" contributed so that the "extended family" might be extended even further.

Finally, congregational autonomy is not to be understood as precluding efforts toward achieving doctrinal unity among far-flung congregations. Even given the unique nature of apostolic leadership in the early church, we learn something of this from Paul when he tells the Corinthians, "This is the rule I lay down *in all the churches*" (1 Corinthians 7:17). And again he warns, "If anyone wants to be contentious about this, we have no other practice—nor do the churches of God" (1 Corinthians 11:16).

If congregationally we are free and independent of all others, no congregation is free to depart from the apostolic teaching to which all congregations will be held accountable. This is why we periodically come together from our various congregations to search the Scriptures and to discuss issues of mutual concern. It is in the spirit of mutual edification that we participate in annual Bible lectureships at church-related universities or in other retreats and workshops—and certainly in gospel meetings in local congregations which those from other congregations may drive some distance to attend.

In earlier chapters I've been a bit rough on some of the "brotherhood papers" for what I believe are often attitudes unbecoming brothers, but if they took to the high road of loving confrontation, even those papers could have their place in facilitating dialogue among us. As do "brotherhood books"—like this very book and others—which are written for the extended family.

Although no local congregation is to be a watchdog over any other local congregation or group of congregations, individually and collectively we are still our brothers' keepers. We owe it to each other to contend for the faith in both our immediate and extended families.

What we must be careful never to cross is the line between mutual edification, on one hand, and usurping the responsibility given to local churches and their spiritual leaders, on the other. If perhaps conscience prevents us from joining together in close-family fellowship, we must nevertheless honor the collective conscience of each and every other congregation.

In fact let me put it as boldly as I can: *All congregations of be-*

lievers who share "in Christ" fellowship are to be regarded as local bodies of Christian brothers and sisters. Though we have every right (indeed an obligation) to teach each other the way of the Lord more perfectly, we have neither right nor obligation to require that any congregation answer to us.

One of the wonderful things about our large annual lectureships and workshops is that we come together as individual brothers and sisters in Christ, almost completely unaware of what we all happen to believe and practice in our various congregations back home. How am I to know if someone is from a congregation that is non-institutional, or insists on women wearing veils, or believes in the "one cup," or even uses musical instruments? Praise God that once or twice a year we can meet beyond the constrictive bounds of conscience to talk openly about matters of conscience!

Well, almost openly. A conspiracy of silence does dampen some of our lectureships (both on the left and on the right) when someone strays too far from the party line. "Party line" is code for just another way that we attempt to override congregational autonomy by making sure everyone within "our group" walks in lockstep with everybody else. At that point we've abandoned the spirit of mutual edification and simply imposed a creed.

Ironically, such creeds are often imposed regarding some of those very gatherings of the extended family. The issue here is not whether good things or bad things happen at a given lectureship. (I myself have been critical of some of these programs, even while participating in them.) The point is that there is no biblical authority for ostracizing congregations (or, worse yet, orchestrating secondary boycotts against anyone who joins with them) simply because they participate in some common effort with which others cannot participate in good conscience.

Oddly enough, some of those who most demand congregational autonomy for themselves are the least likely to grant it to others. We have a number of brothers out there who are not content to shepherd the flock that is under their care. Some of these guardians of the faith are never satisfied until they have donned papal robes to become overseers of the entire flock, exercising discipline over whole congregations and removing lampstands with all the authority of Christ himself!

It's time we paid more than lip service to congregational autonomy. God's shepherds have enough to do without having to worry about officious intermeddlers! Elders, surround your flocks with the Word and with prayer, and don't be swayed by wolves on the outside who pass judgment without having the accountability which you alone bear.

The Hardest Part of Family Fellowship

More than once now I have talked about the importance of table fellowship. It's a buzzword, really, for *koinonia* fellowship. Nothing more epitomizes the local congregation than the many ways in which it calls the family to the table. The Lord's table. The "covered dish" table. The dinner table.

I would like to say that the closest we come on any regular basis to sharing *koinonia*-like fellowship is in our weekly observance of the Lord's supper. Unfortunately, our experience around the Lord's table can hardly be compared with first-century *koinonia* fellowship. We have turned the fellowship meal (with all that having such a meal would entail) into a rather perfunctory ritual, done not just weekly but *weakly!* Far too often, what we do together in formally passing around the bread and the cup is not likely to bring us closer, or to tear down walls, or to build each other up.

As intended, the Lord's table should be table fellowship of the highest order. As Paul puts it in his First Corinthian letter (10:16-17), "Is not the cup of thanksgiving for which we give thanks a participation in the blood of Christ? And is not the bread that we break a participation in the body of Christ? Because there is one loaf, we, who are many, are one body, for we all partake of the one loaf." Interestingly, what begins as *koinonia* fellowship (the shared cup and bread) actually ends up being a picture of our "in Christ" fellowship.

Yet as we are reminded by the first-century Christians, table fellowship is to be experienced through more than simply the Lord's supper. For those on-fire Pentecost Christians, *koinonia* fellowship meant having table fellowship "from house to house." Eating together was a sign of their unity. The sharing of food was symbolic of their shared faith in Christ.

In fact, table fellowship was so important to New Testament Christians that Paul enjoined its refusal as a means of bringing wayward brothers and sisters back to faithfulness. Remember the man in Corinth who had his father's wife—the one who Paul said should be "put out of their fellowship"? He wasn't talking about "in Christ" fellowship (something we neither grant nor take away), but *koinonia* fellowship (something we *do* grant and *can* take away).

That Paul was speaking of withdrawn table fellowship as a means of discipline is confirmed when he writes (in 1 Corinthians 5:11), "You must not associate with anyone who calls himself a brother but is sexually immoral or greedy, an idolater or a slanderer, a drunkard or a swindler. *With such a man do not even eat.*"

Of course, if withdrawing table fellowship is going to have the desired effect, there must have been an enviable ongoing table fellowship to begin with. What hope do we today have of sending a message like that when table fellowship is so woefully out of vogue?

For the moment the point about *koinonia* fellowship is that we may have "in Christ" fellowship with a brother yet not share *koinonia* fellowship—either because *we* have had to withdraw "the right hand of fellowship" (Galatians 2:9), or because *he* himself (like Demas) has decided to break fellowship with his family.

It was *koinonia* fellowship which the prodigal son gave up when he left his father's table. That the father threw a feast when his lost son finally returned is not a coincidence. The renewal of table fellowship in that story symbolizes the renewal of *koinonia* fellowship which takes place whenever a wayward brother in Christ returns to the fold. Although he never stops *being a brother*, fellowshiping him *as a brother* has to be put on hold until he himself once again considers being part of the family to be important.

Sometimes a parent must say to a child, "Leave the table until you straighten up." It's a matter of discipline. For the child's own good. For the good of other children at the table.

And that brings us to the next chapter, in which we will explore the flip-side of fellowship: *disfellowship*. Of all the responsibilities given to a local congregation, none is more onerous and fraught with problems than what to do about a brother or sister who stands in need of discipline.

When is discipline appropriate? What form should it take? With what attitude should it be done? Off we go once again into deep and troubled waters. Since we are brothers, shall we talk about it over lunch?

Congregational Fellowship

- God has chosen to place his children in small family groups for intimate *koinonia* caring and sharing.
- There is no biblical precedent for "church hopping and church shopping."
- Each congregation, under its elders and deacons, is independent and autonomous—alone responsible to God for how it works and worships.
- Only God can "remove lampstands" from individual congregations.
- Table fellowship in its many forms is crucial to body fellowship within the immediate family of local congregations.

PART III

RETHINKING SACRED COWS

We do everything by custom, even believe by it; our very axioms—
let us boast of free-thinking as we may—are oftenest simply
such beliefs as we have never heard questioned.

THOMAS CARLYLE: SARTOR RESARTUS

CHAPTER TEN

THE LOVING DISCIPLINE OF DISFELLOWSHIP

*Discipline is demanded of the athlete to win a game. Discipline is
required for the captain running his ship. Discipline is needed for the
pianist to practice for the concert. Only in the matter of personal
conduct is the need for discipline questioned.*

GLADYS BROOKS

In article after article in 1984, newspapers all across America
gave unprecedented publicity to the "Church of Christ." There
was high-profile coverage even in *Newsweek*. It's the kind of
publicity you couldn't pay for. If before the articles appeared people hadn't previously been aware of the "Church of Christ," they
were certainly aware of it afterwards.

But it was hardly favorable publicity—at least in the eyes of a
world blinded to the realm of the spiritual.

You may remember what the tabloid headlines were all about.
Marian Guinn, a 36-year-old registered nurse and divorced mother
of four, had filed a lawsuit in 1981 against the elders of the
Collinsville (Oklahoma) Church of Christ, alleging invasion of privacy and the intentional infliction of emotional distress. The suit
arose when the elders read a letter to the congregation, citing
Guinn for the "sin of fornication" and calling for the members to
withdraw their fellowship from her.

It was a case of good intentions going sadly awry. Not just the
matter of church discipline but also what had begun as a praise-

worthy example of true *koinonia* fellowship. From the moment she walked through the door, Guinn had been extended the warmest of receptions by the congregation, who eagerly—even sacrificially—looked after her needs and the needs of her children during a particularly difficult time in her life.

However, it all turned sour when the elders were told that Guinn was illicitly involved with a former mayor of Collinsville. Confronted by the elders, Guinn admitted that she and the man were involved sexually. Over a year went by and it was evident that the relationship had not ended. After a second warning, the elders informed Guinn that disciplinary action would be required if she did not publicly repent. This warning was met with pleas by Guinn that no statement be made to the congregation. Yet no step was taken toward any public acknowledgement of wrongdoing.

It was then that the case took an interesting twist. Anticipating disciplinary action by the church, Marian Guinn submitted a letter to the elders (drafted by her lawyer), saying "I withdraw my membership immediately." Less than two weeks later, the elders read to the church the letter that eventually landed them in court.

From the very beginning the case was never going to be resolved in the church's favor. The jury, having no understanding of the nature of church discipline, rendered a predictably secular verdict against the church and its elders, awarding actual and punitive damages in the amount of $390,000.

A later appeal ended in a ruling against the church on the rationale that the church had no jurisdiction over a person who was no longer a member of the congregation. It was thought that voluntary association with an ecclesiastical body could be ended without having to submit to any lingering action by that body.

Lessons from the Guinn Case

As a case study, Marian Guinn's suit was almost worth the high price it cost to maintain Christian integrity. What we can learn from the case rises far above what I'm afraid many congregations have learned from it—namely, to avoid church discipline at all cost for fear of buying a lawsuit. Rather than be cowered by the courts, we must take a page from Peter and "obey God rather than men."

What I think we learn first of all is how different the scriptural view of discipline is from the one generally understood in the world. The Oklahoma Supreme Court in particular displayed complete ignorance about the nature of a spiritual family. A member of the family doesn't just "resign" when the going gets tough. Nor does a family's interest cease the moment one of its members walks out the door.

Note that the letter to the congregation asked *them* to withdraw fellowship from Marian Guinn, not the other way around. Withdrawing fellowship is not the same as excommunication, whereby the communicant is barred from participating in church sacraments. Notwithstanding her "letter of resignation," the family had a spiritual obligation to shun Marian socially in the hope that their actions would cause her to reconsider what she would be missing without their *koinonia* caring and sharing.

That very *koinonia* closeness distinguishes this case from others, where members of the congregation have long withdrawn themselves from the assembly of the saints and from the *koinonia* fellowship associated with it. In those cases fellowship has already been broken. In those cases letters of disfellowship are like closing the gate after the sheep are already out. What chance is there that a person is going to be brought back into the fold by the prospect of having fellowship denied him when he has already voluntarily given up that very fellowship? If family fellowship is not prized, its loss can hardly be used as an incentive for turning around one's life.

Blind to the spiritual implications of biblical disfellowshiping, all the court in the Guinn case could see was a technical line between membership and non-membership. Ironically, the court would not even draw that line among its own members. As a former Director of Professional Conduct for the Oregon State Bar, I can assure you that "resignation under fire" is no barrier to discipline of a lawyer who has breached the bar's rules of ethics. Nor would it be a defense to a military court-martial. Just imagine the reaction if a soldier about to be charged with insubordination were to say, "I hereby resign from the forces. You no longer have jurisdiction over me!"

That the world would have a double-standard is no surprise. The distance between the way the world thinks and the way Christians ought to think is demonstrated in the comment of one of the jurors, who said quite matter-of-factly, "He was single, she was single, and this is America." In other words, no one has any right to judge anyone else. Sadly, of course, such is also the thinking of more and more Christians. Perhaps this attitude goes a long way toward explaining why we have so few congregations today which practice the biblical imperative of withdrawing fellowship where warranted.

A corollary was also suggested in the Guinn case: It's all a matter of privacy—as in *right* of privacy. *Newsweek*, for example, quoted Marian Guinn as saying, "What I do is between God and myself. I don't need the church to work as a medium for me."[1]

Was Guinn absent when the Bible class studied First Corinthians? Had she never read Titus or Second Thessalonians? Or was she simply ignoring the Scriptures' plain teaching about congregational fellowship, which sometimes demands its withdrawal? (Guinn had, in fact, witnessed a withdrawal proceeding before her own case arose.)

In a culture which worships privacy as a sacred value, it is little wonder that disfellowshiping has gone out of style. *Privacy* is short for *personal autonomy*—or simply for the freedom to do what we like without the risk of consequences or censure. Hence Guinn's terse bottom line: "It was none of their business."

When congregational fellowship is properly understood, saving brothers and sisters from spiritual peril is their *very* business!

---

1. "A Premium Price on Casting Stones," *Newsweek*, March 26, 1984, p. 58.

If any action by the Collinsville elders might be second-guessed, it would have been their decision to send copies of the letter to four sister congregations. Not that any so-called right of privacy was thereby violated, but rather that the principle of congregational autonomy doesn't easily lend support for such action. (Unless perhaps the other congregations themselves inquired regarding her character in the process of extending her the right hand of fellowship.)

As an act of congregational fellowship, withdrawal itself is distinctly congregational. Church discipline pertains only to the immediate family, not to any other congregation. The outer boundary of disfellowshiping is the outer boundary of whatever *koinonia* fellowship existed in the first place—the kind which Marian Guinn had been so blessed to receive from her brothers and sisters in Collinsville before she decided to inflict her own brand of emotional distress on those who had loved her enough to discipline her.

Which Sins Warrant Discipline?

Where discipline is biblically warranted, we have no choice but to administer it. The only questions are: When is it warranted, and how is it to be administered?

In the several passages which instruct us about church discipline, we learn that discipline is in order when a brother or sister refuses to listen to the church regarding resolution of conflicts between one member and another (Matthew 18:15-17); when immorality becomes a public shame on the church (1 Corinthians 5:1-13); when someone is divisive (Titus 3:10); and when a brother lives in idleness contrary to the apostles' teaching (2 Thessalonians 3:6). Undoubtedly, this list is not exhaustive but merely suggestive of any number of similar situations which merit action on the part of the church against one of its members.

What all of these circumstances have in common is a dual threat—to the erring Christian personally and to the church corporately. That combination of factors, therefore, becomes the criteria for identifying the kind of behavior warranting discipline.

To engage unrepentantly in any behavior that is soul-threatening cannot help but draw the attention and concern of those whose very reason for existence as a spiritual family includes guarding against anything that might put one's eternal relationship with God in jeopardy. For the one whose soul is at risk, church discipline is a wake-up call. It's a bucket of cold water in the face. It is tough words for someone we care about—tough love when nothing else will break through the barrier of denial.

This is why Paul said of the man in Corinth who was sexually involved with his father's wife, "...hand this man over to Satan, so that the sinful nature may be destroyed and his spirit saved on the day of the Lord" (1 Corinthians 5:5). Rehabilitation is the aim. Reinstatement is the goal. In fact, if the man to whom Paul referred in his second letter to the Corinthians (2:5-11) is the same brother from whom they had earlier withdrawn, then we see a wonderful example of how that aim was achieved. Discipline giving birth to repentance opened the door for forgiveness and love.

But not all sin affects the whole church in the same way. Otherwise we would be required to disfellowship the preacher whose pride is as big as his pulpit; the good brother who is prone to gossip; the sister whose life is consumed with materialism; the man who makes no effort to tell others the good news of Christ; the woman whose manner of dress is less than modest; the elder who lords it over his flock; the deacon who is given to gluttony. In short, we would have to disfellowship everyone in the church, including ourselves.

When the Congregation Is Put At Risk

By their very nature, however, some sins directly threaten the spiritual welfare of the whole congregation. For example, immorality (particularly sexual immorality) which is open and unchallenged lowers the standard for everyone else. If notorious immorality goes unchecked, then the rest of us can easily get the idea that we too can get away with acting beneath ourselves. Because the temptations of immorality are so strong, we need all the external reinforcement that we can get. Standing alone, we're as good as dead. So anyone who opens the church door to the devil is a danger not only to himself but to the whole family.

This then is a second reason why Paul (in 5:6) ordered withdrawal from the man in Corinth until he repented: "Don't you know that a little yeast works through the whole batch of dough?" Discipline is intended not only to accomplish rehabilitation for the erring brother or sister but also to convey a message of deterrence for the entire church family. You can be sure that when Ananias and Sapphira lied to the Holy Spirit and were immediately "disfellowshiped" by falling down dead, Luke wasn't exaggerating in his report that "great fear seized the whole church and all who heard about these events"!

Still a third way in which the church is affected when cancerous sin is not excised from the body has to do with its reputation in the community. The eyes of a sinful world are always on the church, looking for imperfection. Actually, looking for an excuse. "If not even the church can be pure," says an onlooking world, "then why should we even try?" So Paul reminds the Corinthians that the particular sin they have been covering up would be shameful even among the pagans. To harbor such a man as a brother in good standing was simply to confirm the world's belief that Christians are a bunch of hypocrites.

Even if some sins are more "in-house" than others, they may nevertheless have serious consequences for the family. Where, for example, one brother has sinned against another brother in the congregation, it is not just a private matter between the two of them but a family matter as well. Dissension within the family always weakens its ability to function as it ought. And that is particularly true when the brother in the wrong refuses to abide by a family council on the matter. So Jesus says he should be shunned "if he refuses to listen even to the church..." (Matthew 18:17).

Never is that threat more imminent than when someone in the family becomes intentionally divisive. Now we have dissension *with an attitude!* So Paul says, if the brother doesn't get the point after two clear warnings, then "have nothing to do with him" (Titus 3:10). Otherwise, the family is going to be split wide open and destroyed.

Nor is the idleness of the brother to whom Paul referred in his second letter to the Thessalonians (3:6,14) just a matter of individual laziness. The idleness Paul was concerned about had apparently resulted in some brothers' and sisters' not pulling their share of the family load. They were freeloaders who had become a burden on the church. Worse yet, they had become "busybodies" (verse 11). Therefore, because their laziness and meddling in others' affairs had led to a corporate problem, corporate discipline was in order.

These same factors are also reflected in Paul's listing (in 1 Corinthians 5) of idolaters, slanderers, drunks, and swindlers as brothers and sisters warranting church discipline. Having thus illustrated the category of sins worthy of church discipline, Paul leaves it to us to deal with other sins of like kind which have both personal and corporate repercussions. In each instance cited in Scripture, the person in need of discipline was not just someone who happened to believe what others did not: he was one whose life or teaching had become harmful to the group as a whole.

This last point simply has to be underscored: In the absence of some divisive crusade leading to dissension and strife, *mere differences in doctrinal understanding are not a cause for disfellowship,* nor the fact that someone has left (typically) a more conservative congregation for a "liberal" congregation. Discipline has to do principally with character problems, not conscientious differences among the family of God.

How Is Discipline To Be Administered?

Once sin warranting discipline is identified, the next question is how to go about administering the discipline. If we begin by focusing on Jesus' teaching in Matthew 18, we see a three-step process. "If your brother sins against you, go and show him his fault, just between the two of you....If he will not listen, take one or two others along, so that 'every matter may be established by the testimony of two or three witnesses'" (18:15,16). Here Jesus is simply restating the requirement of the laws of Moses for corroboration and verification.

As a lawyer, I am impressed with the procedural fairness of spiritual discipline. Even in the family of God, there is to be no rush to judgment. No speculation. No room for someone to be railroaded on the strength of first appearances. If we exercise caution before sentencing a person criminally, how much more caution ought we to exercise before "handing him over to Satan"! If disfellowshiping is the business of the church, it is *serious* business.

In those cases where the first and second warnings are ignored, the final step is the family council. As Jesus said, "If he refuses to listen to them [the offended brother and his witnesses], tell it to the church" (18:17).

Of course, it is not always necessary for the first two steps to take place. When the sin is so notorious and public that by its very nature the church has already "been told," then it is time for the family to get together and do whatever is necessary to deal with the situation. That was the case in 1 Corinthians 5, where members of the congregation were quite well aware that the man was sleeping with his step-mother, but were closing their eyes, hoping the scandal would just go away.

Whether first step or last, the family council is the point at which discipline is to be administered. "If he refuses to listen even to the church...," then no longer fellowship him (18:17).

Have We Missed the Boat?

It is here at the point of full family participation where we may have missed the biblical pattern in a significant way. Accustomed as we are to representative government and instructed as we are to submit to the leading of the elders, we invariably translate "tell it to the church" as "tell it to the elders for their decision." But is that Paul's intent?

If we take his words at face value, Paul is telling us to have a special gathering of the family to confront the brother with his sin. Not an elders' meeting but a family council. Not yet another private rebuke but a quite public assembly for the specific purpose of showing the family's solidarity and mutual intent should repentance not be forthcoming.

Can you imagine the impact upon a brother or sister who is confronted with that much tough love all at the same time? Surely only the most hardened of sinners could be untouched by such love...if love it is that motivates the occasion, as clearly it must be.

"Telling it to the church" *in the presence of the sinner* also avoids the traditional "letter of disfellowship." Where did we ever get the idea for letters? (Do Paul's letters ever mention letters?) Letters are distant and impersonal. They don't begin to capture the spirit of personal confrontation.

Nor will it then be necessary for the elders to read a letter to the congregation. The congregation itself will already have "read the riot act" to the sinner. Right then. On the spot. In his presence.

If the sinner refuses to listen to the family council's plea for repentance, then the entire body is put on notice of what must be done and, more importantly, of *why* it must be done. After all, it is the entire congregation which will be called upon to withdraw fellowship. And for that to be effective the whole family need to buy into the decision for *themselves*—to participate in the process; to affirm the need for such drastic action.

Do you not find it interesting that Jesus spoke of "the church" before the inaugural Pentecost with which we identify the beginning of the church? It is not without significance that, long before that celebrated Pentecost, Israel was spoken of as "the congregation" ("the church") in any number of contexts—none more important than when related to congregational discipline.

In fact, we are given a model of congregational "disfellowshiping" of the ultimate kind in Leviticus 24:10-16. In that case the man was guilty of blaspheming God, an offense worthy of death under the law. "Then the Lord said to Moses: 'Take the blasphemer outside the camp. All those who heard him are to lay their hands on his head, and the entire assembly is to stone him.'" Substitute "shunning" for "stoning" and we see that God wants the whole congregation to participate.

The end of the passage tells us why the entire assembly was to stone the offender. The Lord further instructed Moses to "Say to the Israelites: 'If anyone curses his God, he will be held responsible; anyone who blasphemes the name of the Lord must be put to death. The entire assembly must stone him. Whether an alien or native-born, when he blasphemes the Name, he must be put to death.'"

Involving the entire congregation was an exercise in deterrence. Discipline was to be accompanied by a sermon—and who could possibly miss the message!

For all of the above reasons, it's high time we put the *congregation* back into *congregational discipline*. Elders may need to take the initiative when discipline is in order, but everyone in the immediate family is to share actively in the decision-making process.

Where Tough Love Is Toughest

We've spoken several times about what has been called "tough love." It's tough, first of all, because it puts someone we love in the difficult situation of being isolated from those who genuinely care about him. And surely that is tough.

But I can tell you personally that "tough love" may be equally tough on those who are forced to administer it. For starters, the chances are very good that one's noblest motives will not be appreciated by the recipient. To shun is to reject. To reject is to give every appearance of not truly caring.

More difficult still is the position we are put in when someone who ought to be shunned socially is in our daily presence as a co-worker or other associate. How can we shun that person without being rude? How are we supposed to "refuse to eat" with the sinner when the whole gang is going out to lunch together?

Most difficult of all is the dilemma of being related to the person to be shunned. Suppose he or she is my spouse, or sibling, or child? Am I to cut off my own family member? How, practically, do I do that? The in-fellowship wife is hardly in a position not to eat with her disfellowshiped husband!

Oddly enough, these very real dilemmas might well be addressed in an obscure passage which I have never heard discussed from the pulpit or elsewhere. It's that enigmatic postscript to the story of Naaman the leper and his healing (2 Kings 5:18,19). Remember this conversation? Naaman said to Elisha, "But may the Lord forgive your servant for this one thing: When my master enters the temple of Rimmon to bow down and he is leaning on my arm and I bow there also—when I bow down in the temple of Rimmon, may the Lord forgive your servant for this." Elisha's simple response, "Go in peace," indicated his appreciation of the difficulty of the situation and his approval of Naaman's intended action.

Sometimes we are forced by circumstances to exercise judgment that is not always strictly consistent with other judgments and commitments we have made. Even considering that family harmony is to be subordinate to obedience (Matthew 10:34-39), I wonder if God hasn't set us in physical families so that there would always be *someone* we can turn to, *someone* with whom there continues to be an open door for encouragement to do the right thing. Maybe even to act as a subtle reminder of the importance of fellowship with one's spiritual family. But I speak my own opinion here. We have no direct authority to lean on.

The trouble with this "family exception" (if there is one) is that it can end up affecting the spiritual family's decision about whether to shun the sinner. If the physical family is the least bit influential in the congregation, it can mean that no formal shunning ever takes place. In deference to the sinner's family, the spiritual family might simply do nothing. What could be seen as a slap to the sinner could also be regarded as a slap to the sinner's family. And so church discipline never happens.

When that is the case, tough love turns out to be misguided love. Rather than offend, we can end up "loving" someone right into hell. Is that what the sinner's family wants? Is that what any of us wants? Surely the congregation has no option but to proceed, even if the physical family keeps the door slightly ajar—always with its own reminder that the loved one's continuing sin leaves him in jeopardy of eternal punishment.

Is Discipline in Order Where There Is None?

The problem with trying to duplicate the biblical model of congregational discipline is that today we very often have congregations which are simply too big for anything like that to happen. Too big to know each other by name. Too big to share in close *koinonia*. Too big to be aware of spiritual needs. Too big to know of sins that warrant discipline. Too big to convene a family council of the entire body. Too big, impersonal, and uncommitted to be faithful to God in exercising the kind of loving discipline he has called us to exercise.

It's not just the size of our congregations but also the "first stone syndrome." Many of us are so compromised by our own sins that we feel we are in no position to cast the first stone. Speaking for myself, who am I to discipline anyone else? I have met the sinning brother, and he is me! When discipline is ignored long enough, there is hardly anyone left to whom Paul can say, "Brothers, if someone is caught in a sin, *you who are spiritual* should restore him gently" (Galatians 6:1).

The result is that the Collinsville experience is the exception rather than the rule. For most congregations today, withdrawing fellowship is but a theoretical possibility. Rarely if ever is it practiced.

At this very moment I can think of any number of congregations where it is "business as usual" despite the fact that members of the body are living with husbands or wives they have no biblical right to be married to; or are living together outside the bonds of marriage; or are known in the community at large to conduct shady business deals; or are notorious for drunkenness. And that's only the short list.

Are we then any different from the Corinthians, who Paul said were "proud" in turning a blind eye to scandal in the church? Shouldn't we rather be filled with grief and put out of our fellowship those whose lives are bringing the body of Christ into disrepute? As long as we continue to tolerate "sin in the camp," our boasting about how loving and spiritual we are only disguises the truth: how very unloving and unspiritually-minded we have become.

The time is ripe for some serious soul-searching, congregation by congregation. Most church families are so lax regarding spiritual discipline that we have compounded the scandal of sin by the scandal of indifference. Right now would be a good time to have a family meeting and talk about this public disgrace. Our lampstands are as tarnished as our reputations.

For the moment, forget the notorious sinners among us. We who have neglected our duty to exercise biblical discipline are the ones who first need to repent! If it is not yet time for judgment to begin with the family of God in terms of mutual discipline, then it will soon be time for a far more fearful judgment to begin with the family of God!

CHAPTER ELEVEN

FALSE TEACHERS OR
FALSE TEACHING?

Prophets were twice stoned—first in anger,
then, after their death, with a handsome slab in the graveyard.

CHRISTOPHER MORLEY

Arriving in middle Tennessee last fall to hold a weekend meeting, I was greeted by a full-page ad in the local newspaper denouncing me as a false teacher. The headline read: "WHICH WILL YOU BELIEVE AND FOLLOW?—the teaching of F. LaGard Smith or the teaching of Jesus Christ and the Bible?" My immediate reaction, of course, was to leave F. LaGard Smith (whoever he was) in the dust and follow Jesus! What kind of a choice was that?

The first of twenty polemic paragraphs minced no words: "Hundreds in this area do not intend to support F. LaGard Smith as he preaches at a local Church of Christ. Many doctrines he holds do not represent churches of Christ, both here and elsewhere."

Among many other things, I learned to my surprise that "SMITH DOES NOT BELIEVE THAT WATER BAPTISM PUTS ONE INTO THE KINGDOM;" and "SMITH DOES NOT BELIEVE IN THE REALITY OF HELL WHICH IS CLEARLY TAUGHT MANY TIMES BY JESUS AND THE APOSTLES." Wow, I always *thought* I did!

But then I might be hiding what I believe even from myself. You never know, because "If you hear him preach, you probably will not hear him teach false doctrine because he knows where he is and he is afraid to preach his false doctrine in this area." Rats! Somehow I'd been found out. But then what threat did I pose? If I was purposely going to hide my heresy, what did they have to fear about my being in town that week end?

And here I was without any possible defense. My credentials as a false teacher were pretty much confirmed in one sentence: "He is a lawyer and teaches law at Pepperdine University." Lawyer? Pepperdine? What more evidence did one need?

The most amazing thing was that the lion's share of their concern came from my book *Baptism: The Believer's Wedding Ceremony.* After painstakingly writing for months to convince the denominational world of the necessity of faith-prompted adult immersion for the remission of sins, I travel to Tennessee only to discover that I believe in faith-only salvation, infant baptism, and the charismatic working of the Holy Spirit.

No wonder they were so upset. No wonder they said, "If we could meet him in a public discussion we could expose him for what he really is—a false teacher!" Sounds like a dangerous fellow to me. I, for one, am ready to heed their call: "Let us plead with you, dear brother, stand up for Jesus. Stand against false teachers and false religions. Have nothing to do with them (II Jn. 9-11; Rom. 16:17-18; Eph. 5:11)."

Context, Context, Context!

The article was so bizarre I hardly knew what to think. It was as if I had written one book, and they had read an altogether different one. Obviously they had gone to my book looking for error and—surprise of surprises—found whatever they wanted to find! It hardly mattered that I stood for things quite opposite from what they wanted me to stand for. Factual accuracy was no obstacle in the search for dirt. With some folks, it never is.

What they had done was to take no more than a dozen paragraphs with which they disagreed and let them color how they viewed everything else in the rest of the book. Of course, that required taking what I said out of three different contexts. The first context was the overall, central, obvious, compelling message of the book: the absolute necessity of baptism for salvation, redemption, and kingdom fellowship. (The very message you have already seen in *this* book.)

The second desecration was of the immediate context of each section with which they disagreed. They simply lifted one suspicious sentence here and another controversial sentence there. None of the qualifying statements or disclaimers or further explanations were supplied for those who had not read the book. Revealing those, of course, would have alerted the reader to a quite different perspective, and that would have prevented the kind of tabloid reporting which makes it so easy to twist a person's teaching beyond all recognition.[1]

More serious still, they had deftly managed to merge together quite separate issues and thereby come up with patently ludicrous conclusions. This breach of logical context is always a formula for disaster, whether done by those on the right or those on the left. And it's being done regularly by both. There seems to be a pervasive inability today to make a careful distinction between issues. Issue A might affect issue B, or perhaps be affected by it. But until issues A and B are first seen in their own distinct contexts, there can be no clarity of thought.

Where Honest Differences Exist

Peel back the various levels of disinformation in the article and what remains is that my detractors disagree with me on at least three basic issues. First, whether God's sovereignty on the day of Judgment permits or precludes his granting clemency to those who have not obeyed the gospel in its fullness. Second, whether the

1. Having been on the receiving end of such distortion, I have redoubled my own efforts to ensure the fair representation of each writer or speaker cited in this book.

Holy Spirit works in any way other than through the written Word. And finally (an issue raised apart from my book), the nature of eternal punishment in hell.

Each of these is a specific, identifiable issue over which reasonable men may differ. However, we must be careful in dealing with those differences. To suggest that God has the right to grant clemency at the final Judgment is not to say that infant baptism or faith alone without baptism gives anyone any hope of salvation. God's revealed plan of salvation and God's inherent sovereignty to judge are two distinct issues. (Fuller discussion follows in the next chapter.)

Nor does affirming that the Holy Spirit works apart from the written Word mean that one believes in charismatic "gifts of the Spirit." It is a leap in logic that can only be made by someone who enjoys theological bungie jumping. I believe in the indwelling of the Holy Spirit (as "the gift of the Holy Spirit" Peter promised at Pentecost to those who were baptized), but I do not believe that we today have the spiritual gifts of healing, tongue-speaking, or prophecy. Only a blurring of two distinct issues can justify someone saying of my position, "This is the holy roller concept of years gone by, but is still with us today under the title 'charismatic.'"

Finally, there is an equally yawning gap between believing that the nature of eternal punishment in hell may be something other than continuing, conscious burning and not believing in the reality of hell itself. Forcing a connection between the two is as illogical as it would be for me to say of those who deny the indwelling nature of the Holy Spirit that they don't believe in the reality of the Spirit. In each case the issue is not *reality* but *nature*.

What's so frustrating in situations like this is that we can't even agree on what we're supposed to be disagreeing about! We don't just have differences; we are not even on the same playing field! To be honest, having honest differences is clouded by the fact that those differences are not being dealt with honestly!

False Teacher, or Teaching Something False?

Perhaps most subtle and most insidious of all is the bogus connection which is automatically made between *false teaching* and *false teachers*. Suppose for a moment that I am wrong in my understanding of each of the above issues. Completely wrong. Does that make me a false teacher? Automatically to make such a linkage is again to confuse two very separate issues.

Even on its face it simply couldn't be true. Equating false teaching with false teachers would mean that everyone who has ever taught something that is doctrinally incorrect is a false teacher. Because of our ever-growing, ever-changing understanding of God's Word, it would mean that we were a false teacher last year but not this year. Who knows what we will be next year?

More likely still, it means that whoever disagrees with us on any point of doctrine is a false teacher. And therein lies the greatest danger.

In fact, therein lies one of the easiest ways to win any debate: the *ad hominem* argument. If you can successfully discredit *the person*, it can appear that you have successfully discredited *his case*. Hence statements like "We have only touched the hem of the garment with reference to the unscriptural things done and taught by F. LaGard Smith."

The label "false teacher" (or "false prophet") is laden with baggage. It carries a connotation altogether different from the mere assertion that a particular teaching is wrong. The tag "false teacher" moves us from *the impersonal* to *the personal*; from *teaching* to *teacher*; from *doctrine* to *personality*; from *scriptural error* to *one's character*.

Not Without Consequences

Most crucial of all—when a person is a false prophet, significant biblical consequences are deemed to follow. As in "marking," shunning, and refusing fellowship. In the case of a false teacher, we are no longer talking about a withdrawal of fellowship by a single congregation but an inter-congregational shunning throughout the entire extended family. Let me give you an example.

The terse letter I received from a congregation in northern Alabama cancelling my upcoming meeting with them was like a bolt out of the blue. Hadn't they begged me to come, saying, "We really need you"? Hadn't I made room in my already over-booked schedule to accommodate them? But then apparently rumor made its way to the elders that I was a false teacher, and suddenly I was *persona non grata*.

Had the elders read my book? No. Did they bother to call me and ask what I actually believed? No. All it took was for someone outside their congregation to wave the label "false teacher" in their faces, and immediately I was a spiritual leper. It didn't even seem to matter that the topics they had asked me to speak on had nothing whatsoever to do with the contested issue.

If you've never been a victim of the "false-teacher" syndrome, I'm here to tell you that nothing is more pernicious in its consequences. Like the Eveready bunny, the consequences keep on going and going and going. Once a person has been wrongly marked as a false teacher, it is almost impossible to remove the label. There is a permanent staining of one's reputation. You might as well just call him a wife-beater or child-molester. Whatever its actual merit, "false teacher" is a label that sticks.

It is also a charge easily made but terribly difficult to defend. How do you go around to every congregation where the rumor has spread and tell your side of the story? Considering the gravity of its impact upon one's place and reputation in the kingdom, no more serious charge can be leveled against a teacher. Given what's at stake, therefore, the term "false teacher" is not to be thrown around lightly.

Looking Closely at the Text

When folks are willing to vandalize the context of books written by men, the odds are pretty good that they are also willing to vandalize the context of God's Word itself. Such is the case in the libelous newspaper article which referred the reader to three passages in support of the call for me to be shunned as a false teacher. A closer look at each of these passages reveals just how carelessly scriptures are being bandied about to support false charges about false teachers.

Ephesians 5:11. "Have nothing to do with the fruitless deeds of darkness, but rather expose them." Is Paul talking about fruitless *teaching* or fruitless *deeds*? The entire context (from 4:17 to 5:20) has to do with behavior, not teaching. Listen to what Paul says: "You must no longer live as the Gentiles do." "Live as children of light." "Be very careful, then, how you live." Not a single word about teaching doctrinal error. As we shall soon see, ungodly behavior is almost invariably associated with the false teacher, but in this passage Paul is clearly not talking about false teachers.

Romans 16:17,18. "I urge you, brothers, to watch out for those who cause divisions and put obstacles in your way that are contrary to the teaching you have learned. Keep away from them. for such people are not serving our Lord Christ, but their own appetites. By smooth talk and flattery they deceive the minds of naive people."

Once again we look in vain for an inspired imperative to shun as false teachers those with whom we happen to disagree on some doctrinal matter. As before, we are confronted here with a character problem. The person Paul is describing is not just *teaching* something, but *doing* something. He is a busybody causing division. He is deliberately preying on the minds of simple Christians so as to deceive them. (What could be more divisive than a full-page ad in the local paper trying to orchestrate a boycott among sister congregations of the Lord's church? What could be more deceptive than repeatedly quoting a brother out of context?)

2 John 9-11. "Anyone who runs ahead and does not continue in the teaching of Christ does not have God; whoever continues in the teaching has both the Father and the Son. If anyone comes to you and does not bring this teaching, do not take him into your house or welcome him. Anyone who welcomes him shares in his wicked work."

At last we are no longer talking about behavior, but teaching. Yet there is not a more potentially self-serving passage in all of the Bible than this. Taken out of its context, "this teaching" (from which someone else departs) can mean anything anyone wants it to mean. As typically used, it means any teaching with which you or I happen to agree. In such a case the person who departs from *our* teaching is not continuing in "*this* teaching" and therefore is not to be fellowshiped!

The only problem once again is the context. When we go back to verse 7, we find out exactly whom John was referring to as those who were "running ahead" of the teaching of Christ. "Many deceivers," says John, "who do not acknowledge Jesus Christ as coming in the flesh, have gone out into the world. Any such person is the deceiver and the antichrist."

Does this sound like doctrinal differences over head coverings, or cups, or classes, or instruments, or footwashing, or orphans homes, or divorce and remarriage, or the indwelling of the Holy Spirit, or any of the other issues we might find being discussed in our brotherhood papers?

In the larger context of John's three letters, verse 7 would include not only false teaching about the person of Christ but also rejection of ultimate truth and the need to obey the commandments of Christ. (See 2 John 1-4; 1 John 2:4-6.) Even so, John's reference simply couldn't be further from the kind of differences of understanding which we have among ourselves along a broad front of doctrinal concern in our attempts to honor both Christ and his teaching.

Why then have we branded so many of our brothers as false teachers just because they have reached a different conclusion regarding one issue or another? Have they denied that Jesus Christ came in the flesh? Have they repudiated the fact that ultimate truth lies in Christ and his teaching? Are they denying any need to obey the commandments of Christ?

Not Preachers, But Impostors

We are put on notice by John's letter that not all false teaching makes a person a "false prophet." In his first letter (4:1-3), John spells it out even more clearly: "Dear friends, do not believe every spirit, but test the spirits to see whether they are from God, because many false prophets have gone out into the world. This is how you can recognize the Spirit of God: Every spirit that acknowledges that Jesus Christ has come in the flesh is from God, but every spirit that does not acknowledge Jesus is not from God. This is the spirit of the antichrist, which you have heard is coming and even now is already in the world."

As used in the New Testament the label "false prophet" is virtually always tied to teaching which destroys the very core of the personhood and mission of Jesus Christ. Not once is the term "false prophet" used in connection with conscientious disputes among brethren over what Christ and his apostles have taught us to do. By our very passion to seek the truth and expose error we proclaim our allegiance to the Lord's leading. We are not antichrists—not even the "antis," whether anti-Sunday school or anti-orphans homes.

We would get a much better handle on false prophets if we thought of them as what they really were: *impostors*. It was Jesus himself who made that clear when (in Matthew 24) his disciples asked him about the sign of his coming and the end of the age. Jesus cautioned: "At that time if anyone says to you, 'Look, here is the Christ!' or, 'There he is!' do not believe it. For *false Christs* and *false prophets* will appear and perform great signs and miracles to deceive even the elect—if that were possible" (24:23,24).

Don't ask me how, but these *false Christs* could actually work miracles and do other signs that would deceive folks. The same had been true of false prophets before Jesus' day. God said through Isaiah, for example, "I am the Lord...who foils the *signs* of false prophets and makes fools of diviners" (Isaiah 44:24,25).

No wonder John calls them "deceivers." No wonder Jesus warned, "Watch out that no one deceives you. For many will come in my name, claiming, 'I am the Christ,' and will deceive many" (Matthew 24:4,5).

Among other deceivers was Elymas, "the Jewish sorcerer and false prophet" (Acts 13:6-10). Remember when Paul "looked straight at Elymas and said, 'You are a child of the devil and an enemy of everything that is right! You are full of all kinds of deceit and trickery. Will you never stop perverting the right ways of the Lord?'"

The deceit didn't stop with false prophets claiming to be Christ. Paul warned the Corinthians (in 2 Corinthians 11:4-15) about some phony "super-apostles," saying, "For such men are false apostles, deceitful workmen, masquerading as apostles of Christ. And no wonder, for Satan himself masquerades as an angel of light."

And then there were the "false brothers" of the type who, said Paul, "infiltrated our ranks to spy on us" (Galatians 2:4). They too were impostors.

Deceivers. Miracle workers. Performers of signs. False Christs. False apostles. Antichrists. False prophets. Impostors, impostors, impostors!

In each of the cases mentioned, the false prophets are *impostors*—men out in the world posing either as Christ or as one of his apostles. They are not just some brother in Christ who happens not to see eye to eye with me on every point of doctrine.

False Teachers in the Church

Referring historically to false prophets who mingled among the genuine prophets of God, Peter predicted that likewise "there will be false teachers among you" (2 Peter 2:1). Tell us more, Peter. What false doctrines will they be teaching? It's the same story we've seen before: "They will secretly introduce destructive heresies, *even denying the sovereign Lord who bought them*...." And they will also be deceivers. "In their greed these teachers will exploit you with *stories they have made up*" (2:3).

Paul tells us they will also blaspheme, as did Hymenaeus and Alexander (1 Timothy 1:18-20). And they will cast aspersion on Christ's own resurrection by teaching "that the resurrection has already taken place"—as Hymenaeus did, together this time with Philetus (2 Timothy 2:16-18).

Are the high-profile preachers among us whom some have tagged as false teachers coming anywhere near to denying the sovereign Lord? Are they making up stories? Are they blaspheming God? Just because they teach doctrine that many believe to be error does not make them the kind of false teachers that the Bible itself describes.

This is not to say, of course, that these preachers are immune from criticism for what they promote. (Even in this book, I have taken issue with several of our leading lights whom I believe are teaching error.) Without question, there is a time to rebuke those who teach false doctrine (1 Timothy 1:3), but interestingly enough this particular rebuke is likely to be most appropriate for those brethren who seem to delight in finding false teachers behind every disputed issue, whatever the issue may be.

Just listen to how Paul describes such a man (in 1 Timothy 6:3-5): "If anyone teaches false doctrines and does not agree to the sound instruction of our Lord Jesus Christ and to godly teaching, he is conceited and understands nothing. He has an unhealthy interest in controversies and arguments that result in envy, quarreling, malicious talk, evil suspicions and constant friction between men of corrupt mind, who have been robbed of the truth and who think that godliness is a means to financial gain." Know any brethren like that? I do.

The Character Issue

That last line about financial gain brings us to what may be the most telling test of all regarding false teachers. It's the character issue. Common to both false prophets and false teachers are not just their false doctrine but also their ungodly character. Jesus said, "Watch out for false prophets. They come to you in sheep's clothing, but inwardly they are ferocious wolves. By their fruit you will recognize them" (Matthew 7:15,16).

In three unusually strong passages, Paul, Jude, and Peter all tie false teaching directly to the character issue. In Titus 1:10-16 Paul speaks of some rebellious people who were "ruining whole households by teaching things they ought not to teach—*and that for the sake of dishonest gain.* Even one of their own prophets has said, 'Cretans are always liars, evil brutes, lazy gluttons.' This testimony is true. Therefore, rebuke them sharply, so that they will be sound in the faith...."

Interesting tie, isn't it, between being doctrinally "unsound" and being morally corrupt?

Jude joins the chorus on this note, calling for his readers to contend for the faith, "for certain men whose condemnation was written about long ago have secretly slipped in among you. They are godless men, who change the grace of God into *a license for immorality* and deny Jesus Christ our only Sovereign and Lord" (Jude 3,4). Not only are these false teachers antichrists, but they are also immoral.

Just how immoral are they? Jude (in 5-19) says they pollute their own bodies; reject authority; slander celestial beings; profit from the gospel like Balaam; are ungodly; are grumblers and fault-finders; follow their own evil desires; boast about themselves; flatter others for their own advantage; are divisive; and do not have the Spirit.

Do those whom we accuse of being false teachers today come anywhere near falling into this category of ungodly folks? If not, we owe them an apology.

Peter's assessment of false teachers (2 Peter 2:1-19) is equally damning—a veritable laundry list of character flaws. Says Peter of these spiritual pretenders, they—

Follow the corrupt desire of the sinful nature
Despise authority
Are bold and arrogant
Slander celestial beings
Blaspheme God
Are creatures of instinct like brute beasts
Carouse in broad daylight
Revel at feasts
Have eyes full of adultery
Seduce the unstable
And are greedy like Balaam

How much clearer could it be? Being a "false teacher" is not simply about *doctrine* but about *character* as well.

Time for a Turn-around

Here's a quick reality check. Just think about all the preachers you know, especially ones with whom you might have sharp differences. Do they carouse in broad daylight? Do they slander celestial beings or despise authority? Are they greedy like Balaam? Do they seduce the unstable or revel at feasts? Be completely honest. Are they creatures of instinct like brute beasts? Do they follow the corrupt desires of the sinful nature? If not, how much further can these men be from Paul's description of false teachers!

Yet lock all the preachers you know or have ever heard about in a room together and it wouldn't take long for doctrinal dissension to break out. *Serious* doctrinal dissension! *Deep* ecclesiological rifts! With that much disagreement, they can't all simultaneously be right. Somebody has to be teaching something false. Does that mean any or all of them are false teachers?

Brothers, we are not impostors pretending to be Christ himself. And sinful though we all are, we are not ungodly purveyors of the gospel. We are fallible men of faith, incomplete in our understanding, prone to error, and wrong about any number of things. But we are not false prophets, and we are not false teachers.

Actually, I can think of one preacher who falsely claims to be an apostle. And I'm sure we all know some spiritual leaders who are greedy in the way of Balaam or perhaps are "bold and arrogant." But without further evidence, the preachers on the other side of the fence from ourselves do not qualify as false teachers.

Brothers, it is time to stop this business of loosely smearing teachers and preachers with the labels "false teacher" and "false prophet." Can we not meet each other honorably on the field of battle? How can we possibly engage in dialogue and debate when the other side is denouncing us (even publicly before outsiders) as a false teacher? How can we ever hope to reach an accord on other matters of doctrine when we can't even agree on what Scripture teaches about false prophets?

The grand irony is that what I have said in this very chapter has undoubtedly only confirmed in the eyes of some that I am indeed the false teacher they perceive me to be!

A Case Study

But this chapter is not just about me. It is about a brotherhood capable of libel, slander, and character assassination against any number of righteous, conscientious men with whom others have disagreed. I think in particular about a godly man greatly wronged—a spiritual giant whose last years are being wasted in ignominy. Sadly, a younger generation no longer even remembers him. For those of us who do, 94-year-old Homer Hailey is still a towering man of God.

For some eleven years Homer taught for (then) Abilene Christian College before moving on to Florida College, where he served as head of the Bible Department for twenty-two years. In the wake of the controversy over church organization, he became a widely-respected teacher among the "anti-institutional" or "non-cooperation" congregations. Homer's early writings in particular received wide acceptance both within and beyond the churches of Christ. Among his most well-known books are *Attitudes and Consequences*, *That You May Believe*, and *Prayer and Providence*, as well as excellent commentaries on Job, Isaiah, the Minor Prophets, and Revelation.

After all these books on which many of us cut our teeth, Homer is still writing. After all the sermons upon which many of us modelled our own, Homer is still preaching. After all the classes where we sat at his feet, Homer is still teaching a class each week in his home.

But Homer is alone now. As of this writing, Homer has just lost his beloved wife, Widna, and his son, Gordon, within less than a month of each other. Not that you would know it from Homer's typically upbeat countenance. It is not in Homer's nature to wallow in self-pity.

Nor would he want it known that he is still hurting from another kind of loneliness that he has felt for many years now. A loneliness that comes from being disfellowshiped. Oh, no, he wasn't kicked out of any local congregation. There would have been no reason for anyone to withdraw fellowship from such a stalwart brother.

But Homer did make one big mistake. He wrote one book too many. Or at least the wrong book. Or at least a book in which he might have been wrong. Or partially wrong. Or maybe not wrong at all, but definitely on the other side of the fence from some other folks. And for this one mistake, Homer was immediately castigated as a false prophet!

To this day Homer continues to be shunned by a large segment of congregations among whom he was once regarded as a pillar of the church. He is no longer welcomed with open arms at the annual Florida College lectures. Former students of his who learned much of what they know from his keen scholarship and insight now treat their aged mentor as if he were a blaspheming Hymenaeus or Alexander.

I find it interesting that the offending book was on the subject of divorce and remarriage. Surely it ought to tell us something to know that few subjects have been as controversial, sharply dividing conscientious brothers and sisters on both sides. It is not exactly as if Homer Hailey was out there alone in some cosmic orbit of theological error. Any number of preachers, elders, and other brothers and sisters would agree with his basic position, if perhaps not all of his arguments.

As with other authors, his problem was having a paper trail. Put one foot wrong in black-and-white print, and it's three strikes, you're out! If we had ten times as many writers among us, we would automatically have ten times as many false prophets among us!

More interesting still, those who would most pride themselves in objecting to anyone's putting asunder what God has joined together in marriage (something with which Homer himself would agree) were the very ones who so eagerly put asunder what God has joined together in the family of Christ. One "mistake" and there was a spiritual divorce. No forgiveness. No forbearance. No margin for error. No benefit of the doubt. No credit for years of faithful service. No brotherly kindness. No love.

And talk about your ironies. This dangerous, heretical man is the very same man who more than any other person in the Lord's body on earth today has lived with the true prophets of old. Nobody knows them more intimately. Nobody has more closely molded his own life to theirs. Nobody else has written about them with as much insight and intensity.

And now to be reduced to being a *false* prophet!

I tell you, brothers, there ought to be some serious weeping and wailing over this disgraceful sin against one of God's finest. On the Day of Judgment this cruelty will not go unanswered. If God grants this great servant sufficient breath for it to happen, there ought to be hundreds of cards and letters flooding into his hands begging for forgiveness. Not just his, but God's.[2]

---

2. For those who might wish to correspond, Homer Hailey's address is 760 Las Lomitas Rd., Tucson, AZ 85704.

Yet in some ways Homer Hailey is the easy case. Outside a relatively small circle, he no longer has the name recognition he once did, especially to a younger generation. His story is simply a parable. It is today's high-profile preachers and writers at the center of doctrinal controversy who present the more urgent case. They are the current candidates for being wrongly tagged as "false teachers." For their sakes, and for the sake of the kingdom, we simply have to get away from the simplistic conclusion that anyone who teaches anything false (as we see it) is therefore a false teacher.

It is not just a matter of semantics. Such false charges have a chilling effect on our mutual search for God's will. Who dares speak the truth as he sees it when the price to be paid is being tarred as a false teacher by any who disagree?

If after all this you still think that saying "he's wrong in what he's teaching" is the same as saying "he's a false teacher," take a long walk with a shunned spiritual giant I know and feel the burden of his broken heart. Then perhaps you'll understand why Scripture uses "false teacher" sparingly and with precision. It's not just a label. Loosely applied, it's a libel.

So it is to Homer Hailey and to all the other Homer Haileys, past and present, who have ever been falsely accused of being a false teacher that this chapter is dedicated. Slandering God's servants and withdrawing fellowship from those whose understanding of Scripture doesn't match up with our own thinking is itself false teaching of the worst sort.

CHAPTER TWELVE

THE PROSPECT OF
ETERNAL FELLOWSHIP

If I ever reach heaven I expect to find three wonders there:
first, to meet some I had not thought to see there;
second, to miss some I had expected to see there;
and third, the greatest wonder of all, to find myself there.

JOHN NEWTON

At one of our annual lectureships, a number of folks were waiting for me to autograph a newly-released book. It was nice to think that there was interest in the book. I've been to some book signings so poorly attended that I actually ended up buying more books from the store than the total of my own books sold that day!

As I was concentrating, head down, on writing an inscription for the next person in line, suddenly I was aware that two fellows had rudely pushed themselves to the front of the line and were accosting me with questions about the issue of God's sovereignty (which I briefly mentioned in the previous chapter).

Not exactly thrilled with their timing or attitude, I gathered as much self-control as possible and said, "Now is not really the time to discuss it. All I'm saying about the final Judgment is that God has prerogative to determine our eternal destiny."

Whether it was from momentarily being put off or perhaps feeling the rebuking eyes of the people who had been waiting patiently in line, the two of them backed off slightly as if to leave. I think that I shall never forget what I heard next. One of the fellows, obviously feeling the need to make a closing argument, said boldly and firmly: "God has no prerogative! He has no prerogative!"

Thinking later about the incident, what this brother had said reminded me of Shirley MacLaine on the beach at Malibu—arms outstretched to the ocean waves, yelling, "I am God! I am God! I am God!" Can you imagine what God must be thinking as he looks down from heaven at this blasphemous woman? Compared to God, is she not but a grain of sand on the beach?

And here was a brother who I'm sure would have upbraided Shirley for her blasphemy, yet who apparently hadn't stopped to consider that he himself was treading precariously close to denying God his rightful place as Sovereign of the universe.

Just think about those words: *God has no prerogative! He has no prerogative!* Dare we even think such a thought?

Why Would Anyone Say Such a Thing?

Oh, I know exactly what the brother had in mind—that God has made promises about our salvation which give us assurance of the hope that lies within us, and warnings about eternal punishment that give us every reason to urgently tell the disobedient of impending doom. But neither his promises nor his warnings rob God of his divine prerogative. In fact, it is God's very prerogative that is the source of both his promises and his warnings. Without the prerogative to judge, God would be in no position either to promise eternal life or to threaten eternal death.

I also appreciate the concern that lies behind such a statement. To say that God has prerogative could imply a final Judgment characterized by whim and caprice—further suggesting that our hope of eternal salvation is not really all that secure and that "the lost" might not actually be lost after all.

Someone might point us immediately to the Great Commission: "Whoever believes and is baptized will be saved, but whoever does not believe will be condemned." Those words certainly don't appear to give much elbow room for anything like discretion on that Great Day. If a person is looking only for black and white, it doesn't get much more black and white than the Great Commission.

Keeping Separate Issues Separate

Here again, however, we encounter the need to think critically and carefully about separate, distinct issues—about "issue 1" and "issue 2," not some confused mixture of 1 and 2 looking more like "issue 12." The black-and-white truth that "our God is a consuming fire" would certainly seem to preclude another black-and-white truth that "God is love." But we all acknowledge that God is in fact *both*.

Similarly, a person seizing upon passages which point to God's grace and mercy could easily dismiss other passages which clearly speak of God's harsh judgment, and *vice versa*. The whole truth about God is not found in either extreme but at the point where those two truths intersect.

That's *intersect*, not *merge*. By merging together two separate, distinct issues, Christians on both ends of the spectrum have lost perspective about the final Judgment. An incomplete, partial perspective is all you can get when two truths become less than the sum of their parts.

On one side of the spectrum is the question we're being asked more and more these days: "What kind of God would look at the sincere seeker and say that because of a technicality he is forever lost in hell?" To say that God is abundant in love and steadfast in mercy does not give us the complete picture about the One who will judge us. It ignores what this same God has said about disobedience and its consequences—not to mention example after example of harsh punishment for failure to do *precisely* as God has required.

By joining together the two separate issues of God's *character* and God's *judgment*, the conclusion is drawn that, given his divine mercy, God *will in fact pardon* those who sincerely seek him regardless of whether they have complied with his plan of salvation.

On the other end of the spectrum is the mentality of those who would insist that "God has no prerogative!" Simply to say that God has set forth the eternal consequences awaiting those who are disobedient does not tell us the whole story about a God who is known as much for his mercy as for his judgment.

By joining together the two separate issues of God's *commandments* and God's *judgment*, the conclusion is drawn that, given his commandments, God *will in fact condemn to hell* those who have not fully complied with his plan of salvation regardless of the sincerity of their faith commitment to Christ.

The truth is that neither of these two extremes is right. Somewhere between the black-and-white truth of God's commandments and the black-and-white truth of God's character is the equally black-and-white truth of God's divine prerogative which leaves us unable to say what *in actual fact* God will do with each soul that stands before him.

God's ultimate judgment of mankind will be determined at the point where God's commandments and God's character intersect. It is not an intersection any of us have ever driven through. None of us knows that intersection. Therefore, not one of us has any right to pronounce a judgment which only God can pronounce.

What we *can* do (and *must* do) is obey God's commandments, teach God's commandments, and warn others pursuant to God's commandments.

What we *cannot* do (and *must not* do) is assume either that God's commandments preclude a granting of divine mercy or that God's mercy will necessarily and invariably override threatened punishment.

Judgment and Clemency

To use a human analogy is always to draw but a tenuous conclusion. Our human experience can never guarantee a perfect parallel with the divine. Yet it may be helpful, if for no other reason than to define terms and concepts, to look at our own system of criminal justice by way of comparison.

The lawyer in me wants to stand up and object whenever I hear someone say that the sovereign Judge of the universe has no prerogative. Prerogative is what judges have! That's what makes *me* a lawyer and *them* judges. I can argue the law all day long, but at the end of the day the judge has discretion to enter a judgment notwithstanding the jury's verdict; or to dismiss the case in the interest of justice; or to suspend the imposition of a sentence required by law for violation of the criminal code.

There is nothing about the discretionary role of a judge which nullifies either the law or the penalties attached to that law. Ours is not a system of *law* but a system of *justice*.

Even beyond the justice system itself we are familiar with a form of prerogative known as *clemency*. Simply by virtue of his office, a king, president, or governor has the right to pardon someone who has been duly convicted and sentenced under the law.

While we would hope that such a pardon was granted only for good cause, it doesn't have to be. Merely consider President Ford's grant of a pardon to Richard Nixon. Was it deserved under the law? Did Nixon do anything to justify such a pardon? Was there universal support for its being granted?

Whether dispensed wisely or unwisely, the granting of clemency is an act of mercy, pure and simple. One can neither demand it under color of law nor complain that the law makes no specific provision for such clemency. The law and its administration has one role; sovereign clemency another.

What's more, clemency is never deserved. Had there not already been some finding of guilt (formally in court or informally in the court of public opinion) clemency would never be extended. The issue is not guilt or innocence. Guilt is presumed. Clemency is extended for its own sake—sheerly because, in mercy, the sovereign chooses to grant it.

Of the prerogative of human clemency there can be no doubt. Virtually all governmental institutions both at home and abroad presuppose it. The only question is whether God himself has such prerogative either as Judge of mankind or as Sovereign of all creation. After all, God is not only the Judge, but the Lawgiver as well. Would his granting of clemency violate limits which he has set upon himself through his own laws of order, consistency, and truthfulness? Would it be inconsistent with his holiness?

I suggest that one answer to the question of divine clemency is found in a dramatic expression of mercy associated with Jesus' own crucifixion. We see it in Jesus' conversation with the criminal on the cross who asked Jesus to remember him when he came into his kingdom. Jesus' response, "I tell you the truth, today you will be with me in paradise," was an act of divine clemency. The criminal himself had said to the other insulting criminal: "We are punished justly, for we are getting what our deeds deserve." Clemency can never be claimed as a matter of right; nor, unlike our own salvation, can it be expected as a matter of promise.

For that very reason we must be careful not to transform clemency into a more generalized rule of justification. That is why (among other reasons) "the thief on the cross" is such a bogus argument for faith-only salvation. Not only was water baptism physically impossible at that moment, but what we were witnessing in that incident was clemency, not justification.

Frightened by God's Prerogative

There are several reasons why talk of possible clemency might make us nervous. To begin with, it might appear to give the pious unimmersed false hope. But what person in his right mind would knowingly refuse to be baptized merely in the hope of receiving a clemency never promised and with every scriptural indication being to the contrary! Besides, any *knowing refusal* would hardly seem to evidence the kind of heart that might elicit an act of clemency.

We may also get nervous because with the possibility of clemency we lose a sense of predictability. Just when we were sure about who is going to heaven and who is going to hell, suddenly we are reminded that eternal destiny is still in God's hands, not ours.

I'd like to believe that what concerns us most about that lack of predictability is the question of our own salvation. If that were the only thing disturbing us, we could turn to any number of passages for reassurance that our salvation is secure. The writer of Hebrews, for example, puts it in the strongest possible terms (6:16-19): "Because God wanted to make the unchanging nature of his purpose very clear to the heirs of what was promised, he confirmed it with an oath. God did this so that, by two unchangeable things in which it is impossible for God to lie, we who have fled to take hold of the hope offered to us may be greatly encouraged. We have this hope as an anchor for the soul, firm and secure."

God does not dangle before the righteous the prospect of eternal life, only to snatch it away at the last minute like some cruel joke. Of course we ourselves can drop the ball. Peter reminds us to "be all the more eager to make your calling and election sure. For if you do these things, you will never fall, and you will receive a rich welcome into the eternal kingdom of our Lord and Savior Jesus Christ" (2 Peter 1:10,11).

Together with Paul we can say with confidence, "I know whom I have believed, and am convinced that he is able to guard that which I have entrusted to him for that day" (2 Timothy 1:12)

Will We Turn Green—or Red—in Heaven?

But I wonder if what disturbs us most regarding lack of predictability is not our own salvation but the prospect that we could be wrong about the eternal destiny of others. Almost as if, like Jonah (4:1-3), we would be *disappointed* if God were to save others besides ourselves. Or even upset. Possibly even red-faced with anger.

It wouldn't be the first time that such an attitude has surfaced.

The Pharisees simply couldn't bear the thought that anyone other than themselves might have God's approval. Not after all they had invested in being the exclusive recipients of God's favor! Not after all the work they had put in!

So Jesus told them the parable of the vineyard workers (Matthew 20:1-16). You'll recall that the landowner hired some men in the early morning to work in his vineyard, agreeing to pay them a denarius for the day. That same afternoon the landowner hired other men as well. When it came time for the workers to be paid, those hired in the early morning noticed that those who were hired late in the day were being paid the same as themselves—one denarius. At such obvious inequity, they grumbled: "You have made them equal to us who have borne the burden of the work and the heat of the day."

The landowner's response is all about God's prerogative as owner of the vineyard: "Friend, I am not being unfair to you. Didn't you agree to work for a denarius? Take your pay and go. I want to give the man who was hired last the same as I gave you. *Don't I have the right to do what I want* with my own money?"

There was never any question but that God would uphold his end of the bargain. Payment was never in doubt, and the promised denarius was in fact paid. What bothered the early workers (representing the Pharisees here) was that the landowner was exercising his prerogative to cut others in on the same deal. That was something they had never bargained for. It didn't seem right. Wasn't fair.

But of course it *was fair*. Their problem, and the problem which the Pharisees had—first with Christ's disciples and later with the Gentile Christians—was not a claim of unfairness but sheer jealousy. The landowner knew exactly what their problem was: "Or are you envious because I am generous?"

To say that God has prerogative regarding eternal destiny could mean that God might ultimately save some folks that we would never expect to be saved—perhaps folks who weren't as clear about doctrine as they might have been. It's not enough that we will be given eternal life just as we were promised. We want to make sure that no one else reaps the benefits extended to us through God's grace.

What kind of an attitude is that? Do we really want people to end up in hell? Is there some reason why we wouldn't want *everyone* in heaven if that were possible? Isn't that the very reason why we evangelize—to take as many people to heaven with us as we can?

Sadly, we know from the word "go" that "wide is the gate and broad is the road that leads to destruction, and many enter through it" (Matthew 7:13). You can forget any notion that God's clemency might end up being some kind of universalism in which the doors of heaven are thrown wide open for all. That would make a mockery of Judgment and hell. At best, ours is a hampered salvage operation—a desperate race against time to point the relatively few willing souls to the smaller gate and to the "narrow road that leads to life."

Minding Our Own Business

I can't help but also think of that wonderful exchange between Jesus and Peter following Jesus' resurrection (John 21:15-23). After asking Peter three times if he really loved him, Jesus told Peter that he would live to a ripe old age, giving him plenty of time to do the work to which Jesus was calling him. Peter then saw John standing behind them and asked, "Lord, what about him?"

Jesus' response to Peter is all we really need to know about the eternal destiny of others: "If I want him to remain alive until I return, *what is that to you?* You must follow me."

To put it as bluntly as Jesus did to Peter, how God will exercise his prerogative on the Day of Judgment is none of our business! Our business is to follow Jesus. To "go and make disciples of all nations, baptizing them in the name of the Father and of the Son and of the Holy Spirit, and teaching them to obey everything" he has commanded us. Our job is to tell them in no uncertain terms that "whoever believes and is baptized shall be saved, but whoever does not believe will be condemned."

We are merely messengers. We are not the Judge.

To us has been given the *message* of God in all its authoritative completeness and finality. "The things revealed belong to us and to our children forever, that we may follow all the words of this law" (Deuteronomy 29:29). The message is ours to live by. It is ours to teach and to proclaim. It is ours to warn others about—those who are ignoring the dire consequences of Judgment and eternal punishment in hell.

But to us has not been given the *mind* of God as if we ourselves were God. "The secret things belong to the Lord our God" (Deuteronomy 29:29). His mind is not ours to appropriate. His unrevealed thoughts are not ours to speculate. His infinite knowledge is not ours to know fully until that day and hour when "all will be made known and all mysteries shall cease."

If we reduce the God of creation to nothing more than the revealed message, then we have misunderstood that very message. What that message tells us about God is that he is the great God of the universe and the almighty Sovereign over the nations, with every power and authority inherent within such sovereignty. And that he is the great and mighty Judge who will judge justly, however he judges.

> Oh, the depth of the riches of the wisdom and
>   knowledge of God!
>   How unsearchable his judgments,
>   and his paths beyond tracing out!
> 'Who has known the mind of the Lord?
>   Or who has been his counselor?'
>   (Romans 11:33,34)

How dare we then say that God has no prerogative! It is *we* who have no prerogative to dictate to God whom he will save and whom he will condemn.

A Paradox of Possibilities

At this point in the book I am fully aware that what I'm suggesting in this chapter will seem to some readers as if I am nullifying everything I have said in earlier chapters about the utter futility of salvation apart from immersion. And in truth it is a great paradox we are dealing with here. But the mere fact that two truths *seem* to be contradictory does not necessarily make them so. For example, I am the same person I have always been even though I don't have a single cell that I had when I was ten years old. Or consider the more divine paradox of a virgin becoming the mother of Jesus. Or the ultimate paradox: God in human flesh.

So when we speak on one hand of the absolute necessity of baptism in order to enjoy present kingdom participation, and on the other hand of the possibility at the Final Judgment of being admitted into heaven without having been baptized, it may at first seem contradictory and absurd. But if we place into their own separate contexts God's plan of salvation and his divine sovereignty, we are faced simultaneously with two paradoxical truths.

Touching close to the issues at hand, consider the paradox encountered when the following two statements are read in tandem:

"For nothing is impossible with God" (Luke 1:37)

"It is impossible for God to lie" (Hebrews 6:18)

Does the latter statement nullify the former, or the former nullify the latter? Of course not. We readily acknowledge that, in their proper contexts, they are both true.

The same goes for the seeming incongruity between these statements by Paul and James:

"A person is justified by faith apart from works"
(Romans 3:28 NRSV)

"A person is justified by works and not by faith alone"
(James 2:24 NRSV)

Once again, careful attention to context resolves the seeming paradox, inconsistency, and conflict.

The two distinct contexts we are dealing with in this book are 1) the revealed plan of salvation, in which baptism plays an indispensable part along with faith and repentance; and 2) Final Judgment, in which God's sovereign power includes the prerogative to exercise (or not exercise) divine clemency for those who have failed to comply fully with the plan of salvation. Although crossing the boundaries of these two concepts appears to involve an inherent contradiction, the paradox is that, within each of the separate contexts, both positions remain completely true.

Given these distinct contexts, the exercise of divine clemency at the Final Judgment is only a *present possibility*, not a *future actuality*. It would be a mistake of the highest order to assume a kind of backward causation—to think that what might potentially happen at the Final Judgment changes in any way the divinely-revealed plan of salvation. If God wants there to be unbaptized believers in heaven, that is up to him. All we know and all we can preach is what we read in the Book. And from what we can read in the Book, there is no such thing as salvation, redemption, or justification apart from penitent, faith-prompted immersion.

Restoration Reflections

I am not a great believer in citing restoration leaders in support of any proposition. Their own plea—"Back to the Bible"—would militate against citing them as authority for any matter religious. But because I know that some readers may have particular difficulty with the ideas presented in this chapter, I will share the following discussion from Alexander Campbell's writing. If nothing else, it will demonstrate that what I've presented in this chapter is not wholly outside the stream of restoration thought.

Responding to Andrew Broadus in the *Millennial Harbinger* in 1831, Campbell makes a clear distinction between the present "kingdom of grace" and the heavenly realm. Campbell begins by summarizing Broadus' query:

> ...but what comes of all the pious Catholics, Greeks, Protestants? The Greek and Roman Church say, 'We believe in one baptism for the remission of sins'; and they believe that infants are sinners, and therefore the former immerse and the latter sprinkle them; and that is baptism with them. All christendom either immerse or sprinkle.... 'What havoc does baptism for the remission of sins make among all these!!'
>
> I simply say, they are not in the kingdom of grace; because Jesus said, 'Except a man be born of water and of the spirit he cannot enter the kingdom of God.' *But he may accept the will for the deed, and admit them into the future kingdom, such of them as are merely mistaken, who are disposed to obey, or who think that they have obeyed, as he may accept infants and idiots into the future kingdom without faith or baptism.* [Emphasis mine.][1]

In so saying, Campbell left open the possibility that God might save some who are not in the present kingdom of grace. On what basis? Solely upon the divine prerogative which inheres in the Sovereign of the universe. For Campbell, the universal, singular plan of salvation was one matter; God's final judgment, a separate matter altogether.

---

1. *Millennial Harbinger*, October, 1831, p. 44, 45.

As to the former, Campbell was in no doubt:

> I have repeatedly asserted and shown that regeneration
> has respect only to the present kingdom of grace in its
> scriptural import, and that faith and baptism are
> indispensable to admission into it; also, that the terms
> justified, sanctified, pardoned, etc. have respect to the
> present enjoyment of salvation.

Only at the risk of eternal condemnation do we dare move the boundary stones of the kingdom of revelation. But the boundaries of the heavenly Jerusalem remain God's to determine.

Implications for Eternal Fellowship

All of this has been a long, roundabout way of saying that eternal fellowship in heaven may well be a surprise. On that "great gettin' up morning" when heaven dawns, we are going to look around and see "a great multitude that no one could count, from every nation, tribe, people and language, standing before the throne and in front of the Lamb" (Revelation 7:9). What a rapturous fellowship it will be!

Will there be people among that multitude who have never been baptized for remission of sins? You can count on it! Abraham, Moses, and Elijah—all unbaptized—will be there to meet us. And maybe, God willing, even some among our own family and friends who have never been immersed. Will we be outraged if they are there? Will we be disillusioned with God if they are *not* there?

Will there be souls in heaven who never attended a Church of Christ? No doubt about it. Deborah, Daniel, and David will be telling us stories about how they used to worship God in the days before Christ and his apostles. And maybe even some brothers and sisters in Christ who worshiped down the street from us. Should we snub them because they never associated themselves with us? On the other hand, would we have any right to snub God if he decided that baptized believers forfeited their salvation by remaining in doctrinally rebellious denominations?

Will some of God's singers in heaven have been used to singing with an instrument? Absolutely. Asaph, Heman, and Jeduthun (appointed by David to accompany the temple singing with harps, lyres, and cymbals) will likely be in that heavenly chorus. And maybe some of the hymn writers of more modern times who wrote their songs of faith to be accompanied by instruments. Will we refuse to sing with them if they step up on the risers in the throne room? Or, if it turns out differently, will we shake our heads disapprovingly at God for having chosen not to honor their faith solely because in this one area they preferred to "sacrifice" rather than to "obey"?

Speaking of people who might be missing from heaven, will there be people whom we know in the church who won't be there? Almost certainly. For we are told that some "who have once been enlightened, who have tasted the heavenly gift, who have shared in the Holy Spirit, who have tasted the goodness of the word of God and the powers of the coming age" (Hebrews 6:4,5) will not find their names listed in the Book of Life.

Unlike in other areas, thankfully, we haven't yet been seduced into believing Calvin's notion of "once saved, always saved." Apostasy *is indeed* a possibility! So it doesn't matter that a person may have been biblically baptized. It doesn't even matter that he might still claim some association with the "Church of Christ." If he has fallen away, then he has made his faith and immersion into Christ as if they were null and void. Having despised his "in-Christ" fellowship, he has cut himself off from the eternal life promised to the family of God. By his own choice, he has disinherited himself.

We might think that someone has fallen away, while God sees it differently. Or we might think that someone has *not* fallen away, while God knows otherwise. Either way, only "God, who knows the heart" (Acts 15:8) knows for sure.

If heaven holds surprises, of one thing we can be certain:

Everyone who is supposed to be there will be there, and no one who is not supposed to be there will slip in under the curtain.

So it is inconceivable that we might complain to God that he has made some mistake either in including those we think ought not to be saved or excluding those we expected God to welcome with open arms.

When you think about it, the odds are pretty good that anyone who *would complain* won't *be there* to complain! That thought alone ought to give us pause when we are tempted to make anticipatory complaints even before the Day of Judgment.

One thing which does intrigue me is how God has planned for us to experience the joys of heaven despite our knowing that some of our loved ones and friends aren't there. Any number of us ache even now at the loss of those we hold dear who have passed from this world without committing their lives to Christ. How, we ask, could we ever be happy in heaven while they are condemned to the punishment of hell? But somehow, someway we must trust that God has solved the problem long before we ever thought about it.

Whatever doubts or questions we may have in this life, when we finally see our Lord face to face, there will be no question about whether God exercised his divine prerogative as we might have predicted or desired. If I read John's Revelation right, we will all be too enthralled in praising the Lamb to worry about what kind of sheep the Shepherd ultimately welcomed into his eternal fold!

The Perfect Fellowship

Call me an idealist. Call me a perfectionist. Or just call me picky. But when it comes to Christian fellowship I go about, like Diogenes holding his lantern, looking for the perfect fellowship. And, of course, I never find it. Everywhere I look I find fallible Christians just like myself—a guaranteed recipe for imperfection. If the doctrine is right, the spirit is wrong. If the spirit is right, the doctrine is wrong. Woe is me! Of all men I am most miserable!

For that reason, Christian fellowship as it ought to be is what

I most like about the prospect of heaven. I realize that lots of folks are a bit skeptical about being in heaven for an eternity. ("But what will we *do* in heaven through 'endless years the same?'") What we will *do* "when time shall be no more" doesn't bother me. All I can think about is the end to my search—finding *the perfect fellowship!*

Heaven for me will be the perfect sharing; the perfect caring. An unending, extravagant table-fellowship around the banquet table of the Bride. Unlimited, unbounded, never-ceasing *koinonia* fellowship with the whole extended family of God. No more reluctant enclaves of difficult conscience fellowship. No more agony over disfellowshiping wayward brothers and sisters from the immediate family of a local congregation. No more doctrinal squabbles. No more division. No more petty infighting. No more slander of brothers and sisters. No more venomous brotherhood papers. No more wondering, "With whom can I share my faith in Christ?"

After all the frustration of fellowship I have experienced in this life, heaven for me will mean the bliss of peace and harmony. Unity and love. Joy and praise all around. I tell you, brothers and sisters, the eternal fellowship of the saved is what I long for. How sweet, how heavenly will be the sight of those who love the Lord!

When fellowship is no longer an enigma but a divine puzzle with every piece perfectly in place, "That will be glory, be glory for me!"

EPILOGUE

*Worshiping together is a more personal thing than riding trains
or attending movies together. Tolerance is not enough;
it must be real brotherhood or nothing.*

FRANK T. WILSON

OPEN LETTER, OPEN HEART

Nothing is more difficult in the cut and thrust of doctrinal dialogue than taking issue with a friend. Yet sometimes the greater good of the kingdom requires a tough and tender testing of understandings, particularly when one's personal views have been made public and have had considerable influence throughout the extended family.

In the pages which follow I want to share with you a letter which I have sent to my friend and brother, Max Lucado. It's about his recent book, *In the Grip of Grace*.[1] It's a difficult letter—a letter I hoped I would never have to write to anyone, least of all to a friend.

I am painfully aware from personal experience that a letter shared publicly has every potential for tyranny and abuse. It is, after all, a one-sided conversation risking the danger of taking the other person's thoughts out of context without the benefit of explanation or clarification.

Even the normal disclaimer ("We've offered him an opportunity to respond, but he refused to reply") is often little more than a calculated comment on how indefensible the other person's position is. Having myself been among those who "refused to reply," I know that there are any number of reasons why choosing not to make a public reply might be in the best interests of the kingdom. To his credit, it would not be Max's style to get embroiled in

---

1. Max Lucado, *In the Grip of Grace* (Dallas: Word Publishing, 1996)

polemic debate. I am the cross-examining lawyer; Max, the ever-inspiring poet.

So why go public in this case? More than anything, it was for lack of better options. In Max's own words, *In the Grip of Grace* contains "watershed, historic thoughts"—a kind of ninety-five theses tacked on the church door, as it were.

Because substantial portions of the book have already had significant impact on our thinking about baptism and fellowship in the churches of Christ, any considered response would have to cover the book as a whole. Unfortunately, such a comprehensive analysis could hardly be anonymous. Even the slightest reference to one of Max's well-known illustrations, in particular, would have given away his identity and hinted of devious sniping on my part.

Nor did it seem fair to lob cold, argumentative barrages from a distance as if Max and I somehow didn't know each other. In fact, knowing Max personally gives perhaps the keenest insight into why the current issues have come to the forefront. Christian fellowship and unity are deeply personal issues welling up from within the sensitive hearts of a growing number of fellow Christians just like Max. For that reason if for no other, the last thing I would want to do is to "write him up," as seems to be the standard practice for tabloid journalism in the church.

Was there any way, then, to demonstrate how two brothers can have serious doctrinal differences without expressing rancor toward each other? What follows is an effort to do just that and to encourage tough and tender dialogue among all of us on the crucial issues which so deeply divide.

The issues at stake are far more important than personalities. It's not a question of either *Max* or *LaGard*, or anyone else for that matter. As Paul told the Corinthians, who were so intent on forming personality cults, "I have applied these things to myself and Apollos for your benefit, so that you may learn from us the meaning of the saying, 'Do not go beyond what is written.' Then you will not take pride in one man over against another" (1 Corinthians 4:6).

So in the words which follow, I have likewise applied the things in this book to myself and Max for your benefit. Given the eternal consequences of what is at stake, I simply had to be tough. But what dare I say to the tender heart of a gentle, gifted servant of God?

Dear Max,

I've just finished reading your recent book—again. The promo piece on the inside flap is right: *In the Grip of Grace* is indeed your most theologically challenging book to date. You continue to amaze me with your imaginative, breezy style of writing—this time, turning Paul's own most theologically challenging treatise into an easy-to-understand, powerful *tour de force*.

I hope I don't sound like a groupie to tell you some of my favorite lines:

> David and Jonathan were like two keys on a piano keyboard. Alone they made music, but together they made harmony.

> We'll celebrate the empty tomb long before we'll kneel at the cross.

> Circumcision proclaimed that there is no part of our life too private or too personal for God.

But you already know that I'm not writing you to stroke your ego. As I told you in my earlier note, I am deeply concerned about where you are leading us in our thinking about Christian fellowship. I know that Christ's call for unity among believers has become a genuine passion for you in recent years. You've spoken about it from your own pulpit, at the Pepperdine lectures, at the Evangelical Christian Publishers Association banquet, and, in Atlanta, at the special Promise Keepers rally for church leaders. Much of what you presented on those occasions has now found its way into your book.

I also know that you have agonized for a long time over the matter of Christian unity and particularly its implications regarding baptism. I'll not soon forget that special day when Ruth and I had tea with you and Denalyn at that cozy little place in Bourton-on-the-Water. It hasn't escaped me that the name of the place was "Small Talk." What irony! It was anything but small talk we engaged in that long afternoon. It was deep. Heavy. Difficult. As I recall, tea gave way to tears.

As a fellow author I doubt if there is anyone who resonates more with something you said almost in passing in your book. What was it...? "I wonder if people will agree, if they'll approve, if they'll appreciate all the long, painstaking, tedious, exhausting, tortuous hours I am humbly putting into these watershed, historic thoughts?" Here it is...coming up on 2:30 in the morning...and I'm experiencing all the writer's tortures you described.

But it's not just a matter of sharing your pain in a way that few others can. It's those other words that haunt me: *"these watershed, historic thoughts,"* as you put it. Haunting, first, because I know how far you've travelled in your own thinking to get to the point where you are now. It's like shifting gears in your old pickup. Or maybe more like turning a corner. You've come a long way from being a relatively unknown "Church of

Christ" missionary in Brazil to a best-selling Christian author and speaker pleading on a high-visibility platform for unity among believers in all denominations.

Yet it's not just your own private "watershed, historic thoughts" that most trouble me. It's knowing that your personal thoughts have in turn become watershed, historic thoughts for the churches of Christ. Never in a million years would I ever have guessed that we, of all people, would be sliding down the slippery slope of baptism theology by calling for unity with believers who have never been immersed or whose only baptism was as an infant. *Watershed*, indeed. *Historic*, to say the least.

You are not, of course, on a one-man crusade. What I've come to call "the quiet revolution" is being pushed by a lot of folks along a number of different fronts. But as I'm sure you must be aware, an increasing number of preachers out there are being led into their own "watershed, historic thoughts" by what you've said and are passing them along to others in sermon after sermon.

I know you would be the first to join me in hoping that it's not simply a case of saying, "If Max Lucado believes it, how could it be wrong?" Frankly, I don't know what gives me greater cause for alarm: that possibility or the more likely probability that they've actually found your arguments to be convincing. In that case I have my work cut out for me re-digging some ancient wells.

Of course if you are right on the issue of fellowship, there'll be some well-deserved stars in your crown. At the very least, Christian unity is always a noble idea. The right idea. And I assure you it gives me no pleasure to come off sounding as if I'm opposed to it. But if either of us is wrong on this one (and it's possible that we could both be mistaken in some respects), then we have much to answer for. Lots of folks are listening in on our not-so-private musings.

In your gracious Foreword to *Meeting God in Quiet Places* you said candidly of my writings: "We haven't always agreed with him—but we have always been prompted by him." Max, I hope you are still open to being prompted. Unfortunately, I know that it's a bit more difficult for those of us who write books to continue to be open once our thoughts are typeset and published for all the world to see. At the very least, then, I just hope that this effort to sharpen each other's swords can be of some value to those whose own thoughts are not yet in print.

United with Each Other, But Not with Christ?

The most encouraging aspect of our differences is that there is still so much common ground. When you get to Romans Chapter 6, for example, you are—as the British say—*spot on!* What could be clearer than the way you presented Romans 6:2ff (p. 114): "Did you forget that all of us became part of Christ when we were baptized?" From that one statement alone, I would have thought that the bounds of Christian fellowship would be clearly delineated so as to include all those who have "become part of Christ" *when they were baptized.*

What then are the implications for those who aren't baptized? Surely the only conclusion can be that they are not part of Christ and therefore have no fellowship in him. Yet in the rest of your book you appear to be arguing quite to the contrary. Have I missed something?

Consider also your own questions on the following page: "Have we forgotten what life was like before our baptism? Have we forgotten the mess we were in before we were united with him?" Here too the matter of fellowship in Christ seems clearly linked to both baptism and being united with him. Before baptism, not united; after baptism, united. Before baptism, no fellowship; after baptism, fellowship.

I can't help but be struck by the thread running throughout these words: *United. Union. Unity. Unity movement.* How are we to have unity with each other if we have not first been united with Christ? And how— by this passage, certainly—can we be united with Christ apart from baptism?

In each instance you state the premise correctly (even elegantly), only to draw conclusions elsewhere that simply don't follow. The bizarre result is that you inevitably end up including within the circle of Christian fellowship unbaptized believers who are neither "part of Christ" nor "united with him." Can you understand why I'm so puzzled?

Does Something Really Happen in That Water?

Even at what I think is your point of departure from biblical immersion (baptism as merely a symbol), there is still a kernel of truth. As long as we all know what we are talking about you are certainly right to say (p. 115), "Please understand, it is not the act that saves us. But it is the act that symbolizes how we are saved! The invisible work of the Holy Spirit is visibly dramatized in the water."

As for being symbolic, you're right. Baptism is one of those pictures worth a thousand words. It speaks volumes about Christ's own death, burial, and triumphant resurrection, with which we identify by way of re-enactment in a watery grave. It's a perfectly-performed charade of the good news. A divine pantomime.

So is it symbolic? Yes, and beautifully so! Is it *only* symbolic? Not a chance. Certainly not from what you yourself have already indicated so clearly about baptism's role in our "becoming part of Christ" and "being united with him."

Baptism doesn't just *stand* for something; it *does* something. Given all the things that Scripture says happen *because of* immersion (new birth, sonship, forgiveness, salvation), baptism is its own "watershed, historic" moment in the life of a believer.

Never has that moment been more clearly articulated than by one of your co-authors in *In Search of Wonder*. The way Jack Reese puts it is almost breathtaking:

> Something happens in baptism. An old person dies; a new person rises. The one who was not a Christian becomes a Christian; she is forgiven, a new creature in a new relationship. And the Holy Spirit is given as a gift. Something actually happens.[2]

If as Jack says *something actually happens* in baptism, then it is more than merely symbolic. It is an act of covenant. A transaction. A divine trysting place in which the Spirit of a gracious God and the heart of an obedient man or woman are merged together in holy union.

What then shall we say of the act of baptism? Does it save us? No, not if we think that by doing *anything* (even believing on Jesus) we could ever merit salvation because of something we ourselves have done. But since

---

2. Ed. by Lynn Anderson, *In Search of Wonder* (West Monroe, LA: Howard Publishing, 1995), 123.

baptism is God's chosen means by which he imparts his saving grace to the willing believer, it was altogether fitting that Peter should speak of baptism "that now saves you."

Is Peter talking about what we do when we go through the motions of the ritual? No way! He's not talking about how *we* work in baptism but about how *God* works in baptism.

And, oh, how he works! When a person goes down into the water, God scrubs the sinner's sins away! When a person comes up out of the water, the Holy Spirit hugs a risen saint!

Hear your own moving, compelling words again, Max: "Remove your shoes, bow your head, and bend your knees; [may I provide the emphasis?] this is a *holy event.*"

And so it is! Not just a reminder of an event, but the event itself.

Symbol, Or Substance?

Yet look what happens in your book. From that spectacular mountaintop view of baptism you climb down to an almost apologetic, minimalist view of the act. Tracing back from the middle of your book to the beginning (pp. 47-50), your robust depiction of a life-transforming baptism turns out to be but a shadow of its former self. Now suddenly baptism is nothing more than a symbol of something that God has already done.

Do you not recognize the quick shift you've made from present tense to past? Even the fledgling writer knows that using the past tense robs the present of its punch and excitement. Baptism is a "here and now" event, not a "then and there" event. It's not a memorial service but a delivery room. Someone has died, yes, but someone else—someone new—is just being born. Right now. This instant.

That's why baptism as merely a symbol doesn't work. What delivery room was ever just a symbol? When you compare baptism to circumcision, and then to your wedding ring, and finally to your varsity football jacket—in each case you're talking about past-tense symbols.

This is so tough. Where to begin? We have about a zillion separate issues to deal with, and the temptation is to just throw them all into a theological blender. But unless we're careful, we're not going to get *pure* doctrine, only a blended glob of *puree* doctrine.

Maybe it would help then to begin with something else we agree on—that beyond all doubt baptism is predicated upon that which God has already done. "For God so loved the world that he gave his one and only Son, that whoever believes in him shall not perish but have eternal life" (John 3:16). God loved us before we ever left our mother's womb. God loved us when we grew up and spit in his face. Without God's love and Jesus' death on the cross, our getting wet would be...well, just getting wet.

For that matter, not even our *faith* would mean anything if God hadn't already done something. As is true of our love, we also *believe* because he first loved us. Does that also make faith nothing more than a symbol?

Are Baptism and Circumcision on the Same Shelf?

There are any number of problems as I see it with comparing baptism to Jewish circumcision and saying that both are just religious symbols. Clearly there are certain similarities, but there are also significant differences.

When God established his covenant with Abraham, he said, "You are to undergo circumcision, and it will be the sign of the covenant between me and you" (Genesis 17:11). Without question, then, circumcision was a sign. A symbol of God's more-than-slightly-one-sided contract with Israel. But it was a national symbol, not an individual thing. Wasn't for Gentiles. Wasn't for little girls. Wasn't something the eight-day-old boy chose for himself. And—most important of all—it wasn't prompted by the youngster's personal faith in God.

By contrast, baptism couldn't be more universal, genderless, classless, and individual. When we clothe ourselves with Christ by being baptized into him (Galatians 3:27-28), "there is neither Jew nor Greek, slave nor free, male nor female, for you are all one in Christ Jesus." (Talk about a basis for unity!)

Nor could baptism be more personal and faith-motivated. I confess I've never considered it before, but why do we never read about someone being circumcised and then "going on his way rejoicing" as did the exuberant Ethiopian eunuch? Apart from the obvious, I suppose, circumcision was not something that was internalized at the moment of its occurrence. Until a Jew grew to the point where he appropriated the significance of the symbol for his own life, it was only an external "tattoo" worn as a symbol of national pride.

In fact that is Paul's very point about circumcision in Romans chapters 2 and 3. For the unrighteous, unbelieving Jew, the external symbol had never become an internal reality. It was all form and no substance. Worse yet, as you so vividly point out, Paul then lambasted them for turning what should have been a symbol of submission into a symbol of smug superiority.

Now you've got yourself a parallel with baptism.

Or rather *with our attitude toward it.* What the Jews did with circumcision we too can do with baptism: empty it of its power and meaning. Get wet but dry off. Rely on the fact that we've "been there, done that." Sniff at those who haven't experienced it, while leading lives that can't hold a candle to theirs.

This is the "rock-stacking legalist" you described, who thinks that he must earn salvation by "do and do, rule upon rule." This is the "finger-pointing judgmentalist" you wrote about, whose only sense of spiritual security comes by knocking everybody else's misunderstanding of what it takes to become a Christian.

A person's high-handed attitude is the bad guy here. If substance and attitude are important, form is not unimportant. ("You should have practiced the latter without leaving the former undone.")

Properly regarded by the person you describe as the "grace-driven Christian," baptism does things that circumcision never did. That's where I believe you hung your varsity football jacket on the wrong peg. Or perhaps talked about the wrong jacket. Your point, of course, was that merely wearing your old high-school football jacket wouldn't entitle you to go back out on the field and play with those much younger, fine-tuned athletes. The jacket is just a nostalgic symbol of days gone by.

Hence you said, "It alone doesn't transform me, empower me, or enable me....Neither does your baptism...." Had you been referring only to circumcision (or to a "showcase" baptism or to infant baptism), your varsity jacket analogy would be a good one. But that is precisely how baptism is different from circumcision. Baptism *transforms* (from death to life, and from condemnation to forgiveness). It *empowers* (through the working of the Holy Spirit). It *enables* (by uniting us with Christ and making us a part of him).

The only time that Paul or any other inspired writer even mentions baptism and circumcision in the same context is in Colossians, chapter 2—and that by way of a contrast. Paul reminds the saints in Colosse that when they were "buried with Christ in baptism" and "raised with him through their faith in the power of God," at that moment they were "circumcised" in a way that before had never been possible with a circumcision "done by the hands of men." Abraham's circumcision sliced off a bit of human flesh. The "circumcision done by Christ," says Paul, is "the putting off of the sinful nature."

Call baptism a symbol if you wish. For that it is. But never since the cross itself and the empty tomb has any symbol been so transforming, empowering, or enabling. "When you were dead in your sins and in the uncircumcision of your sinful nature, God made you alive with Christ. He forgave us all our sins!"

In that light, Max, put your football jacket aside for the moment and try another one on for size. Remember that old faded brown corduroy jacket you borrowed from me while you were touring in the Cotswolds? You didn't need it to keep warm, and you sure didn't want it just to make a fashion statement. Not that jacket! The fact was, your hotel wouldn't let you eat in their dining room without a jacket, and you'd forgotten to pack one.

No jacket, no dinner. They weren't being rude. Just trying to keep us scruffy Americans from spoiling the local landscape. So what did you do? Get huffy and say, "Just because a guy is wearing a jacket doesn't necessarily mean he's got class"?

No, what you did is honor their request. You borrowed a jacket and put it on. And it wasn't just a symbol of class or style. It actually got you in where you couldn't have gotten without it.

In this case your jacket wasn't just symbolic. It was instrumental, as is baptism, through which Paul says we "have clothed ourselves with Christ." Having no righteousness of our own, we borrowed Christ's righteousness and put it on. And, with that, "all things are ready; come to the feast!"

In his bombshell British book, *The Normal Christian Birth*, evangelical David Pawson, put it this way: "Baptism isn't just *like* a bath; it *is* a bath. It is not just *like* a burial; it *is* a burial." And here comes the best line of the day: "The 'sign' actually accomplishes what it signifies."[3]

The way you have described baptism as merely a symbol is like being honored with a ceremonial "Key to the City" that is so big it couldn't unlock anything. The way the New Testament describes baptism as a symbol is more like a new CEO at a press conference being handed a master key to the corporate headquarters. That key actually does what it symbolizes. Like baptism, it opens doors.

Sign and substance, simultaneously.

Ring, or Vows?

For all the same reasons, Max, I believe your wedding ring analogy also fails. Certainly you are right when you say (p. 48), "Were I to lose the ring, I'd be disappointed, but our marriage would continue. It is a symbol, nothing more." Some people don't even exchange

---

3. David Pawson, *The Normal Christian Birth* (London: Hodder & Stoughton, 1989), 51.

rings when they are married. So obviously a ring doth not a marriage make.

The reason your marriage would continue without your ring is that it is the *marriage*, not the ring, that is the bond of your relationship with Denalyn. As I urged in my book by the same name, baptism is the believer's wedding ceremony. What makes a marriage is the exchange of vows. The pledge of faithfulness and purity. The promise, "til death us do part."

As you quoted Peter in that absolutely "spot on" middle section of your book, baptism is *"the pledge of a good conscience toward God"* (1 Peter 3:21). "No casual custom. No ho-hum ritual," you wrote.

I distinctly remember a day barely four years ago when I gave up my bachelorhood and became a married man. Prior to that day, I had come to love Ruth and had committed to her to be wed. But we were only engaged, not married. She was still Ruth Batey, not Ruth Smith. On May 1, 1993, at 2:00 in the afternoon, we exchanged our vows and turned to face a joyous gathering of family and friends as husband and wife. Mr. and Mrs. LaGard Smith.

Beyond merely being symbolic of the love and commitment which already existed, the wedding ceremony was a transaction which initiated a new relationship. It was a watershed moment legally, morally, and spiritually. A bright line of entitlements and obligations. A bright line of benefits, blessings, and burdens.

I also distinctly remember a Sunday morning in 1958 when I pledged my love to Christ and was led down into the waters of baptism by my father. Coming up out of the water, I was greeted by a joyous spiritual family as a fellow Christian and newborn brother in Christ.

My baptism was more than merely a symbol of the belief in Christ which I had acknowledged all throughout my youthful years. At the point of belief, I was not yet a Christian. Baptism was a transaction which initiated a new relationship. It was a *blood*-shed, *water*-shed moment. A bright line of entitlements and obligations. A bright line of spiritual benefits, blessings, and burdens.

I appreciate that those who champion salvation by faith apart from baptism would insist that penitent belief itself is a watershed moment, its own bright line. Yet as much could be said of the day I met and fell in love with Ruth—July 4th. The question is not whether *some kind* of a new relationship is formed or whether—as perhaps with the new believer—one's life is radically transformed. The question is whether we are *in Christ.* Whether we are *united with Christ.* Whether we are a *brother or sister in Christ* in fellowship with all other brothers and sisters in Christ.

It is not just any bright line that we are after. What alone matters is the bright line which God has drawn. Whom has God forgiven? Whom has God saved? That is the person who is my brother in Christ.

Leaks in Your Fellow-Ship

Part of your particular genius, Max, is your ability to paint word pictures. Nobody does it better. And of all the pictures you've ever painted, none has been more clever or mindsticking than the picture of what you call "God's fellow-ship" (pp. 159-170). It's a masterful play on the word. Of Christian fellowship you write, "We each followed him across the gangplank of his grace onto the same boat." What an inspired first stroke of the brush! What an opening line!

Whereupon you proceed to talk about all the

"disharmony among the crew" who are arguing about classic questions of theology. Everywhere you turn on deck, there is controversy over "once-saved-always-saved," or predestination, or premillennialism, or tongue-speaking, or the legitimacy of clergy, or worship style, and on and on. Nothing but squabbling and infighting.

What does the Captain of the ship think about all this disunity among his crew? He prays that they will all get along together and love each other. Isn't that exactly what we hear Jesus saying in John 17? And I'm telling you, Max, every fiber of my being says, "Yes!" "Yes!" "Yes!"

But it just won't float, Max. No matter how much you or I would like for it to, your boat simply won't float. Beneath the surface of your illustration are holes big enough for whales to swim through.

From the outset your argument for Christian unity assumes that everybody on board is a Christian—that each one is in fact both *on board* and *a member of the crew*. You refer to them as "brothers and sisters"; the Father's "kids"; part of the "one flock"; "Christians" who "share a common Savior" and who were "covered with the same grace." If all of that were true, then your case for unity and mutual fellowship would be absolutely watertight. But when all these believers came across that gangplank of grace, there was not the slightest mention that any of them even got their toes wet in the process.

Whatever happened to baptism? There's not a hint of it—not even as a symbol. In fact, what do you do (p. 169) when it comes to defining a Christian? You fudge, Max! "Where there is faith, repentance, and a new birth," you say with finesse, "there is a Christian."

A new birth? Do you mean *baptism*? Does the mere

mention of baptism destroy the picture? What you and I both know, of course, is that it does. Not everybody who believes has been baptized. It would mean that not all who call themselves Christians are on board the ship. And when the whole idea is to get everybody on board, that just won't do.

To make wide-open Christian fellowship happen on this scale, you have to throw baptism into the brig. It can't be allowed out on deck. It might accuse some of the crew of being stowaways. Nor can it be allowed below deck, because "just as a ship has many rooms, so God's kingdom has room for many opinions." Even, presumably, about what it takes to become a Christian. With cabins reserved for all the different denominations, whatever Scripture teaches about baptism has to be reduced to the lowest common denominator. Make that *the lowest common denomination.*

At that point what else can we say other than what you said: "When I meet a man whose faith is in the cross and whose eyes are on the Savior, I meet a brother."

A brother who is not yet born? (John 3:5) A brother who is not yet a son? (Galatians 3:26-27) A brother who is not yet saved? (Mark 16:16; 1 Peter 3:21) A brother who is not united with Christ? (Romans 6:5) Apart from being the kind of brother we always wish we had but didn't, what kind of a brother would this be?

When the Heart Tugs for Fellowship

Max, you're wearing your heart on your sleeve. I think I know something of your heart. (It's a heart I love.) And I think I know what's pushing your buttons. It's all the spiritually-minded, godly people you're surrounded by who haven't been biblically baptized.

In that soulful 16th chapter you count your blessings and name them one by one. It's the Brazilian Pentecostal preacher who taught you about prayer and the Southern Baptist who helped you understand grace. It's Anglican C. S. Lewis, Catholic Brennan Manning, and Presbyterians Steve Brown and Frederick Buechner. It's James Dobson, Chuck Swindoll, and Bill Hybels. How could all these men *not* be your brothers!

Don't think I don't feel exactly about them as you do. Some of them have been the wind beneath my own wings. They've taught me, encouraged me, tested me, and—in the fervor of their own faith—even rebuked me.

There are others too that you didn't mention. Particularly the many dedicated, faith-filled people you and I both know in Christian publishing. (There we go again..."Christian" publishing.) They're publishers who literally invest in our thoughts. They're editors who not only unsplit our split infinitives, but who suggest ideas that well up from the depths of their own faith in Christ. How could all these believers *not* be on board the ship?

What about the audiences you and I speak to? I know some might question it, but we both proclaim the Word wherever we are invited. I think, for example, of Bill and Gloria Gaither's "Praise Festival" each year in Indianapolis. Thousands of believers sit at our feet to learn more about the Lord. They're just as hungry to be nourished from the Word as those to whom we speak at Jubilee, Abilene, and Pepperdine. How could all those godly seekers *not* be part of the crew?

And what of our faithful readers from every stripe and denomination? The ones who are kind enough to write and tell us what a difference our books have made in their lives. I dare say you'll never forget that couple who knocked on your door at home, wanting to thank

you for writing the book their son had read just before
he was killed in the Gulf War.

As you say, Max, how could all these fruit-bearers
not be part of the orchard?

Taking a Closer Look at the Fruit

Our problem is that we are called to be fruit in-
spectors but aren't usually very good at it. It's a problem
we come by honestly. To Eve the fruit looked good. Surely it was acceptable. But from God's perspective the fruit
was not acceptable, and obedience was the true fruit of
which Eve should have partaken.

It's simply not true (p. 168) that "the Master says
examine the person's faith. If he or she has faith in Jesus
and is empowered by God, grace says that's enough."

Only man says that's enough. Only man is still
tempted to take good-looking fruit and do unauthorized
things with it. Only man presumes that a person is di-
vinely empowered apart from receiving the Holy Spirit
through baptism. Only man confuses being spiritually-
minded with being Spirit-filled.

Would it help at all if I suggested there are any
number of couples out there who love each other and
are committed to each other but who cohabit without
the benefit of a wedding ceremony? Would we, or the
law, consider them to be married?

Would it help if I pointed to the righteous, faith-
filled Cornelius who still needed to be saved? Or to the
sincere Ethiopian seeker on the road to Gaza who still
needed to be baptized?

I also wonder if it is really true that *our* acceptance,
that *our* tolerance is the key to unity in Christ, as you
seem to suggest (p.165)? This may seem an odd, politi-
cally-incorrect question these days, but does tolerance

have anything at all to do with who is a child of God and who is not?

Max, I know good and well that you don't believe we come to God on our own terms. How then could Christian fellowship be decided on our terms—on our own subjective feelings about the spiritual state of all the wonderful, godly people we know and love?

If it would be wrong for us to impose baptism when God hasn't, is it any less wrong for us *not* to insist on baptism when God has? If we are being judgmental by insisting that baptism is essential to Christian fellowship, we are being equally judgmental to insist that it is not essential. Either way, we're making a judgment.

What Happens at the End of the Voyage?

The good news is that you and I don't have to make the Final Judgment. It is a separate and terribly complicated issue, but your question (p. 50) is legitimate enough: "What kind of God would look at the sincere seeker and say, 'You dedicated your life to loving me and loving my children. You surrendered your heart and confessed your sins. I want to save you so badly. I'm so sorry, your church took communion one time a month too many. Because of a technicality, you are forever lost in hell'"?

I too believe in a God of grace. "What then shall we say? Is God unjust? Not at all! For he says to Moses, 'I will have mercy on whom I have mercy, and I will have compassion on whom I have compassion'" (Romans 9:14-15). Our God is a great God! (If he can save me, he can save anybody!)

Maybe it's just what I want to believe, but my guess is that there will be some surprises at the Judgment. Whatever happens, I am fully persuaded that God will

sort out with righteous justice our eternal fellowship in
the kingdom to come. Even if we mess up Christian fellowship here on earth, God will straighten it out in the
end. The Shepherd knows his sheep.

Yet you and I surely agree that there is a broad way
that leads to eternal destruction. Pat Boone's early hit
song notwithstanding, not everybody's "gonna get religion in the morning." Not *everybody* is "gonna have a
wonderful time up there." Not even everyone who says
of Jesus, "Lord, Lord." Nor, for that matter, everyone
who has been biblically baptized.

There are other caution lights to observe about
your question. As for a God of technicalities, I can't help
but think about a sacrificial, but disobedient King Saul;
and David and Uzzah, who thought they had a better
idea about how to carry the ark of God; and Naaman,
who initially scoffed at the idea that there was any need
to baptize himself seven times in the Jordan. Naaman in
particular could teach us an invaluable lesson about the
benefit of observing God's "technicalities": not in the
rivers of Damascus but in the Jordan. Not five times. Not
six times. But seven.

Even in the New Testament, what could be more of
a technicality (should one wish to call it that) than the
fact that the men in Acts chapter 19 had not received the
Holy Spirit because, despite their baptisms, they had not
been immersed into the right name? Whoever came up
with this line was dead right: God is in the details.

What kind of a God would banish to hell the pious
but unimmersed friends we know and love? All I know
is what I read. The same Bible that records Jesus saying,
"I am *the* Way, *the* truth, and *the* life—No one comes to
the Father but by me," records Jesus saying "Whoever
believes *and is baptized* will be saved...."

Max, you've got your stern before your bow. You're asking what will happen at the end of the voyage, when what counts at the moment is obeying the Captain's orders. If at the end of the voyage the Captain wants to save some whom we might not expect, that's his prerogative. He's the Captain.

Our sole responsibility is to do whatever he tells us to do and to pass those orders along to anyone else who wants to sign up for the crew. Would we be doing them any favors to bring them along as stowaways only to find out at the end of the voyage that the Captain has *not* saved them? How should we think the Captain would feel about *us* if we were to tell everybody else that it's O.K. to ignore his orders?

As hard as it is for us to grasp the thought that there are friends and colleagues who live and think perhaps even more Christianly than we do, yet still are not biblical Christians—still not saved, still not forgiven, still not brothers and sisters in Christ—even so our quandary is no cause for open mutiny. It's not our ship. We don't make the rules.

What I think we must do, faced with the enigma of Christian fellowship, is to give renewed thought to what it means to be Christlike. If the many spiritually-minded believers we know and love truly are Christlike, then why would they not want to follow Jesus himself down into the waters of the Jordan to fulfill all righteousness. "Now hear this! Now hear this!" comes the call from the bridge. If baptism was so important for our sinless Savior, how could it ever be unimportant to us?

Keep that great heart of yours, Max. And keep the vision of Christian unity alive. Make it live, Max, make it live! But I beg you to tell our "Christian" friends about redemptive, saving baptism. It's you, of all people, they'll listen to! Don't hide it under a bushel of good intentions. It may bring harmony, but not unity. Unity comes only one way. Not just from being *like Christ*, but from being *in Christ*. Not just *imitation*, but also *justification*.

Your picture of God's loving fellow-ship has such great potential. Among those whom God has washed in the blood of Christ it's time to end all the squabbling and set sail. But from what I've read in your book, I beg you not to weigh anchor just yet. It's those words from Isaiah (33:23) that concern me:

> *Your rigging hangs loose:*
> *The mast is not held secure,*
> *the sail is not spread.*

Is our fellow-ship seaworthy as we launch out into the next millennium? Could it possibly be missing a rudder?

Your brother, as ever,
LaGard

Having now myself gone public through the pages of this book, and having written my own letter of reply to Max, I invite similar responses from any who might wish to continue the dialogue. The crucial issues raised in this book need all the collective attention we can give them. Nothing but good can come from an honest, open searching of the Scriptures on the nature and boundaries of Christian fellowship.

If nothing else comes from the writing of this book, I pray we will have been reminded that speaking truth in love, without slander or rancor, is the only hope we have of maintaining unity of the Spirit in the bond of peace.

So in the warmth of Christian fellowship, come let us reason together. Open and honest; tough and tender.

May the grace of the Lord Jesus Christ,
and the love of God,
and the fellowship of the Holy Spirit
be with you all.

Discussion Questions

Chapter 1 — A Clear and Present Danger

1. Were you previously aware of what LaGard has called "the quiet revolution"?

2. In what different ways might one refer to "faith-only" salvation?

3. What do the following terms mean to you: sect; denomination; non-denominational; inter-denominational; ecumenical?

4. In what ways have you seen or heard the term "church of Christ" used in a denominational sense, rather than as the universal body of Christ?

5. How does one's view of baptism affect one's view of unity among the "Christian community," and *vice versa*?

6. How do you view the relative importance of doctrinal purity and Christian unity?

7. If you believe baptism to be "essential," to what is it essential?

8. How has our culture contributed to the way we view issues like baptism and Christian unity?

9.   Has your own thinking been influenced by Christian radio and television, or popular Christian music, or Christian books written by authors outside the churches of Christ?

10.   To what extent have your ideas about Christian unity been affected by friends and family who are not members of the churches of Christ?

11.   What questions about Christian fellowship are most worrisome to you?

12.   How do you see biblical fellowship—mostly bright lines, or mostly fuzzy?

CHAPTER 2 — THE GHOST OF FAITH-ONLY ARGUMENTS PAST

1. Have you heard any talk of "faith-only" salvation in your own congregation or in others?

2. In what ways have the churches of Christ been known for their exclusivity relative to other churches?

3. In your own mind, what do you do with "all the wonderful, Spirit-filled, Jesus-like, prayerful believers who don't go to church where we go and weren't baptized like we were baptized," as the preacher put it?

4. Thinking specifically about Romans 15:7, whom are you supposed to accept in the same way that Christ has accepted you?

5. What does the following statement mean to you: "In matters of doctrine, unity; in matters of opinion, liberty; in all things, love"?

6. In what way has our thinking on Christian initiation and Christian unity been shaped by restorationists like Campbell and Stone?

7. Is there some truth in the preacher's statement that "faith in Christ alone is what brings salvation"?

8. Can we simultaneously maintain our historical view of baptism and the view which says that unbaptized believers are saved?

9. Is baptism a matter of "work," or is it a matter of "grace"?

10. Does unity result from a correct view of baptism?

11. On what basis did Paul make his plea for Christian unity in 1 Corinthians 1:10-17?

12. To whom was Jesus directing his call for Christian unity in John 17:20-26?

CHAPTER 3 — NOT BY OVERNIGHT EXPRESS

1. What evidence, if any, do you see of biblical illiteracy in the church?

2. How would you rate the level of spiritual maturity in the teaching which is done in you own congregation?

3. Being brutally honest, how would you characterize your own level of biblical literacy?

4. What are the relative merits of small congregations and mega-churches?

5. What factors are involved in the growth of your own congregation?

6. To what extent is your congregation youth-driven?

7. How important to understanding and applying the Scriptures is the particular hermeneutic one chooses?

8. What differences are likely to result from an objective view of Scripture as compared with a subjective view?

9. Is there a connection between how a person views doctrine pertaining to church organization and worship and doctrine pertaining to moral issues?

10. Do our unique "identity markers" (like *a cappella* singing and baptism for the remission of sins) get in the way of evangelism?

11. In what ways is our fellowship with those outside the churches of Christ affected by the culture around us?

12. In what ways is our fellowship with each other affected by the culture around us?

CHAPTER 4 — UNCOMMON COMMON CAUSE

1. With what believers outside the church have you joined in common cause?

2. Why have we in the church been so far behind other believers in the battles over issues like abortion, gay rights, and euthanasia?

3. What common cause do we have with Promise Keepers?

4. Is there any difference between Promise Keepers and other movements or organizations as it relates to Christian fellowship?

5. How does the Promise Keepers' use of the "sinner's prayer" square with Scripture relative to how a person becomes a Christian?

6. Have you seen any ways in which your own congregation has been influenced in its thinking by the Promise Keepers movement?

7. What is the difference between *association* and *fellowship*?

8. What dangers or potential for good are presented by unity meetings with other churches?

10. Are unity meetings among restoration movement churches a good idea?

11. Is it ever acceptable to use the term *Christian* apart from references to biblically baptized believers?

12. Is there any danger in using the term *Christian* relative to those who are not truly Christians?

CHAPTER 5 — UNIVERSAL FELLOWSHIP: THE FAMILY OF MAN

1. What things do we have in common with all of humankind?

2. Why is it good to remind ourselves that we are part of the family of man?

3. In what way are we our brother's keeper?

4. What incidents in the life of Jesus remind us of universal fellowship?

5. In what way are we not to be yoked with unbelievers (2 Corinthians 6:14,15)?

6. Is it wrong to pray for those who are not Christians?

7. Is it wrong to have close friends who are not Christians?

8. What is the significance of having table fellowship with someone else?

9. In what ways do we have table fellowship every day with people who may have little or no faith?

10. Do we have a double-standard in the way that we talk about and treat our friends who are not Christians?

11. How can we honor the faith of fellow seekers without compromising principle or doctrine?

12. How can we use the faith of others as a bridge to evangelism?

Chapter 6 — Faith Fellowship: Like Family

1. Do you know anyone who is *like family*? If so, what might he or she teach you about what LaGard has called "faith fellowship"?

2. What have you learned about worship or service to God from those outside the church?

3. What do you think the wider "Christian community" could most profitably learn from the churches of Christ?

4. What problem does it pose for you personally or for the church at large that there are brothers and sisters in Christ who do not produce the kind of fruit witnessed in those outside the church?

5. What did Jesus mean in Mark 9:38-41 when he said that "Whoever is not against us is for us"?

6. Should we pray that God's blessings would rest on those who are not Christians but are devout believers in Christ?

7. In what way would the world be different if every person were a believer in Christ even if not strictly a Christian?

8. Is it right for us to sing hymns written by men and women who were not Christians?

9. Have you ever found that you have a closer relationship with a believer outside the Lord's body than with some

brothers and sisters in the church? If so, what conflicts does that pose?

10. Should we prefer the company of worldly members of the church to spiritually-minded believers outside the church?

11. Are you able to speak frankly with your believing friends about the need to be fully joined with Christ?

12. Are you able to speak frankly with worldly brothers and sisters in Christ about the need to be fully committed in their faith?

CHAPTER 7 — "IN CHRIST" FELLOWSHIP: THE EXTENDED FAMILY

1. What quite different worship experiences have you had with those who are brothers and sisters in Christ—perhaps from another country or culture?

2. Has your congregation been blessed with a diversity of fellow Christians (racial, economic, educational, generational, etc.)? If not, is it because diversity is not wanted?

3. How is "in Christ" fellowship determined?

4. Can we be in fellowship with someone who is not in fellowship with God?

5. Can we be out of fellowship with someone who is in fellowship with God?

6. Are there any biblically-baptized believers that you are ashamed to call your brother or sister in Christ? Why?

7. Are all biblically-baptized believers Christians?

8. What does the parable of the lost son (Luke 15:11-32) tell us about "in Christ" fellowship?

9. What does it take for a brother or sister in Christ to fall away from salvation?

10. Is an "erring Christian" still a brother or sister in Christ?

11. Why are those who have been baptized thinking they are already Christians such a difficult case with regard to fellowship?

12. To what degree have your experienced *koinonia* fellowship among the extended family of Christians?

CHAPTER 8 — CONSCIENCE FELLOWSHIP: CLOSE FAMILY

1, What kind of issues have divided the church, and why those particular issues as compared with others?

2. What theological litmus test must be passed before a person can become a Christian?

3. What theological litmus test must be passed for one to continue being fellowshiped as a Christian?

4. What do we learn about separate enclaves of conscience fellowship from New Testament references to Jewish and Gentile Christians?

5. What principles can we glean from Romans 14 and 15 about maintaining fellowship despite differences in doctrinal understanding?

6. When we must go our separate ways because of conscience, what can we learn from the disputes between Paul and Barnabas (Acts 15:36-41); Abraham and Lot (Genesis 13:7-12); and Joab and Abner (2 Samuel 2:12-29)?

7. Which, if either, is more reprehensible: division or divisiveness?

8. How is a party spirit different from conscience fellowship?

9. Which, if either, is the greater sin: doctrinal error or ungodly attitudes in correcting doctrinal error?

10. What can we learn about "close family fellowship" from the fact that Israel was divided into tribes?

11. How can we maintain conscience and unity simultaneously?

12. What problems are we likely to encounter if some congregations among the churches of Christ give open acceptance to those who have never experienced biblical baptism; and how shall we resolve those problems in the spirit of unity?

CHAPTER 9 — CONGREGATIONAL FELIOWSHIP: IMMEDIATE FAMILY

1. How would you describe *koinonia* fellowship?

2. What is there about the fellowship of your own congregation that has blessed you most?

3. What is most lacking in the fellowship of your own congregation?

4. What kinds of struggles have you had with questions pertaining to fellowship in one or another congregation?

5. If you have ever considered leaving a congregation, was it a matter of conscience or was it your personal comfort zone that was being threatened?

6. How do we know where to draw the line between conscience and preference?

7. What is the purpose of having an "immediate family" in Christ?

8. What role do elders and deacons play in the fellowship of the local congregation?

9. How might our current practice of choosing a congregation differ from the church in the days of the apostles?

10. Is the ease with which one becomes a member of a

congregation responsible in any way for the ease with which one can leave a congregation?

11. Is withdrawing fellowship from one or more congregations a biblical practice?

12. What is the relationship of the local "immediate family" to the larger "extended family" of Christians, especially with regard to such things as annual lectureships, church-related universities, brotherhood papers, etc.?

CHAPTER 10 — THE LOVING DISCIPLINE OF DISFELLOWSHIP

1. What fundamental difference is there between church membership as seen in Scripture and church membership in the eyes of the court in the Marian Guinn case?

2. What two primary reasons are there for disfellowshiping, and which, if either, is the more important?

3. Why is the disfellowshiping of those who have already left the church so futile?

4. Does your own congregation have the kind of *koinonia* fellowship which, if it were withheld, would be a good incentive for one who is disfellowshiped to be brought to his senses?

5. What effect should disfellowshiping by one congregation have on sister congregations?

6. Which sins merit disfellowshiping, and why those sins rather than others?

7. In what various ways is the "immediate family" affected when individual members sin?

8. What does Scripture teach us about the procedure to be followed in withdrawing fellowship from a brother or sister?

9. What do you think of LaGard's suggestion that the biblical process of disfellowshiping involves a "family council"

where the wayward member and the entire congregation are present?

10. What is involved in "withdrawing fellowship?" What does it mean to "shun" a brother; or "have nothing to do with him", or "with such a one do not even eat"?

11. How should one's own physical family treat the brother or sister in the church who has been disfellowshiped?

12. Would you say that your own congregation is either too eager or too lax in the matter of withdrawing fellowship?

CHAPTER 11 — FALSE TEACHERS OR FALSE TEACHING?

1. Why is context so important when we are reading Scripture or even a book written by man?

2. Why is it so important to keep distinct issues separate when engaging in doctrinal discussions?

3. What immediate problem do we encounter if we say that anyone who teaches something false is a false teacher?

4. In what way is labeling someone a false teacher an *ad hominem* argument?

5. What scriptural consequences are to follow if a person truly is a false teacher?

6. What practical consequences follow when someone is wrongly accused of being a false teacher?

7. In what way were the false prophets of Scripture impostors?

8. Are there any false prophets or false Christs among us today?

9. Wnat role does the character issue play in one's being named a false teacher?

10. Do many, or any, of those who have been named as false teachers today merit that label on the basis of bad character?

11. Is someone a false teacher just because he teaches a doctrine you believe to be false?

12. How should we regard those who falsely accuse others of being false teachers? How do you think God regards them?

Chapter 12 — The Prospect of Eternal Fellowship

1. Does it make you uncomfortable to think that God has prerogative to judge as he sees fit on the day of Judgment?

2. Do you believe that your hope of salvation is secure in the promises of God?

3. Do you agree that God has the right to grant clemency to those who have not fully obeyed the gospel?

4. What is the difference between clemency and justification?

5. Would it be a violation of God's character for him to save someone who has not fully complied with his plan of salvation?

6. What does Matthew 7:13 tell us about the nature of final Judgment?

7. Is it wrong for us to say what God will or will not do in fact on the day of Judgment? Why?

8. Does the prospect that God might grant mercy to those who have not fully obeyed the gospel lessen in any way our obligation to teach and warn them regarding God's commandments?

9. How would you feel if in heaven you discovered people you had not expected to meet, or did not find people you thought would be there?

10. In what way should our present experiences with spiritual fellowship prepare us for heaven?

11. What do you most look forward to about heaven?

12. What fellowship do we have even now with God, Christ, and the Holy Spirit?

EPILOGUE—OPEN LETTER, OPEN HEART

1. If you have read Max's *In the Grip of Grace*, what were some of your own favorite lines or thoughts?

2. In what way has Max made you more fully appreciate God's grace?

3. What is right about Max's call for Christian unity?

4. In what way are Max's words "watershed, historic thoughts"?

5. In what way is baptism symbolic?

6. Does anything beyond symbolism happen in the act of baptism?

7. What are the differences between the significance of baptism and the purpose of circumcision?

8. Is it possible that our attitude toward baptism can become legalistic?

9. What impressed you one way or the other about Max's analogy of God's "fellow-ship"?

10. Is there a significant nuance in Max's reference to "faith, repentance, and *a new birth*"?

11. What is your reaction to Max's statement: "When I meet a

man whose faith is in the cross and whose eyes are on the Savior, I meet a brother"?

12. Do you find it tough to think that people who seemingly bear the fruit of the Spirit might be lost because they haven't been biblically baptized?